# Carschooling

# Carschooling

## Over 350
### Entertaining Games & Activities
### to Turn Travel Time into
### Learning Time

DIANE FLYNN KEITH

PRIMA PUBLISHING

Published by Prima Publishing, Roseville, California. Member of the Crown Publishing Group, a division of Random House, Inc., New York.

PRIMA PUBLISHING and colophon are trademarks of Random House, Inc., registered with the United States Patent and Trademark Office.

Carschooling is a registered trademark of Diane Flynn Keith.

*Interior illustrations by Nathaniel Levine.*

**Library of Congress Cataloging-in-Publication Data**
Keith, Diane Flynn.
    Carschooling : over 350 entertaining games & activities to turn travel time into learning time / Diane Flynn Keith
        p.    cm.
    Includes index.
    ISBN 0-7615-3684-1
    1. Educational games.  2. Games for travelers.  I. Title: Carschooling.
LB1029.G3 K45  2002
371.33'7—dc21                                                        2002071473

02 03 04 05 06 BB 10 9 8 7 6 5 4 3 2 1
Printed in the United States of America

First Edition

**Visit us online at www.primapublishing.com**

*To Nick and Chad Keith, my reasons for Carschooling.*

*To Cliff Keith for tireless support, vehicle maintenance, and for loving the driver.*

*To my mom, Jan Flynn, and her "invisible brake."*

*To my dad, Carol Flynn, for Sunday family drives, and for packing—and then repacking—the car.*

*And to The Fog Lifter, clearing the path for safe travel on the road ahead.*

# CONTENTS

# ACKNOWLEDGMENTS

M Y APPRECIATION and profound gratitude must be expressed to the fantastic people whose support, encouragement, and contributions made this book possible, including:

★ My husband, Cliff, and our sons, Nick and Chad, who inspired this book and gave me the gift of time that I needed to research, write, and edit. Thank you for listening to hundreds of audiotapes and for enduring short stops, potholes, and detours in the pursuit of education.

★ All of the ingenious parents who are members of the Carschooling e-list or who have attended Carschooling workshops—their contributions of real personal stories, ideas, activities, and resources are the foundation of this book.

★ My carschooling "experts," Katy Hunt, John McChesney, Marnie Ridgway, Leslie Pitts, and Jane Williams, whose creative ideas infuse this book with exceptional educational opportunities in the car.

★ Mary, Michael, and Lennon Leppert for providing a national venue for *Carschooling* in *The Link Homeschool Newspaper* and an introduction to Prima Publishing.

★ Shannon Noll and the Education Staff at Happy Hollow Zoo in San Jose, California, for clearing a space for me to work amidst the inspiring sights and sounds of lemurs, crickets, and macaws.

★ Rebecca Kochenderfer for Monday afternoon brainstorming sessions.

★ Barbara and Rachel Phillips for ongoing support, encouragement, and friendship, and for providing invaluable assistance in the implementation of Carschooling workshops.

★ Teena Bennett for competent and friendly office support and workshop assistance.

★ Linda Joy Kattwinkle and Evelyn Davidson for providing top-notch legal advice.

★ The terrific staff of Prima Publishing including: Jamie Miller, acquisitions editor; Andrew Vallas, project editor; Pat Henshaw, publicity manager; Stacey Curran, sales and marketing; and countless others.

★ Finally, I'd like to acknowledge my own siblings, Carol Flynn and Brad Flynn, for sharing the backseat on memorable family excursions.

My heartfelt thanks goes to each and every one of you. You're the best!

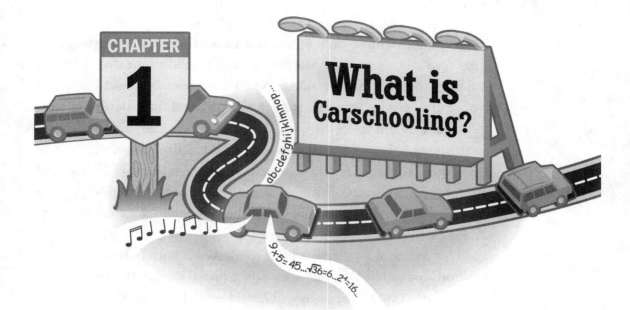

# CHAPTER 1

## What is Carschooling?

CARSCHOOLING IS all about turning travel time into learning time. Parents today cite their children's education as a top priority. Some supplement traditional schooling in public or private schools with after-school activities and curricula. Others homeschool their children to provide optimum learning environments. What all parents have in common is that they spend a lot of time in the car with their kids commuting to classes, field trips, tutoring sessions, libraries, and enrichment programs—not to mention running everyday errands.

All parents complain about wasting time in traffic jams. All kids grumble when there is nothing to do in the car and evoke the universal whine, "Are we there yet?" What if parents could use the time spent in the car to enhance their children's education with fun activities, resources, and games designed to improve skills in math, science, history, reading, grammar, and more?

As a homeschooling parent, I spend a lot of time in the family car with my two sons. I cart them around to science, music, and gymnastics lessons, to libraries, to friends' houses, to homeschool park days for recreation and socialization, and I take them on numerous field trips to distant points of interest. I have logged more than 218,000 miles in the car with my kids. When I mentioned this to a friend whose children go to public school, she revealed that she also spends inordinate amounts of time in the car running the kids back and forth to school, volunteering as a designated driver for school field trips, and taking her kids to various after-school activities and school-related social gatherings. We shared ideas about how to make the journeys more tolerable for antsy kids and to maintain the driver's sanity.

Our solutions were similar in that we had both discovered methods for enhancing our kids' education while on the road. Tracy D. of Texas concurs. She says, "I have learned that cars are not only places for listening to tapes but also can be places for experiments in solar oven cookery, pretend orchestra conducting, bug collecting in or on the car, and nature studies. One of my favorite memories of carschooling was when my son and I were driving through the inner city of Austin, Texas. We saw a vulture trying to eat an opossum road kill, but three mocking birds would not let it. They dive-bombed and pecked the vulture whenever it landed near the carcass. We just stopped the car in a parking lot and watched until the birds drove the vulture out of the neighborhood. My son and I were fascinated by this event since we had never before seen a vulture in our downtown area, or one being chased by tiny birds. My son was inspired to write a story about the incident that he titled 'Goldy Vulture and the Three Mocking Birds.'" You can see that educational opportunities are abundant when you are in the car and on the road. Just as I have turned our dining room into a homeschool, I have turned my automobile into a carschool. I began to ask other parents if they used time in the car to learn. Carschooling mom Tammy said, "We listen to the news on the radio and then discuss it. We have also found that car time is a great time to pass on family history, telling old family legends and jokes." Many parents said that their carschooling included homework and workbook assignments, art projects, and listening to audiotapes. Photini H. of South Dakota shuttles her kids to a variety of co-op classes. She said, "We listen to an audiotape of Shakespeare's plays on our way to drama class and an audiotape on physics while driving to science class. That way, our carschooling ties in with what we are learning in the classroom." Rebecca Kochenderfer, coauthor of *Homeschooling for Success* and cofounder of www.Homeschool.com, uses travel time with her son in this way: "We've had great luck listening to audio versions of classic books in the car. My son has a vision disorder and, although he is an excellent reader, reading makes his eyes tired. So he listens to audiobooks in the car. We listened to an audio version of *Jane Eyre* and the original *Tarzan* book while on one 10-hour car ride. Because of the audiobooks, I think the kids liked the car ride almost as much as the visit to Legoland!"

Some families I interviewed played games like 20 Questions, or looked for alphabet letters and numbers on license plates; others revealed unique activities their families enjoy and some interesting carschooling experiences. Delaine N. of California shared this memory: "One of our favorite carschooling experiences was when we visited Fossil Rim, a drive-through animal park near Fort Worth, Texas. We opened the rear windows so the kids could get a good look at the animals as they dropped feed (that the park ranger provided) on the ground. For nine miles, the gazelles, zebras, moose, giraffes, ostriches, and more came up to greet us. The taller animals seemed accustomed to sticking their heads completely into the car windows without any encouragement from us to get their treats! At one point we were surrounded by three to four giraffes. They took turns swooping their heads down through the window into the backseat and sticking out their long black tongues to reach for the kids' feed cups. The kids were squealing (partly with intimidation but mostly with delight) because they had never before been so up-close and personal with such exotic animals. It was such a rewarding experience, and it was a day of carschooling at its best!"

I, personally, have been carschooling since my kids were born. I found that lullabies and classical music played on audiotapes when they were very little calmed them as we drove in the car. As they grew, my rambunctious toddlers loved to listen to and sing along with children's songs, Broadway musical soundtracks, and even Spike Jones recordings! Some of the children's music recordings included stories that my children found spellbinding. That convinced me that I was onto something—and I began to find resources for recordings on various subjects while traveling in the car.

As the kids got older and bigger, I found that when they were riding in the backseat and were cramped for space they would often initiate a game of "slug bug"—when you see a VW Bug on the road you get to slug or punch the person next to you. That drove me crazy in zero to 60 seconds! To distract them from punching each other, I would put on an audiobook and it settled them right down. The subjects in the stories would lead to many wonderful discussions in the car as we drove from one destination to another.

I also discovered educational tapes on everything from math to grammar to geography that my children enjoyed as well. We found that subjects requiring rote memorization were easier when set to poetry or music. They learned the multiplication tables from a math rock 'n' roll tape, and the capitals of every state as well as biology concepts from musical audiotapes and CDs. Carschooling for our family eventually evolved into some remarkable unit studies and educational projects that were exclusive to our time spent in the car.

We also played car games that were fun and educational. Frequently, a well-known travel game would metamorphous into a new game as the boys changed the rules or added nuances that were unique to their interests and abilities. Carschooling is about using ideas and resources to help children learn while on the road, but it is also about doing activities that help families spend meaningful time together.

The demands of work and conventional schooling mean that parents and kids spend significant portions of their waking day—seven hours or more—apart from each other. The responsibility of running a home (cooking, cleaning, minor repairs, grocery shopping, laundry, and so forth) means that time at home is often usurped by the realities of day-to-day tasks. Even entertainment devices in our homes (TV, the computer, and electronic games) steal precious hours that could be spent in conversation or activities that help us to know and understand one another and our world better.

The greatest single gift that passes between parent and child is the gift of time and attention freely given to one another. To spend time learning with your children is an investment in their future, the future of the family, and, indeed, the future of our society. The greatest measure of our success as parents is our relationship with our children. Effectively using time spent in the car with them playing fun and interactive educational games, or immersed in earnest discussions about provocative issues of the day, improves communication, builds trust and goodwill, and bonds families together in profound and heartfelt ways.

This book is designed to help families discover inventive ways to make the most of time spent in the family automobile. I have gathered together the unique and creative ideas of carschooling parents, along with resource recommendations that can be used in the car for learning every subject typically required by national curriculum standards, so that you can start carschooling and get on the real "Information Highway!" When you use the games and activities suggested in this book, keep these guidelines for successful carschooling in mind:

★    Games and activities are supposed to be fun for everyone.
     If they're not fun, don't play.

★ Sometimes kids will understand the rules, and other times they won't. Some kids' skills will be better than others. Sometimes having patience with a child who takes longer to comprehend and deliver an answer can be frustrating for parents as well as other players. But please, please, please do not show your frustration and don't allow the other players to tease. Maintain a joyful environment that is full of support, patience, and praise.

★ Keep the rules as flexible as possible. Many of the games and activities here can be adjusted to accommodate a whole new set of rules that your kids make up. Let them. It's all part of the learning process.

★ There is often a wide age range in carschools. Give older players handicaps to make the games and activities fair for everyone.

★ Competitive games with winners and losers are difficult for many children to cope with or understand. If you have such a child, turn competitive games into cooperative games by having everyone do the activity together. Set a goal in a time frame, and once it is achieved everyone wins or gets a treat.

As parents, we want to encourage learning while building self-confidence in a fun and affirming way. Be on your kid's side, and recognize his or her accomplishments. When children experience success, it will produce in them the motivation to learn more. Above all, have fun learning in the car with your family.

# SAMPLE CARSCHOOLING CURRICULA

Carschooling families can cover all of the subjects typically required by national curriculum standards that include English, social sciences, foreign language, physical education, science, math, visual and performing arts, health, and other electives. They tackle academic subjects in traditional and nontraditional ways. Many carschoolers claim that the discussions that ensue as they learn together in the car not only create literate "road scholars" but also lead to enhanced family dynamics, respectful communication, understanding, and bonding. Take a peek at some sample curricula and get a glimpse of how interactive learning not only sharpens and refines academic skills but also improves and nurtures family relationships. Try a sample carschool curriculum the next time you're on the road and see if it doesn't convince you to adopt "Auto Academics."

I have included five different sample curricula, compiled from activities in this book, to cover different age and grade ranges including Preschool and Kindergarten (ages 3–5), Early Elementary (ages 6–9, or grades 1–4), Middle and Upper Elementary (ages 10–13, or grades 5–8), High School (ages 14–17, or grades 9–12), and Family Curriculum (all ages, all grades). Please remember that these ability levels are approximate and are based on traditional academic "norms." It is my opinion that people deviate from standardized norms in significant ways and therefore, all curricula—including the suggestions here—should be tempered by parents' innate understanding of their own child's learning style, ability, interest, and needs gained through years of day-to-day interaction, observation, and experience. I encourage you to use these samples as a guideline to create your own individualized curriculum from the many activities and resources in this book. As with all curricula, it should adapt to your family's changing needs and interests.

I believe parents are the ultimate experts on what is educationally appropriate for their own children. So please feel free to supplement, augment, discard, and change the curriculum samples provided. I also trust that parents who have children with learning differences (including those labeled "gifted") will use parental license to custom-tailor a curriculum that is suited to their child's special needs. The following lists provide a tip-of-the-iceberg view of what is available for committed carschoolers.

# SAMPLE CURRICULA BY AGE AND GRADE

## Preschool and Kindergarten (ages 3–5)

### SCIENCE
A Mobile Bug Collection Box
Clouds: The Ultimate Shape-Shifters

### MATH
More Things to Count
Driving in Circles

### LANGUAGE ARTS
Searching for ABCs
Car Puppetry

### SOCIAL SCIENCES
A Day in the Life of . . .
Memory Boxes

### GEOGRAPHY
Color the States
Inflate the Globe

### VISUAL AND PERFORMING ARTS
Silver Sculptures
Got Rhythm?

### FOREIGN LANGUAGES
Sing Along with Me
Drive-By Foreign Languages

**PHYSICAL EDUCATION AND HEALTH**
Skeleton Hokey Pokey
Off-Ramp Romps

# Early Elementary (ages 6–9, grades 1–4)

**SCIENCE**
Science—Magnified!
How Far Away Is the Lightning?

**MATH**
100 Bottles of Juice on the Wall
Time Is Money

**LANGUAGE ARTS**
If C-A-R Spells "Car" . . .
Paper Bag Story Starters

**SOCIAL SCIENCES**
How Do They Make That?
Clothesline History

**GEOGRAPHY**
Road Navigators
Stamp Out States

**VISUAL AND PERFORMING ARTS**
Black and White Masterpieces
Singing in the Rain—or Sunshine!

**FOREIGN LANGUAGES**
Fairy Tale Foreign Languages
Global Language

### PHYSICAL EDUCATION AND HEALTH
Musical Rest Stops
Car Seat Calisthenics

# Middle and Upper Elementary (ages 10–13, grades 5–8)

### SCIENCE
20 Questions Science Game
Guess the Wind Speed

### MATH
The Grate-Googol Game
Roman Numeral Hunt

### LANGUAGE ARTS
Highway Hangman
Getting to the Root of It

### SOCIAL SCIENCES
The Tour Guide
Historical Marker Countdown

### GEOGRAPHY
Where in the World?
License Plate Photo Safari

### VISUAL AND PERFORMING ARTS
Songs in a Bag
Pass It Along Art

### FOREIGN LANGUAGES
Multilingual Gaming
Translation Game

**PHYSICAL EDUCATION AND HEALTH**
Thumb Wrestling
Mobile Anatomy Lab

# High School (ages 14–17, grades 9–12)

**SCIENCE**
Seasonal Changes
Dipping Up the North Star

**MATH**
Stock Car Game
Pi in My Eye

**LANGUAGE ARTS**
Ghost
Crack the License Plate Code

**SOCIAL SCIENCES**
Decade or Dare?
Rubbing Up History

**GEOGRAPHY**
State Mottos
Compass Capers

**VISUAL AND PERFORMING ARTS**
Picture This
Speak the Language of Music

**FOREIGN LANGUAGES**
Guess the Word
Foreign Tongue Twisters

**PHYSICAL EDUCATION AND HEALTH**

Stop Watch Olympics

Car Dancing!

# Family (all ages, all grades)

**SCIENCE**

Road Raptors

Ear Popping Air Pressure

**MATH**

Round and Round We Go

Coin Toss—Testing the Theory of Probability

**LANGUAGE ARTS**

The Day You Were Born

The Car Mechanic's Cat

**SOCIAL SCIENCES**

Family History in 7 Questions

Brown Bag History

**GEOGRAPHY**

Alphabet States and Capitals

Two Bit Geography

**VISUAL AND PERFORMING ARTS**

Musical Hot Potato

Colorful Knowledge

**FOREIGN LANGUAGES**

Signing Signs

Yummy Foreign Languages

**PHYSICAL EDUCATION AND HEALTH**

Road Sign Harvest Time

Rest Stop Olympics

# A LAST COMMENT ABOUT CURRICULUM

I hope I have demonstrated for you how simple it is to create a curriculum for use in your carschool. Some of you may want to do exactly that; others may want to use the activities randomly in no particular order and without structure at all. This book is intended for both purposes. Most of all, I hope the activities I have compiled will be conducted in a joyful environment, without pressure to perform. Remember that kids love to learn. When given the opportunity to engage in activities that are interesting and fun and that have relevance and meaning to their lives, our children will usually exceed our expectations for learning in every way.

# CHAPTER 2

# Getting Organized

LIKE ALL classrooms and educational settings, your carschool should be well maintained and suitably stocked with tools and resources to help your students learn. Some activities in this book don't require any tools at all, but others call for specific items to conduct the lessons. At the beginning of each subject chapter you will find a list of the tools needed to augment every activity suggested. Some materials are recommended repeatedly and will come in handy for all of your carschool studies. These "Top 12" necessities are discussed later in this chapter along with tips from carschooling families about additional resources and "fun packages" that will enrich your carschool environment.

First, let's turn our attention to maintaining a tidy carschool. You will find ideas for organizing materials so they don't wind up all over the floor of the car. I also have some not-too-messy snack suggestions for your carschool cafeteria. Carschool "professors" provide advice and remedies for behavioral potholes and carsickness detours along the way. I've even included parents' recommendations for the best "educational cars" on the market, as well as some practical add-on features that help to make every vehicle ideal for carschooling. Detroit, are you listening?

# THE CARSCHOOL CUSTODIAN

## Maintaining Your Carschool

One of carschooling's little "givens" is this: If you spend lots of time on the road with kids in the car, the car will have a "lived-in" look. When my family began carschooling, I wasn't prepared for the mess that ensued. At one point, little plastic building blocks, trading cards, papers, pencils, books, electronic game cartridges, and other assorted toys and tools littered the car floor. My car upholstery had a tie-dyed effect thanks to melted crayons and leaky marker pens. Drips from soda and juice containers had left sticky residue on door and window handles. My spilled lattes (even after cleaning) imparted a lingering odor of sour milk for days. Little bits of cracker crumbs, a few stray french fries, and squished Gummy Bears were imbedded in seat belt and car cushion nooks and crannies until an ant infestation forced me to rethink carschool cleanliness. (I was also tired of scrambling to transfer all of the junk from the car to the trunk every time we offered a ride to a friend.) Unlike the local public school, my carschool didn't have a janitorial service that came after hours to tidy up the mess. I was the designated carschool custodian, and, as such, I determinedly employed my kids as a maintenance crew to help keep our mobile classroom spick-and-span.

I began to notice other people's cars. Some were just as bad as ours had been. In fact, one family had spilled raw popcorn on the floor of their car—and it sprouted! I'm all for agricultural studies in the car, but wouldn't a cornfield in the backseat eventually impair the driver's vision and limit passenger access? As one carschool mom in New Hampshire put it, "I have to confess that on the

Oscar–Felix bell curve of car cleanliness, I'm 100 percent Oscar [the slob]. Sand, crumbs, small rubber bands, loose toys, or broken limbs from action figures . . . and yes, an occasional unidentifiable piece of forgotten food is found under my seat."

I continued to observe cars and found many that were impeccably kept in spite of the fact that the families spent a good deal of time on the road. I collected the owners' advice and tricks of the trade for keeping their carschool clean, such as this bit of wisdom from carschooling mom Megan:

Car maintenance is a great opportunity to teach the kids how to be organized—talking to them about what you are doing and why. Like many jobs, this one is easier when you teach the kids gently, but at an early age. Consistency is important, too. I developed a cleanup plan and then stuck to it. I explained it to everyone so we all knew the expectations. Training the kids is the hardest part, but you also have to train yourself to stay on top of it. For example, you need to be aware that someone is done eating something and a wrapper is about to hit the car floor. You must point out where the trash bag is located and ask them to use it. This is something you will need to do repeatedly until their response is automatic—and that can take years. Also, make sure the kids take their stuff out of the car, reminding them that what goes in must come out. Don't let them desert you with a car full of stuff. Make vacuum trips once a week to the local car wash. Raise the kids' consciousness about keeping things neat and try to make it fun!

## Stash Your Trash—And Keep the Garbage Under Control

Used resources accumulate quickly in the limited space of a carschool. Wadded up scratch paper, pencil shavings, and broken crayons, along with empty juice cartons, food wrappers, and nap-kins fill the litterbag to capacity and the overflow competes with your feet for space on the car floor. Carschool sanitation specialist Ruth offered this advice:

> Always keep litter bags in the car to stash the trash. (You can find trash bags that fasten onto the back of the front seats at many stores.) Consider assigning a car student the job of "trash moni-tor" and remind him or her to empty or replace it daily. Make sure that whatever you use for garbage will be easily seen so that it acts as a constant reminder for the students to deposit their scratch paper and empty drink boxes and cans in the bag, keeping the car clutter-free.

## Protecting the Upholstery

Let's face it—cars aren't designed like school buses, with institutional-grade seat covers that can hold their own against everything from unrelenting seat-kicking to spit balls and graffiti. Upholstery takes the brunt of the wear and tear in carschools. Broken pens leave in-delible imprints, sticky hands find relief on cushiony fabric, and food crumbs and road dust compete for every inch of crevice space. Here are some ideas submitted by carschooling parents that may help preserve your car upholstery from total annihilation:

★ To protect car upholstery from food and beverage stains, cover the backseat with a twin-sized, waterproof mattress pad. Cut slits in the pad to allow use of the seat belts.

★ Cover the backseat with a bassinette-sized fitted sheet. A carschool mom named Deanna said, "It's the perfect size and the elastic keeps it from slipping off. On long trips, you can shake it out periodically, and it's easy to remove and wash.

Not only do sheets keep the car seats clean, but they have the extra benefit of keeping the seats cool when the weather is hot."

★ Only allow clear or light-colored beverages in the car, such as water and apple juice, to avoid stains from spills. Carschool mom Aimee had this advice for those who do let passengers drink colorful beverages that stain: "My husband has been known to give the kids those darn squeeze drinks that are bright red and orange! He uses a product called Tough Stuff, and it has gotten almost every stain out of the upholstery."

## Odors and Other Oddities

Car classrooms (like school science laboratories) take on all kinds of peculiar odors garnered from the many activities conducted within. Spills and smears scent the upholstery and carpet in a way that hanging pine tree deodorizers just can't conceal. Here is carschooler Tammy's suggestion for eliminating unpleasant smells:

We don't qualify for the car-looks-new-but-isn't award, but we do have a few tricks in our bag. To take a bad smell out of a car (such as spilled milk), put a whole apple in the car somewhere. A whole apple will do a good job of deodorizing if the job's not too big. The apple shouldn't stay in the car for more than a few days—unless you want to attract fruit flies for a science experiment. There's also a terrific product called Natural Magic Odor Blaster that you can buy at hardware stores. It neutralizes bad odors without leaving a perfume smell, but it has to be reapplied if the smell is rooted deep in the carpet or upholstery.

# ORGANIZATION AND STORAGE

With so many educational tools on board in the carschool, safety is a concern. The last thing the driver needs is an errant gel-pen or double-A battery rolling under the gas pedal, or the view in the rear window blocked by stacks of books, CD players, and educational toys and games. Loose objects in the car can also become airborne if the driver has to stop short—and that could potentially harm someone. What's needed is a place for everything, and everything needs to be in its place. Here are some recommendations by veteran carschoolers on how to organize your gear and keep the car safe and ship-shape.

## Finding and Creating Space for Storage

Storage space is a precious commodity to carschoolers. One area of wasted space that can be conveniently utilized is under the seats. Slim boxes with lids can hold all sorts of resources, and three-ring binders with zippered plastic pockets for storing pens, pencils, erasers, and more can be stowed right under the student's seat for easy access. Optimize the space in your trunk, too. Here are some more ideas from carschool parents for storing carschool supplies:

- ★ Try plastic, rectangular kitty litter boxes to store the kids' stuff under the seats.
- ★ Use a large, rectangular plastic box with a removable lid to store carschool supplies and travel games. The box will fit between the driver and passenger seat in the front of some cars (or you could store it in the trunk just as easily). When the lid is on, it can double as a little table and becomes a handy place to fix sandwiches or snacks on the road.
- ★ Keep small necessities such as wipes, tissue, and first aid gear in the glove compartment.

★   Small toys, games, and books can be relegated to car door
    side pockets.

★   Many carschoolers keep a small basket or box in the back of
    the van or in the trunk of the car to store incidentals such as
    utensils, napkins, plastic trash bags, batteries, and bottles
    of water.

★   Have the kids use their backpacks to bring games, work-
    books, learning supplies, and toys. They can keep them on
    the car floor next to their feet.

## Car Organizers

A number of companies offer pocket organizers for use in the car.
They provide a good storage solution for items that your car students use consistently. Here are a couple of products that have been
recommended over and over again by carschooling parents:

★   The Lillian Vernon Car Organizer is a sturdy, nylon organizer
    that fits on the back of the front car seats. Ten pockets of
    varying dimensions can be snapped shut, zipped closed, or
    secured with a fastener. You can keep games, cards, pens,
    pencils, notebooks, maps, cameras, and even snacks within
    easy reach. The organizer comes in bright primary colors and
    can be personalized with your student's name (to order call
    1-800-505-2250 or visit www.lillianvernon.com).

★   To protect CDs and keep them readily available, store them
    in a CD visor that fastens to the sun visor over the car wind-
    shield and has lined pockets that hold CDs securely. Some
    have mesh pockets that provide storage for car registration or
    insurance papers, as well as items like sunglasses. They are
    available in many stores and from Case Logic (call 1-877-227-
    3347 or visit www.caselogic.com).

## Car Seats and Lap Trays

The lap tray or tray table is an essential piece of equipment for many carschooling families. It provides a hard surface for coloring, writing, and for playing card games. Here are a few products that have been tested and approved by carschoolers.

★ Lap desks with a beanbag bottom stay on the lap without slipping and sliding because the beanbag molds to the student's legs and keeps the tray level. They come in a variety of styles, but all have hard plastic tops for writing. Some have built-in storage bins with tops that slide on and off. The Bean Bag Lap Tray, by Creative Manufacturing, has a detachable beanbag bottom so that it can be machine-washed (Creative Manufacturing carries many variations of lap desks; visit their Web site at www.lapdesk.com).

★ A Taby Tray, offered by One Step Ahead, converts a toddler's car seat into a desk (or a snack tray) with a raised edge around the perimeter to keep things (like crayons) from rolling off the tray. It also has a built-in drink or cup holder. Another great feature is that it meets automotive safety requirements for use in a moving car (order at 1-800-274-8440 or www.onestepahead.com).

★ The Car Seat Activity Panel, also by One Step Ahead, hangs on the back of the front seat. It unfolds (similar to an airline tray table) so that you can write on it, and there are pockets for crayons, markers, and other stuff. The tray table is made of sturdy foam. There's even a built-in night light so kids can use it after dark (order at 1-800-274-8440 or www.onestep ahead.com).

★ The Backseat Organizer with Tray Table, offered by Case Logic, is a combination tray table and organizer that hangs on the back of the front seat. The tray table folds down to use as a desk, and the organizer has two bottle/cup holders, several pockets, and mesh compartments for storage. It is available at many stores or you can buy direct from Case Logic (1-877-227-3347 or www.caselogic.com).

★ The Doodle-Case is a portable, combination plastic case and clipboard that can act as a sturdy desktop for writing letters or drawing while you're in the car. Inside the case are 8 markers, 18 oil pastels, 12 colored pencils, a pencil sharpener, and 20 sheets of paper. It is available from Solutions (order at 1-800-342-9988 or www.solutionscatalog.com).

Carschool mom Jan converted a cookie sheet into a car lap desk by turning it upside down. She said, "It's long enough to cover my daughter's lap, and the added advantage is that it also provides a metal background for her magnetic paper dolls."

## CAR SNACKS AND BEVERAGES

Educational car excursions can really stimulate appetites and work up a thirst. Carschool parents seem to prefer offering students supplements that are bite-sized, not too sticky, and relatively nutritious. Here is a list, as well as some advice, for snacks and beverages that fit the bill while keeping the carschool campus relatively clean:

★ Animal cookies (sweetened with fruit juice, available at health food stores)

★ Bananas (make sure the peel goes in the litter bag)

★ Bite-sized crackers, graham crackers, fish-shaped crackers

★ Bottled water (quenches thirst without sticky or staining spills)

★ Clear beverages such as flavored mineral water, lemon-lime soda, apple juice. For hot summer days, put juice into plastic, flip-top bottles, and *freeze* it the night before a trip; it will stay cold for a long time.

★ Cereals in small, snack-size, zipper-lock plastic bags. For a special treat, string Cheerios or Fruit Loops on a ribbon and knot it at both ends. Kids can eat them without dropping or losing any. Let the kids string their own before your next car trip!

★ Fruit leather (available at health food stores)

★ Granola bars and nutrition bars

★ Peanuts

★ Raisins and other dried fruit

★ Rice crackers (small, bite-sized)

★ Seedless grapes (make sure stems go in litter bag)

★ String cheese

★ Trail mix

★ Turkey jerky

Christy in Canada offers this tip: "We never travel in the car without sippy cups. They have valves in them to release the liquid only when someone sucks on it. Juice doesn't squirt out randomly, and if someone drops a sippy cup—no spills."

# TOOLS AND SUPPLIES

Transforming your car into a place for higher learning is easy. To help you create a comfortable and enriched mobile learning environment, here are some basic tools and supplies carschoolers recommend for your educational journeys.

## For Easy Carschool Cleanups

Learning on the road is messy, so be prepared for cleanups, keeping these supplies on hand:

★ Container of disposable wet wipes or baby wipes

★ Box of tissue

★ Trash bags

★ Roll of paper towels

★ Bath or hand towels (just in case you go where it's wet or muddy)

## Little "Extras" That May Come in Handy on the Road

You won't use these items all of the time, but they are nice to have on hand:

★ Flashlight

★ Cooler for beverages, snacks, medicines, or other things that can go bad or melt (like crayons!) in the heat

★ Blanket (for extra warmth, or to sit on for roadside picnics)

★ Clothes (extra outfit for each child)

★ Portable potty chair (if you have little ones)

## The Top 12 *Essential* Carschool Educational Supplies

Stock up on supplies to prepare your mobile classroom for every educational opportunity that comes along. Here are the basic items that car educators recommend you keep on hand; these items will be referred to repeatedly in subsequent chapters:

1. **Audiocassette or CD player:** This is a must have item for listening to audiobooks and other educational recordings.

2. **Audiotapes and CDs:** Books, stories, and songs on audiotape or on CD are the mainstay of carschools everywhere.

3. **Paper, notebooks, scratch pads, journals, coloring books:** You will need a good supply of paper so that your students can draw, write, and keep game scores.

4. **Writing and drawing tools:** Pencils, pens, colored pencils, crayons, markers, and highlighters will be used over and over again in activities that help the miles pass quickly. Square beeswax crayons (available from HeathSong Catalog) won't roll off lap desks when you're driving. Remember that any type of crayon can melt in the car on a hot day, so keep them isolated in their own containers in cool, shady spots, or put them in the cooler to prevent waxy messes.

5. **Erasers, sharpeners:** Erasers or eraser-tipped pencils for correcting car game scores and tally marks are a must. You'll need a pencil sharpener, too, but get one that has a plastic bubble shield over the sharpener to catch the shavings so they don't wind up on the car floor or permanently stuck in the little grooves of the console.

6. **Books:** For kids who don't get carsick, be sure to bring along books to read.

7. **Activity books and worksheets:** Crossword puzzles, mazes, word searches, and arithmetic workbooks provide practice in language arts and math.

8. **Camera and film:** Keep cameras and film handy (Polaroid, regular, disposable, or digital), and let the kids capture those special moments in photographs while documenting your car curriculum.

9. **Field guides:** Use these guides to identify rocks, trees, birds, flowers, animals, reptiles, and insects. You never know what miracle of nature you'll see while looking out of the car windows.

10. **Magnifying glass:** Talk about a boredom buster! Keep an inexpensive magnifying glass available for each passenger, and let your carschoolers examine everything with it.

11. **A repertoire of car songs:** From "Row, Row, Row Your Boat" in rounds to "This Is the Song That Never Ends," singing in the car is fun for the whole family.

12. **A selection of car games and activities:** This book (that you are holding in your hands right now) offers a wealth of suggestions in many subject areas. Keep it in your glove compartment for inspiration while on the road!

# CAR SICKNESS

Nothing can put a damper on a family road trip like a carsick kid. Car sickness is frequently brought on by the act of reading or doing paperwork while traveling in the car. It is caused because information fed to the brain from the eyes and from the inner ear is out of synch. In a car, passengers (especially those in the backseat) may not be looking at the horizon ahead, so their eyes don't register the movement even though the liquid in their inner ear is being stimulated by the movement of the car. The eyes tell the brain there is no movement, but the inner ear relays the opposite message. The conflicting information to the brain results in nausea for those especially sensitive to the mismatched cues. Kids are especially susceptible to getting car sick, which can result in frequent stops along the way to either throw up or regain composure and settle the stomach. The good news is that kids often outgrow it. Meanwhile, here are some useful preventions and remedies for car sickness that carschooling parents have discovered. Perhaps some will work for you.

## Preventions and Remedies

1. Sit where there is an unobstructed view of the outside horizon; the front seat is ideal. Looking out side windows is not as effective and, in some cases, may exacerbate the problem.

2.  Never read or draw in the car. It takes your gaze off the horizon, causing the eyes to not measure movement, in opposition to the inner ear, which detects movement, resulting in nausea.

3.  Roll the window down. Fresh, cool air circulating in the car will really help relieve some of the nausea.

4.  Plan your trip ahead and allow enough time to provide regular stops along the road. Stopping every 10 to 15 minutes along the way can help the carsick-prone person maintain composure.

5.  Eat a light meal before traveling. Avoid greasy, fatty, heavy foods and meals like burgers and fries. If a snack is needed, try saltine crackers or apple slices. Popsicles (not ice cream) may help to soothe tummies.

6.  Drink water. Avoid acidic beverages like orange juice. Sipping Coke will help to settle the stomach—in fact, you can purchase straight Coke syrup from pharmacies for this purpose.

7.  Eliminate strong odors from the car environment as much as possible. Do not wear perfume in the car. No smoking in the car. Try to avoid congested areas where car/truck/bus exhaust fumes are prevalent.

8.  Try motion sickness wristbands. The bands have small plastic bumps inside of them that press on acupressure points in the wrist to help relieve nausea from motion sickness. They are available at drug stores and some health food stores.

9.  Try over-the-counter motion sickness pills, such as Dramamine (dimenhydrinate) or Bonine (meclizine). Be sure to read the package instructions before purchasing to determine what age they are suitable for—some may not be recommended for young children. Sometimes these drugs can cause drowsiness. If the trip will be educational and you want your students to be alert, look for nondrowsy formulas. Follow the package directions, which often advise taking the medication 30 minutes before you get in the car.

10. Try ginger. Chinese sailors used ginger to quell sea sickness, and scientists have confirmed its effectiveness. Capsules with dried ginger inside or dried ginger chips can be purchased in health food stores. Candied ginger, ginger snap cookies, and real ginger ale have also been shown to be effective.

11. Keep a cooler of ice and fresh water, along with some washcloths, in the car to wipe the face and throat and for cleanup as needed.

## Activities That Don't Make You Car Sick

In addition to the tips for avoiding car sickness, many parents suggested carschooling activities that don't require the "trigger" activities of reading or paperwork. Here are a few of their favorites:

★ Listen to music.

★ Listen to books and short stories on tape.

★ Focus on games that require players to look out the window to find the funniest, strangest, bluest (or whatever) bumper sticker, car, billboard, or some other object. Having fun while learning at the same time may help to take some passengers' minds off the car sickness.

★ Sing songs.

★ Play I Spy, 20 Questions, and other word/talking games.

# PRESERVING DRIVER SANITY

On long car trips, kids' energy is buckled up for long stretches of time and often suddenly bursts from them in a giggle fit, nonstop talking, yelling and shouting, squirming or sliding around in their seats, and even arguments and fighting. That energy can quickly whip into a frenzy that is hard to calm down. Carschooling parents have many suggestions for restoring calm and maintaining behavior that preserves the driver's sanity.

## Strategies for Long-Haul Carschooling Parents

★   Set behavior guidelines *before* getting into the car. Include the kids in a discussion about what behavior is expected and what the consequences for inappropriate behavior will be.

★   Determine seating arrangements *before* you get in the car. Arguments about who gets to ride in the "shotgun" position (in the front seat next to the driver) can be eliminated altogether by determining in advance that whoever has the yuckiest or least liked household chore that week or month gets to ride in the shotgun spot.

★   Have plenty of story tapes to listen to as well as stuff to do like drawing, coloring, and puzzle books. Having lots of options keeps the kids busy instead of bickering.

★   Use the democratic process to determine what to listen to or what games to play. Everyone can vote for their favorite activity, and the one with the most votes is the one that you do first. Then, do each subsequent activity in the order of votes received.

★   Limit time spent playing electronic games in the car. Many parents find that their kids get hyper, frustrated, and ill-tempered if they play for too long a time.

★   Limit foods with lots of sugar or red food coloring. Some parents report hyperactivity immediately after kids eat food or drink beverages containing these items.

★   Impose "radio silence." Insist that the kids keep quiet for a full 10 minutes or 10 miles, whichever comes first. Then reward their good behavior by having them select a game or activity to play in the car.

★ To restore peace and quiet in the car, give everyone a sugarless Lifesavers candy and have a contest to see who can make it last the longest. (You'll be surprised how well this works.)

## Solving the "She's Touching Me!" Gripe

Everyone needs their "space"—a tough commodity to come by in the family car. Kids, especially, are less tolerant of cramped quarters. One of the reasons carschooling families favor vans and mini-vans is because there is more room to separate the kids so they don't start the drive-the-driver-crazy "His arm is touching my side" mantra. Many parents who don't own vans say that placing a box or cooler between the kids can cut down on the bickering over space, as this mom explains:

> I got one of those Rubbermaid cleaning bins that is divided into two sides with a handle in the middle. Originally, the bin was intended just to give both kids a separate place to put their stuff. However, because it sits between the two kids in the backseat, it actually helps to stop the "Mom, he won't leave me alone," or "She's touching me," or "Mom, he took my _____." Each child gets one side of the bin where they can put their own stuff, and they are separated enough that they don't complain as much about the other encroaching on their space.

# FUN BOXES, BAGS, BOOKS, AND BACKPACKS

When it comes to good behavior, some carschoolers have discovered that an ounce of prevention is worth a pound of cure. Planning in advance to have lots of fun things to do can make all the difference. There is something about the element of surprise or reserving something for a special occasion that generates pleasant company. When my sons were little, I kept two large, sturdy, cardboard office supply boxes with lids in the trunk of my car—one for each boy. We called them "Carschool Boxes," and each of the kids personalized his own with stickers and artistic doodles. I always kept an extra outfit, jacket, and towel for each of them in the box, just in case we found some neat wet and muddy place to explore in our carschool travels. (They always had a warm, clean outfit for the ride home.) The box also contained special toys, games, and activity books that the kids used *only* in the car. My kids were so close in age, and their interests were so similar, that in general I bought two of everything to avoid arguments over ownership of an item and whose turn it was to use it. I went through the boxes periodically and removed what wasn't being used and replaced it with new items the kids would enjoy.

Their eyes would light up at the surprise of new things—and even at seeing "old" things they had forgotten were in the boxes. Now that my sons are in their teens, they keep backpacks in the car with their favorite items to occupy their time. However, I still keep a box of surprise stuff—like magazines, books, audiobooks, crossword puzzles, cards, and even small toys like a Rubik's cube to ease the monotony on long trips. It works like a charm.

Other carschooling parents have also discovered the convenience of special boxes, bags, and backpacks that serve the purpose of keeping the students properly attired, well supplied, and that act as boredom-busters on car excursions. Here are a few inspiring examples.

## The Backseat Fun Box

The backseat fun box was invented by a carschooler. His mom, Mary, explains: "My son created 'the backseat fun box.' It was a simple wooden box (18" × 15" × 8") with a hinged lid that closed with a hook and eye. On the bottom he attached a beanbag (like the one on some lap desks) to keep it level, and he attached two cup holders to the front. The top of the box provides a work surface or a place to play cards. It also provides a place to store stuff and hold drinks. The box acts as a great divider so there are no more 'He's on my side' complaints. We don't use it everyday, but it is great for long trips."

## Fun Books

Fun books accompany Lauren's children on their carschool adventures. She said, "Basically it's a thin, three-ring notebook. I fill it with puzzle pages, travel bingo, math tic-tac-toe, writing practice, and dot-2-dot. (These can be found free on the Internet and printed out on your computer.) I include blank pages for drawing and writing, too. Every month we update the pages. They love to do these in the car!"

## Fun Packs

Dee and her carschoolers use fun packs in the car. She describes them as "small backpacks that fit under the car seat where we keep books, markers, paper, a Walkman, handheld computer games, or even those cards that have history and science trivia questions for different ages. I used to fill them and keep them supplied, but once my kids got older, they were able to do it themselves. Those backpacks stopped the 'I'm bored' whine on trips—even short ones!"

## Wacky Wallets and Photo Albums

Carschool mom Carol invented wacky wallets. What are wacky wallets? Carol explains them this way: "I have an old wallet that I fill with real and fake money, family photos, and coupons that I'll never use (but that look important) that I keep in the glove compartment to entertain my 4-year-old when she starts to get fussy on car trips. She loves to go through it and pull everything out and examine it. I also keep a small photo album in the glove box that contains pictures of friends, relatives, and pets that my 7-year-old likes to flip through as a diversion when he gets a little bored or cranky. I replace the photos occasionally so he's surprised each time he opens it."

## Builder's Box

The builder's box is a favorite of Dona's carschoolers on long trips. She said, "I just took a small plastic box with a lid and filled it with plastic, connecting building toys. I would name something for the kids to build—a radio tower, a space satellite, an alligator—and they would proceed to explore engineering and spatial relationships. They learned perspective this way and more about three-dimensional concepts, too."

## Fun Bags and Boxes

Bags with drawstring closures or boxes with lids can be filled with fun activities created especially for car trips. Carschool mom Marti describes how the tradition of fun boxes got started in her family: "My mom used to give me a Fun Box on long car trips. It was a special surprise. It was a Tupperware box full of age-appropriate stuff like Mad Libs, books, art supplies, travel-size games, decks of cards, lots of snacks, and many different flavors of gum to sample. The container makes a nice lap desk to use along the way, too. I couldn't open the box until I was in the car. I've passed the tradition along to my own children who enjoy it as much as I did."

# PREFERRED CAR AND ADD-ON FEATURES

Carschooling families who spend a lot of time on the road learn quickly what features are most advantageous in a family car. If you're in the market for a new or used car, consider these features that are favored by carschooling families.

## Preferred Car: Van or Mini-Van

Most carschoolers prefer vans because of the roominess and storage capacity, as carschooling mom Marti explains: "We love vans! They have a ton of storage. We've managed to seat seven people, our Lab, Newfoundland, and cocker spaniel, our camping supplies, and two kayaks comfortably for a weekend car trip. Some come with tables kids can play games or draw on. We have a porta-potty in ours that we ordered from REI. In bad weather we can all get in via the side sliding door, shut it, belt everyone up, and comfortably walk up to the front seats without getting wet or cold."

## Preferred Features

### Modular Seating

One carschool mom, Luanne, expressed the advantages of modular seating over bench seating best: "We bought a mini-van with center bucket seats that leave just enough 'personal space' to eliminate a lot of the bickering that goes on in the car, like 'He's touching me!' The space has been a sanity saver for sure, and may well have been a lifesaver because I didn't have those arguments going on while I was driving in traffic."

### Air Conditioning with Multiple Controls

Carschoolers prefer air-conditioning systems with separate passenger controls. That way, the driver and passenger next to the driver can maintain separate temperature controls, and the passengers in the backseats can also adjust the temperature to what is comfortable for them.

### Built-In CD/Cassette Player

All carschoolers agree that a cassette player/CD player is essential for learning through listening to music or audiobooks!

### Appliance Plug-Ins

Carschoolers like plug-in devices that work with car cigarette lighters so that they can use electrical appliances on the road. In most cases, major appliances such as televisions, refrigerators, and coolers can be used for up to 12 hours without too much drain on the car battery.

### Portable Toilet

Next to TVs and electric coolers, portable toilets are a popular add-on feature for carschoolers. Sue, a carschooling mom, said, "We have five kids (ages 19, 17, 8, 5, and 3). We've added a camping toilet to our full-size van (right behind the driver's seat). So whether we're on a field trip or just running around town, I don't have to search for clean restrooms."

### Built-In Headphone Jacks for Each Passenger

Some newer cars offer separate headphones for the backseat passengers. This provides more options, enabling some passengers to listen to an audiotape while others listen to the radio or talk.

## Comments on TV/VCR in Cars

Carschoolers had interesting comments on the trend toward TVs in cars. Although parents see the advantage of watching educational videos or movies—especially on very long road trips of four hours or more—they also lament the overuse of TV as a "plug-in drug." They expressed regret at the loss of conversation, games, and other family bonding opportunities that occur when there are no technological diversions in the car. Their ambivalence on this subject is well represented in Jan's comment:

> When we bought a new van recently, we actually turned down a model that was the exact color we wanted because it *had* a TV in it! We decided that our kids probably watch more TV at home then they truly need to. I'd rather listen to the girls talk among themselves as I learn a lot about them that way. I like to see them just sit back and be content to watch the world around them. Being comfortable with solitude is an important skill. I think it's important to be able to "entertain" yourself inside your own mind without the need for outside stimuli. That said, I would still love to know someone I could *borrow* one of those TV/VCR combos from for the really long trips we take across country to visit family and friends.

## A FINAL WORD OF ADVICE

Plan your carschool trips, including your stops, ahead of time. If you know the ride will take three hours in normal traffic without any stops, plan your departure and arrival time to allow for an extra 30 to 45 minutes. That way, if there is bad traffic, or if you simply want to stop and take a break, you won't have to worry about being on time. If you plan extra time, you can take advantage of roadside opportunities for learning that may come up unexpectedly. Younger children (especially toddlers who are developing gross motor movement) may need to take frequent breaks—about 10 to 15 minutes for every 45 minutes in the car. When you stop, have the kids hop, skip, run, and jump to shake all the sillies out. The trip will go much more smoothly when all of you get a chance to stretch your legs regularly. You won't believe how much more relaxed everyone will be when the pressure of time constraints is lifted.

**Carschooling SCIENCE**

**CHAPTER 3**

EVERY ROAD trip is a science expedition! From the gas station to road kill, the car and the highway offer innumerable opportunities to learn about science. Many of the activities recommended here can be appreciated on different levels by carschoolers of all ages. First, stock up on the tools you will need to learn science while on the road. Then, follow the directions for creating a personalized Carschool Science Journal to record your observations. Finally, try the suggested activities. Turn your car sunroof and windows into a portable planetarium. Use 18-wheeler chemistry to better understand the Periodic Table of Elements. Discover that entomology and bug collecting are just a windshield away! Learn about the five senses and map your taste buds at a favorite drive-through fast food restaurant. Be a roadside ornithologist. Practice road-cut geology and find out how the earth was formed. Try some wacky experiments developed by our carschool mad scientist John McChesney. Discover how everyday things that happen in the car, from shivering to yawning, are an opportunity to explore the "Einstein" within you. You are limited only by your imagination!

# SCIENCE TOOLS

Scientists use a variety of tools to observe their environment and record their findings. You won't need beakers and Bunsen burners in your mobile science laboratory, but having the recommended carschool science tools will enable your student to take advantage of any opportunity for discovery that comes along. Not all of the experiments and activities require tools; however, for optimum use of the ideas in this chapter, here is a list of tools (in alphabetical order) to keep on hand in the car.

**Audiotapes, CDs:** Choose biographies of famous scientists, scientific lectures, songs about planets, nature recordings, birdsongs, stories about scientific expeditions, and whatever else you and your children will enjoy.

**Balloons:** Regular or helium balloons are called for in some activities.

**Binoculars:** Provide one pair for each carschooler. When you spot something interesting on the road, there simply won't be enough time to share the binoculars. It will also help to avoid arguments over who gets to use them.

**Bug collection box:** Keep a see-through container with air holes handy for capturing and observing critters.

**Camera and film:** Use a Polaroid, disposable, or regular camera to capture your discoveries on film.

**Carschool Science Journal:** Provide a 2-inch binder with a variety of papers and dividers for each carschooler; the Science Journal is described in detail in the section following this list.

**Disposable plastic gloves:** Use these for specimen collection.

**Erasers, sharpeners**

**Field guides:** These are good resources for identifying rocks, trees, birds, flowers, animals, reptiles, insects, and fish.

**Glue or cellophane tape**

**Lap desk or clipboard:** This is essential to make writing and recording easier while in the car.

**Magnets:** Provide one set of several sizes of magnets.

**Magnifying glass or jeweler's loop:** Provide one for each carschooler.

**Colored pencils and crayons**

**Paper:** Provide various kinds of paper for tracing, sketching, drawing, and writing.

**Plastic bags:** Two sizes, quart-size and sandwich size, are needed for various purposes.

**Plain white self-adhesive labels:** Use to label specimens.

**Periodic Table of Elements chart**

**Rubber bands**

**Scissors**

**Tweezers or needle-nose pliers:** Use these tools for specimen collection.

**Wax paper**

Now that your carschool laboratory is stocked with nifty equipment, it's time to observe, theorize, record, experiment, analyze, investigate, and conduct some road research in your quest for fascinating and fun answers to cosmic questions.

# Carschool Science Journal

Every passenger in the car needs a Carschool Science Journal. You can buy or make whatever seems practical for you and your children. Begin with a 2-inch binder with a clear plastic pocket on the outside cover. Have each carschooler make a drawing (include his or her name) and slip the artwork into the cover pocket to create a personalized cover. Fill the inside of the binder with plain paper for drawing or sketching, lined paper for writing, clear plastic page protectors, page dividers for different subjects, and a plastic zipper pouch to store pencils, erasers, and sharpeners. The Carschool Science Journal will be used to make notes and/or to sketch or draw a picture about something seen or discussed along the way. Here are some additional uses for the Carschool Science Journal:

★ Write down questions that come up in your carschooling travels for which you have no answer. When you get home, help your carschoolers look up the answers (for example, "Why is the sky blue?").

★ Have carschoolers draw or sketch whatever they see in their car travels that really interests them (animals, trees, flowers, leaves, seeds, acorns, pinecones, bugs, tadpoles, clouds, rivers, birds, lizards, rocks, mountains).

★ Encourage carschoolers to make notes about things they discover along the way. Include the name, date, and time it was found, the location where it was found, and any comments that help them to remember information about it.

★ Use the journal for detailed drawings of items your carschoolers observe through a magnifying glass or jeweler's loop (insect wings, leaves, flower petals, your own fingernail, a coin, a cracker).

★ Mount photographs your carschoolers take in their travels. A Polaroid camera is great for this type of journaling as they get instant results and can paste the photos into their journals right away. Some kids will much prefer taking photos of things that interest them rather than drawing them.

★ Mount dried leaves, pressed flowers, feathers, and other items carschoolers collect as a memento of a place visited or something learned along the way.

## Note to Parents

The Carschool Science Journal is a personal diary that your child should be able to use as desired without too much direction and definitely without critical commentary from you. That's why I recommend that you have one of your own! You can set a silent example by recording and drawing in your own journal, but don't dictate what must go into your child's journal or how it should be maintained. Allow your child to experiment with this type of personal record keeping.

# ASTRONOMY

## Portable Planetarium

Traveling at night? Search for familiar constellations, planets, and stars. One carschooling dad told me about his family's experience, "We have always studied astronomy while traveling in the car at night. One helpful tool was *Tapes of the Night Sky* produced by the Astronomical Society of the Pacific. When we played the audiocassettes it was like having a personal astronomer in the car giving us a guided tour of the galaxy. We learned to identify the Big Dipper and how to use it to help locate the North Star and other constellations. The only problem was that we kept pulling over to get out of the car for a better view of the night sky—so it took a long time to reach our destination. We finally used some of the star maps (included with the tapes) and glow-in-the-dark star stickers to create our own night sky on the ceiling of the car. The kids loved having their own portable planetarium!"

*Ready Resources*
Other carschoolers have suggested these resources to encourage an interest in astronomy while on the road:

*Adventures in the Solar System,* by Goeffrey T. Williams and Dennis F. Regan, is an intriguing story on audiocassette about a 9-year-old boy and a transformer robot named Planetron. The robot takes the boy on a planet-by-planet journey that includes scientific facts. The whole family will enjoy listening. (Out of print, but available through your local library, interlibrary loan, or through out-of-print search at Amazon.com. Worth the extra effort to find it.)

*The Magic School Bus Lost in the Solar System,* by Joanna Cole (published by Scholastic, Inc.), is a book about a lovable and nutty teacher, Ms. Frizzle, and her class who board the Magic School Bus to visit the moon, sun, and each planet in the solar system. Sidebars include information on planet size, temperature, environment, and other unique features.

*Rock 'N Learn's "Solar System"* by Brad and Melissa Caudle (ISBN: 1878489607) is geared for ages 7 and up. It comes with either a CD or an audiocassette with entertaining songs that teach planet order, size, atmosphere, moons, and so forth. The tape is about 40 minutes long with separate songs for each planet. It also comes with a book (small, about 30 pages) that has color photos supplied by NASA. It is available at www.hallaudiobooks.com.

## Dipping Up the North Star

The North Star has long been used to determine direction by navigators. It is also known as Polaris or the Pole Star, because it designates the location of the North Pole of the Earth's axis. (The Earth's axis points to the North Star.) Some people think the North Star is the brightest star in the night sky. It is not—and that can make it difficult to find. Challenge your carschoolers to sort through the heavens for the North Star. Then ask them to say what direction they are traveling based on their sightings.

If your carschoolers need some help in their search, explain that a large constellation that is easy to find points the way to the North Star. It's the Big Dipper, also known as the Big Bear or Ursa Major. Ask your carschoolers to locate the Big Dipper—it looks like a giant ladle or a long handle attached to a rectangular-shaped bowl—and find the two stars at the end of the bowl. They are called the "pointer stars." If your road scholars follow them in an imaginary line or arrow pointing upward, it should lead them straight to the North Star, which is the last star in the tail of the Little Dipper. The North Star doesn't ever seem to change position in the sky and can always be found in the same location. Other stars and constellations move depending on the time of year and even seem to revolve around the North Star.

> **From the Information Highway**
>
> It's a beautiful, sunny day. Ever wonder what the sun is made of? It's a big ball of hot gas, about 75 percent hydrogen and 25 percent helium, with a core temperature estimated at 15,000,000° C.

# CAR SCIENCE

## Stormy Weather

Driving in stormy weather can provide many learning opportunities including driver's safety education. Talk to your kids about how vision is impaired by weather conditions and how the roads are slicker and more treacherous in rainy weather. Explain that cars deposit little drops of oil on the surface of the road. When the rain comes, it loosens the oil from the pavement and makes the road slippery. That can cause cars to slide and swerve. Tell them how important it is to adjust the car's speed to maintain safety. These messages early in life will result in safer drivers in the future.

*Ready Resources*

> *Cars and How They Go,* by Joanna Cole (published by T. Y. Crowell, New York, 1983). The author of The Magic School Bus series explains how cars work in the simplest of terms. Written for the very young or the very uninformed.

# Service Station Science

**From the Information Highway**

Do you live where it snows? Why do road crews put salt on the roads in winter? Salt lowers the temperature at which water freezes (32°F) and so prevents ice from forming that would make roads slippery and dangerous for motorists.

Stopping for gas is a great time to get the kids involved in science. Think of the possibilities. How does a car engine work? Why should you check the air pressure in the tires? What is the purpose of the fuel and fluids used in the car? If you don't know the answers to these questions, consider this carschooling story by Lilah in Oregon:

> I don't know anything about cars—except how to drive them. My mechanically inclined children were fascinated by what was under the hood of our car and asked endless questions that I couldn't answer. One day I asked a service station mechanic to check my transmission fluid. The minute he popped the hood of the car open my kids were out of the car and asking questions. He patiently and thoroughly answered all of their questions. What should have been a 1-minute checkup turned into a 30-minute auto-shop class. He enjoyed the opportunity for "show-and-tell" and invited us to come back any time. Just goes to show . . . you never know where you'll find a good teacher or a good education.

Like the service station mechanic, most people who have knowledge about a subject enjoy sharing it with others. All that you need to do is ask.

# Leslie's Glossary of Car Fluids

Carschooling mom Leslie Pitts is a retired auto mechanics teacher. The Pitts family has been homeschooling for 10 years, and it has provided a lot of opportunity to learn and practice auto mechanics on their dirt-bike motorcycles, which need maintenance constantly. Leslie said, "The rewards for knowing how to fix almost any vehicle are great—but the best was when my older son, Geoffrey's, dirt-biking friend paid him the compliment, 'If I were stuck in the middle of the desert with no tools or parts, I'd want to be stuck with Geoffrey. He can fix anything with nothing!'" Teach your carschoolers more about their "ride" using Leslie's handy glossary explaining some of the fluids used in cars. Then play 20 Questions using their new knowledge.

**Gas:** Gas is a liquid fuel that gives off energy when combined with oxygen and then ignited. In combustion engines, which cars have, the proper mixture of gas and oxygen are allowed into the cylinder and then ignited via a spark plug. Contrary to popular notion, there is not really an explosion that occurs to force the piston down, it is really a calculated burn that produces heat; the heat expands the air to push the piston down. The piston is connected to the crankshaft, which—through many other devices including the transmission, drive shaft, and differential (see page 51)—turns to eventually transmit the energy to the driving wheels (some cars are front-wheel driven, some are rear). A chemical reaction is used to create mechanical energy.

**Additives:** Gasoline is clear, so colorants are added to gasoline so that it can be seen. Additives such as MTBE or alcohol are used to help the gasoline burn cleaner. Organic lead used to be added to help make the engine run more smoothly, but it is no longer used because it was found to be poisonous.

**Oil:** The engine, transmission, and differential all use oil as a lubricant, although in different forms. The two characteristics of oil are slipperiness and viscosity or thickness. The main purpose of oil is to keep metal parts from touching each other; it provides a "cushion" on which parts can move next to each other without locking or "seizing up." Without the proper amount of oil in an engine, parts can slide against each other and shave small pieces off. There is virtually no tolerance (or space) between parts, so even the smallest fragment worn off and deposited in the oil can cause a moving part in an engine to either malfunction or totally seize up. There are different grades of oil available in stores, as indicated by numbers like "20/50" or "30" on the labels. This number indicates the "weight" of the oil. Where there is a dual number, as in "20/50," it means that the oil behaves like a 50 weight in the summer (hot conditions), when it would be preferable for the oil not to become too thin due to heat to coat the parts properly, and a 20 weight in the winter (or cold conditions), when it would be preferable for the oil not to be too thick and thus prevent any movement of the parts. The choice of oil depends on the conditions under which a car will be driven. One particular point regarding oil in a car: When the little red oil light lights up, indicating low oil pressure—*stop the car as immediately as it is safe to do so!* Unlike other situations that are not critical, low oil can lead to immediate engine seizure, and is nothing to relax about!

**Antifreeze/Water:** Burning occurs in engines in the cylinders, which makes the car work, but it creates heat that can be dangerous to the engine if not controlled properly. Built into most engines are "jackets" or ports running around all the internal moving parts. These ports allow the circulation of water and/or antifreeze that are delivered by the water pump. A thermostat opens according to the temperature of the engine to allow the right amount of cooling to take place. The cooling is completed in the radiator, through which the water runs and is cooled by incoming fresh air (the radiator is usually in the front of the car where the wind speed is greatest). Although an engine can tolerate a wide range of temperatures (about 32° to 212°F), operating outside that range can damage an engine. When an engine is subjected to freezing or boiling temperatures, it can expand and crack. Water and antifreeze are used to prevent damage from temperature extremes. Antifreeze contains ethylene glycol. It has a freezing point much lower than water and does not permit freezing of the water in the engine. (Note: Antifreeze is poisonous and care should be taken that pets do not ingest it.) When a car overheats, never try to open the radiator to add water. Boiling water under pressure will behave like a geyser and scald anyone nearby. If a car indicates overheating, sometimes it can help to turn on the car heater with the fan set as high as possible (not much fun on hot summer days, which is when cars are most likely to overheat) and coast whenever possible.

**Brake Fluid:** The brake system in modern cars is a hydraulic system, based on the principle that fluids cannot be compressed. Brake fluid is a thin liquid containing no water (which would cause the brake lines to rust). Through a series of devices, such as the master cylinder (which is the brake fluid reservoir), slave cylinder, brake lines, disc brakes and/or drums, when the brake pedal is depressed, the brake fluid is pushed through the system where it eventually exerts pressure on either the brake shoes (primarily rear wheels), which in turn push against the brake drums or, in the case of disc brakes, the pads, which push against the rotors and cause the car to stop. When air gets into the brake lines of a car, it causes the system to malfunction because air is a gas, and gases can be compressed. Likewise, if the brake lines develop a hole, when the brake pedal is depressed, the fluid will be pressed out and onto the ground and not to the brakes, causing complete failure of the system. That is why emergency brakes are created like bicycle brakes—they are totally mechanical and will operate under any condition.

A common condition that occurs when driving down a mountain is called "brake fade" (frequently incorrectly referred to as brakes "burning"). There are two ways this can happen. Brake fluid should actually be changed every couple of years because water from the atmosphere can be absorbed by the brake fluid in the master cylinder, and water has a considerably lower boiling point than brake fluid (212° vs. 400°). At the point where the brake lines carrying the brake fluid press against the brake pads or shoes, there is so much friction created—enough to stop a car moving at high speeds—it can heat up the lines and the fluid in them past the boiling point of water. If there is water in the brake fluid, it will boil, creating water vapor, which is a gas. As mentioned, gases can be compressed, causing the hydraulic system (the brakes) to malfunction; stepping on the brake pedal will not produce the same results as are normally expected. Sometimes the brake pedal can go all the way to the floor without working at all, or just barely stopping the car! Brake pads and shoes, which are intended to wear out and are the most commonly replaced parts in a brake repair, are composed of a number of different things: metal particles, peanut hulls (which replaced asbestos and, although they are not toxic, do not work as well as asbestos), and glue to hold the particles together. The other cause of brake fade originates from the same heat source—the friction of the pads/shoes gripping the discs/drums, but in the case where no water was in the brake fluid, the glue melts, rises to the surface of the brake pad/shoe, vaporizes, and acts as a lubricant. So in a situation where maximum friction is desired, a condition is created where the brake pads/shoes slip by each other instead of gripping each other. The peculiar smell that accompanies braking too much going down a long hill is the vapor of the melted glue. It is best to shift to low gear, in either an automatic or manual shift car, and continually tap the brakes rather than "riding" them.

**Differential:** This is a set of gears that receive the turning drive shaft and transfer the direction of the energy to the wheel axles, thereby spinning the wheels. The most important feature of the differential is that the gears are arranged to allow the wheels to turn at different speeds. This is important because, when a car is turning (and this is best visualized by a car making a tight turn), the wheel on the inside of the turn obviously has less distance to travel than the wheel on the outside of the turn. The differential makes this possible.

# Ear Popping Air Pressure

Carschool mad scientist John McChesney came up with this activity to understand air pressure and why our ears "pop" as altitude changes. Take a cup and stretch a balloon over the opening so it is tight like a drum. Get everyone in the car and head for a tall hill or a mountain. Pike's Peak is perfect! Actually, all you need is about 1,000 feet elevation gain. As you gain elevation, watch the balloon— and at some point you should hear your brain start to leak out of your ears! No, that's not true (unless you are an airhead). Then, turn the car around and go back down the hill. On the way down, chew some gum, swallow some soda, or yawn. Did everyone's ears pop? Did pop's ears pop? Did the yawning or gum chewing make any difference? Did the balloon change shape?

### Explanation

As we travel upward, we find less and less air above us; this means less pressure on our ears and on everything else. The balloon should have pooched outward as you went higher (unless it became so cold that the air contracted). Your ear drum acts just like the balloon but there is one catch . . . the inner part of your ear has a secret passageway that connects to the back of your throat. This passage is normally closed, but if you yawn, swallow, or even chew gum, the passage can open to let air either go in or out. When this happens we hear a "Pop!" sound.

## Up, Up, and Away

Both regular air-filled balloons and helium-filled balloons can be used to demonstrate the physics of acceleration while riding in the car.

Kris Y. of Pennsylvania said that her son's physics teacher encouraged his students to try this experiment in the car to better understand acceleration and motion forces. Have your carschoolers blow up a balloon with air and tie a string to it. Tie or tape the string to the ceiling of the car so the balloon hangs down. Ask carschoolers to predict what will happen to the balloon when the car accelerates.

### Explanation

When the car is picking up speed, your body feels like it is being pushed back into the seat. But what is really happening is that passengers are staying in place and the car, along with the car seat, is moving forward, and it presses you forward. When the car finally reaches a stable speed and stops accelerating, passengers don't feel like they are being thrust back or pushed anymore. Did your carschoolers predict what actually happened to the balloon?

★    ★    ★

CARSCHOOL MAD SCIENTIST John McChesney thinks carschoolers should try this experiment with helium balloons. Buy a few helium balloons, put them in the car, and go for a ride. Make sure the windows are closed and the fans are off. Have your carschoolers leave a couple of balloons free and tie a string to the others, adding some weight to the bottom of one or two of the balloons so they float without touching anything. As the car stops quickly, do the balloons move forward like passengers do? When you make a sharp turn, do they get "pushed" to the outside?

### Explanation

To understand what's happening to the balloons, imagine the back of a truck full of greased bowling balls and you! When the truck comes to a stop, the bowling balls try to keep going straight so they run into the wall of the truck. They also flow all around you, pushing you away from the wall. In this example, you are the helium balloon and the bowling balls represent the air.

# LIFE SCIENCES

## A Full Moon Ride

Take a ride under the full moon with your carschoolers. The world takes on a completely different perspective at night. Driving in the light of the full moon (especially along country or less-traveled roads) lends enough light to see the landscape and possibly to spy some urban nocturnal creatures such as raccoons, skunks, and opossums. You can often see them after 9 P.M. around sewer grates and garbage cans in many towns.

## A Full Moon Caravan

Organize a full moon carschooling adventure to a local park for a full moon walk! Invite other families to caravan with you to a heavily wooded park after dark on the night of a full moon. (If the park officially closes at sunset, get permission in advance from the park ranger to enter the park after hours.) Walk along a trail with your carschoolers, using just their night vision to see nocturnal creatures (an owl, an opossum, a bat, or maybe a raccoon). When you come to a clearing in a meadow, play Moon Shadow Tag (whoever is "it" tries to step on the shadow of someone else). After the game, sit down for some hot cocoa and cookies and see if your carschoolers can identify a few constellations in the night sky.

On the way home, sing moon tunes: "Moon River," "Blue Moon," "Moondance," "By the Light of the Silvery Moon," "Mr. Moonlight," "Shine on Harvest Moon," "Moonshadow," "Moon over Miami," "Mississippi Moon," and "That's Amore" ("When the moon hits your eye like a big pizza pie . . . that's amore!").

## Turn, Turn, Turn

If you travel the same route over a period of a year, encourage your carschoolers to keep a record of seasonal changes. Look for a natural setting along the way (a park, a community garden, a grove of trees, a field, a bay or lake or river), and at the change of seasons stop at your designated "nature spot" and really look around. What do the plants and trees look like? Are there any animals, insects, or birds? Pay attention to the possibility of migrating birds at certain times of the year. Notice what the squirrels are doing. Encourage carschoolers to sketch or photograph the scene and put their illustrations in their Carschool Science Journal. Tell carschoolers to record the date and time near the photo or sketch. Do this four times during the year on or near the change of seasons:

March 23—Vernal (Spring) Equinox
June 22—Summer Solstice

September 23—Autumnal Equinox
December 22—Winter Solstice

Each time you stop, have your carschoolers compare their sketches to their previous records. At the end of one year, carschoolers' photos and sketches will document the history of the change of seasons where they live.

## Ready Resources

In the Lyrical Learning series of workbooks and tapes, carschoolers ages 10 and up can learn about science by singing about it and reinforce their learning with workbook activities. This is an entertaining and effective combination of scientific information and traditional tunes. Sing "The Scientific Method" to the tune of "Dixie," or "Viruses" to the tune of "Yankee Doodle." Or how about "Oh Bacteria" (to the tune of "Oh Susanna")? Available from Lyrical Learning  (8008 Cardwell Hill, Corvallis, Oregon 97330, 541-754-3579). Textbook and workbook are included along with audiotapes.

### Just for Road Scholars

One of the most obvious changes in seasons occurs in the fall when the leaves of deciduous trees turn color and fall off. Evergreen trees remain green and lush. Have your carschoolers collect one specific kind of leaf and do some research on that tree. They can make sketches or photograph the tree at each season and report what they have learned in their Carschool Science Journal. When it's safe to do so, stop along the road and collect some leaves from both types of trees and compare them. Why do the leaves change color?

*(continues)*

### Explanation

You may know that leaves manufacture food for trees. Did you know that most leaves are multicolored—yellow, orange, and green? You can't see the yellow and orange colors in the spring and summer because the green color or pigment called chlorophyll is predominant as it helps the leaf absorb sunlight. Leaves use sunlight and carbon dioxide from the air to produce sugar or food for the plant in a process called photosynthesis. In the fall, days are shorter and there is less sunlight. With less sunlight, the plant stops making food and the green chlorophyll breaks down, revealing the other pigments (yellow xanthophyll and orange carotene) that were in the leaf all along. The absence of chlorophyll along with the cooler weather causes other chemical reactions to take place in the leaf that form the pigment anthocyanin, which produces purple and bright red colors.

## Leaf Coloration Game

As you drive along, have one person look for leaves on trees. That person calls out a leaf color that they see—green, orange, yellow, red, purple, and brown or black. The first player to correctly identify the scientific pigment name for that color gets five points. The person with the most points in five minutes or five miles wins. Make up a silly song or rap to help your carschoolers learn these scientific names for leaf colors:

> green = chlorophyll (klor-o-fil)
> yellow = xanthophyll (zan-tho-fil)
> orange = carotene (kare-o-teen)
> bright red/purple = anthocyanin (an-tho-si-ah-nin)
> brown/black = no pigment

# Science–Magnified!

Observation is a key tool of scientists. A magnifying glass, or a jeweler's loop with a higher magnification power, will help carschoolers see details and things that they didn't know existed. Encourage them to look at everything they can find in the car—hair, clothing, car seat fabric, seat belts, maps, food, fingernails, skin, scabs, dirt, dried up apple, candy, sandwich crusts, paper, wrappers, other people's hands. When you get to your destination, collect more things to examine with the magnifying glass on the way home such as dirt, feathers, weeds, leaves, flowers, seeds, dead bugs, pond scum (sealed in a plastic bag)—anything! Encourage carschoolers to sketch what they see through the magnifying glass in their Carschool Science Journal. This activity teaches two important scientific skills: observation and recording.

Be sure to talk about what your car students see, too. Ask if they see patterns, geometric shapes, symmetrical pieces, fibers, threads, globules, segments, or strands. Give them the vocabulary words (during the course of normal car conversation) to describe what they see. All of the items they describe are components or building blocks that make up the things that they see. Compare and contrast things and talk about how they are similar or different.

Ask the younger carschoolers to sort the things you have collected into categories: for example, put all of the seeds in one bag, all of

## From the Information Highway

Did you ever notice that bugs that splat on your windshield have different colored blood? Bug blood is called hemolymph. It is clear and composed mostly of water. It is tinged with color, depending on what the bug eats. If the blood is green, the bug ate leaves. If the blood is yellow, it ate nectar from flowers. If the blood is black, the bug ate other bugs. Sometimes you will see what looks like red blood in a squashed insect like a fly. That is not blood, but a pigment from the bug's eyes.

the feathers in another, and so forth. Let them play sorting games by type, color, or shape. Then compare similar things under a magnifying glass. Are they really similar, or are they different? Try to explain how they are alike or dissimilar.

## A Mobile Bug Collection Box

Have you ever driven down the road on a sunny day and noticed lots of insects swarming? Sometimes the unfortunate bugs get splattered on the windshield. If they're not too squished to recognize, have your carschoolers try to identify them. One carschooling family in Illinois pulled into a gas station to clean the windshield after driving through an insect swarm and noticed a number of dead, but intact, bugs in the radiator screen of the car. They pulled a few out and put them in a paper napkin for safe-keeping so that they could refer to a field guide when they got home to identify them. The dad, Cliff, said, "From that point on, whenever we traveled long distances we stopped every so often to collect bug specimens from the radiator. We looked up the bugs in a field guide, identified them, and each person took a turn telling one interesting fact about their bug to everyone in the car. The kids used a magnifying glass to examine the bugs—and that kept them busy during travel time as they traded bugs and inspected them."

### Just for Road Scholars

Here are some additional suggestions for bugging out with your carschooler's insect collection.

**Label the Bugs:** Place bugs in clear plastic bags. Keep sheets of plain white self-adhesive labels handy. After identifying the bug, write its name, along

*(continues)*

with the date, time, and place found on the label. Attach the label to the bag. Carschoolers can mount the bugs in a collection box later.

**Sketch the Bugs:** Dead bugs don't move and are easier to sketch. Carschoolers can make simple sketches of each other's bugs in their Carschool Science Journals. Remind them to look at the bugs through the magnifying glass to see intricate wing patterns and other small features.

**Bug Talk:** When you travel to different places, you may notice that *different* types of bugs will get caught in your radiator. Talk about what makes a bug (or any creature) indigenous to a particular area. (*Hint:* Think about environment, weather, food supply, and so forth.)

**Headlight Entomology:** If you are driving at dusk or at night, slow down and try to spot flying insects that come into view in the headlight beams of the car. Carschoolers will see moths, beetles, mosquitoes, and other flying insects. They may also spot active orb-web spiders in the foliage alongside the road. If it is safe, pull over and observe the spiders in their webs.

# Road Raptors

Birds of prey or raptors, such as kestrels, hawks, eagles, and falcons, can often be seen along roads next to open fields. Raptors perch on telephone poles and fences—good lookout posts for food such as field mice, rabbits, and ground squirrels.

As you drive along the highway, enlist your carschoolers as raptor spotters and help them identify the raptors they see. Notice the tail, feathers, coloration, belly, beak, and talons. Use a good field guide to help your carschoolers identify the species based on that information. Even younger children can look at pictures in field guides and match them to the birds they see. Older children and adults can read the information so that everyone in the car can learn a little more about our feathered friends.

One family turned this bird-watching exercise into a game, awarding points for every raptor spied:

1 point for more common birds like red-tailed hawks
2 points for American kestrels
3 points for falcons
5 points for eagles

Extra points were awarded to carschoolers who could tell an interesting fact about the bird. For example, "Red-tailed hawks hunt mammals by *kiting*." If you don't know what "kiting" is—look it up in a field guide or visit a Web site about raptors.

### Ready Resources

The University of Minnesota has a very informative raptor site, visit it at www.raptor.cvm .umn.edu/. You can also visit the Falcon Cam to see nesting peregrine falcons atop the Rachel Carson State Office Building in Harrisburg, Pennsylvania, at www.dep.state.pa.us/dep/falcon/.

> **From the Information Highway**
>
> Raptors can sit on a high voltage wire and not get electrocuted. However, if they touch two wires or a wire and a pole together, a large voltage of electricity would run through their bodies and electrocute them.

## Name That Tune

Bird watching from the car is much easier with binoculars. If you have time, and the road conditions are safe, pull off the road and look at the birds. Some may be startled and fly away, but others will remain perfectly still so that your carschoolers can get a good look.

Encourage carschoolers to take pictures and mount them in their
Carschool Science Journal, noting the species as well as the time,
date, and location. This is a great way to practice the scientific skills
of observation and recording.

Birdsongs are distinctive, and carschoolers can often identify
the species by their songs. Provide audiotapes or CDs of birdsongs
and encourage your carschoolers to learn to recognize birds from
their distinct calls, as Karen T.'s California family is doing: "We just
bought a book with a CD called *Common Birds and Their Songs*, by
Lang Elliott. The book has photos and information about the birds
and would be interesting by itself, but it's the CD with all those
sounds that makes it really special. Each section of the CD identifies which bird it is, and then the sounds follow. We listened to it
straight through the first time to see what was on the CD, and 65
minutes was a little too much bird sound for me—but my cat loved
it! I was envisioning that my son might use it more as a resource
when he wanted to focus on the sound of one particular bird rather
than a background CD to listen to, but who knows?"

## Ready Resources

Here are some resources to get you started on your birding adventures:

★ Bird books and birdsong CDs are available from the Nature
  Sound Studio (www.naturesound.com/) or through organizations like the National Audubon Society (www.audubon
  .org/).

★ You can also find the recorded songs of a variety of birds for
  free at this Web site: www.enature.com.

★ One of the best field guides for birds is *The Sibley Guide
  to Birds*, written and illustrated by David Allen Sibley for
  the National Audubon Society (New York: Alfred A. Knopf,
  2000).

# Road Kill Zoology (Not for the Squeamish!)

Carschoolers use every opportunity on the road to learn about science including road kill. If you have time to stop the car, and it is safe, you can look at a carcass or what's left of it more closely. Vultures and ants frequently pick over the carrion so that there are only skeletal remains, which provides an opportunity to learn about the anatomy of different animals. Simply look at the carcass. *Do not touch it or disturb it in any way.* Dead animals can harbor various parasites, bacteria, and diseases that can be harmful.

Dana, a carschooling mom with three sons, invented the Road Kill Game. She admits that the game sounds gross, but it does keep her boys (ages 4–9) occupied on long car trips: "Points are based on the species of dead animal seen. A common road kill find around here is opossum, so it's worth 2 points. But a skunk is a little more rare, so it's worth 4 points. We also pick a 'special of the day' and make it worth 10 points. If you can't identify it, you only get one point."

## From the Information Highway

Beatrix Potter, the author of *Peter Rabbit*, used to find dead animals and boil the carcass off of them—then reassemble the skeletons and sketch them. It is said that her understanding of animal anatomy from engaging in this activity is what made her drawings so lifelike.

*Ready Resources*

To learn more about how scientists examine road kill and skeletal remains of animals, read the book *Skulls and Bones* by Glenn Searfoss. It is available through online bookstores such as www.amazon.com.

# Nature Collections

Lots of families collect little treasures from nature and use them as a springboard for studying science. Here are some ideas submitted by carschooling parents:

## Seeds, Cones, and Leaves

Sandi, a carschooling mom, explained that her children enjoy collecting natural things on their car excursions. "We collect pinecones, acorns, seedpods, and leaves from each new location we travel to. We use a field guide to identify our treasures. My kids enjoy making leaf rubbings in the car, too."

### How to Make Leaf Rubbings

You will need a hard surface. Lap desks work well. Place the leaf upside down on the hard surface so that the veins are on top. Put a piece of tracing paper over the leaf. Use the side of an unwrapped crayon to rub across the paper that is over the leaf until you see the image of the leaf appear on the paper. You can save the leaf rubbing as is, or cut it out and mount it in a nature journal, with the name of the tree that the leaf is from, along with the date you found it.

## Flowers

Arianna from California expressed that her daughters enjoy picking a flower as a souvenir of each place they visit. They also use field guides to identify the flowers. She said, "The girls enjoy pressing the flowers and mounting them in an album as a memento of every stop along our route. We use large textbooks that we keep in the trunk of the car to press the flowers."

### How to Press Flowers

Lay a sheet of wax paper down and place a piece of white paper (like computer paper) over it. Place the flower on top. (*Note:* Flat flowers are best for pressing. If the flower has a thick stem base you may need to trim it so that the flower will lie flat on the paper.) Place another piece of wax paper on top of the flower, and carefully place the whole thing inside of a thick book. Close the book and put another book or two on top of it. The flower should be pressed and ready in about two to four weeks. It is ready when it is flat, stiff, and dry. It can be mounted with glue on a sheet of paper. Write the name of the flower and the date and location found under it. Place a clear, see-through sheet protector over it, and put it in your Carschool Science Journal.

*Ready Resources*
Here are some additional resources to help you get your carschoolers interested in life sciences:

★    *Explorabook: A Kid's Science Museum in a Book,* by John Cassidy is published by Klutz Press. It contains activities on everything from magnetism to biology and includes tools to use in the activities that are bound into the book, such as a magnet, Fresnel lens, and even agar growth medium. Of course, carschoolers can't do all of the experiments while traveling—but they can do some of them.

★    *Acorn Naturalists Catalog* contains hundreds of resources for studying science. Tools, kits, jeweler's loops, magnifying glasses, videos, books, tapes, and more for the trail, for the classroom, and for carschooling. Call 1-800-422-8886 or visit their Web site: www.acornnaturalists.com

# 20 Questions with Plants and Animals

A truly classic game, 20 Questions can be played by all ages. One person thinks of the object that the other players must guess. The players get to ask 20 questions to figure out the correct answer. The questions must be asked in such a way that they can be responded to with "yes" or "no." Michelle and her carschoolers take turns, letting one person pick an animal or plant and the others ask questions to try to figure it out. As she describes it, "The kids (ages 6 and 5) usually pick something we have recently studied or that they read about in *Zoobooks* (www.zoobooks.com) and *Ranger Rick* (www.nwf.org/rangerrick/) magazines. They love to fool mom and dad by picking plants and creatures that we know little about—so it is a real confidence builder for them."

# THE FIVE SENSES

Human beings have five distinct senses; sight, smell, taste, hearing, and touch. The following activities are designed to explore each of your five senses while traveling in the car.

## Dilating Duo

The sense of sight is one of our five senses. Talk to your carschoolers about their eyesight. How do we see? How do our eyes react to light? Here's an activity two carschoolers can do in the car to demonstrate pupil dilation: Have your carschoolers face each other and look at each other's eyes. One covers his or her right eye with a hand (keeping both eyes open) for about 20 seconds. Then the hand is removed and the other carschooler watches as his or her partner's right pupil shrinks! Take turns so that both carschoolers have the opportunity to see the eyes in action.

### Explanation

The pupils of our eyes get larger or smaller depending on the amount of light available. Pupils dilate (or open wide) when it's dark to get as much light as possible so that we can see. They get smaller when it is very bright or light.

> **From the Information Highway**
>
> Have you ever gotten into the car first thing in the morning or late at night when it's cold? If you have, you probably shivered. Why do we shiver? We shiver to get warm. When we are cold, muscles in our bodies make rapid contractions and that generates heat that warms us up.

## Your Memory Stinks!

Did you know that your sense of smell improves your memory? This activity takes a bit of advance preparation, but it's fun to take along in the car to prove the point.

You will need (1) a shoebox with 8 to 10 items in it that don't have an odor (i.e., a deflated balloon, a paper clip, a spoon, a battery, a cotton swab, a sock, a comb, a roll of tape), (2) another shoebox with 8 to 10 items that have strong odors (i.e., a lemon, a clove of garlic, a cinnamon stick, a tea bag, a flower, perfume, a permanent marker pen, Wintergreen Lifesavers), and (3) enough pencils and paper for everyone.

When you get in the car, pass around the shoebox with the odorless items. Let everyone look at and touch the items. Then put a lid on the shoebox and place it out of sight (on the floor). Give everyone a piece of paper and a pencil and ask them to write down what was in the box to the best of their recollection. Next, pass around the shoebox with the smelly objects in it. When everyone has seen it, put the lid on the shoebox and place it out of the way. Ask everyone to write down what they saw. Compare the lists. You will find that people remember more objects in the box that had items with a distinct smell.

### Explanation

The centers for memory and smell are close to each other in the brain—so the recollection of an odor can trigger a memory.

## Drive-Through Taste Test

You have taste buds on the front, back, and both sides of your tongue that distinguish the tastes of sweet, sour, salt, and bitter. The next time you go to a drive-through restaurant, have carschoolers use their lunch to figure out which taste buds on their tongue control those tastes. You can use these lunch items for this activity: soda pop (not sugarless kind), french fries (and a packet of salt), dill pickle chip, and iced tea (no sugar or artificial sweetener).

Have carschoolers put their straw in their soda and then pull it out and touch a drop of soda to each section of their tongue. Ask which part tastes the sweetness of the soda and have carschoolers make a note of it. Next have carschoolers dip a french fry lightly in the salt packet and touch it to each section of their tongue. Ask which part tastes the salt and have carschoolers make a note of it. Do the same with a dill pickle chip (from their hamburger) and ask which part of their tongue tastes the sourness. Then, have the students put their straw in the iced tea, pull it out, and touch a drop of tea to each section of their tongue. Ask which part tastes the bitterness of the plain tea. Ask the kids to make a map of their tongues' taste buds in their Carschool Science Journal by drawing a picture of their tongue showing the location of the sweet, sour, salt, and bitter sections.

## The Sound of Sirens

Hearing is an important sense for drivers. It helps to be able to hear traffic, horns, trains, trucks, and other vehicles. Have you ever noticed that the sirens on ambulances and fire trucks sound different as they pass you on the road? The sound waves are close together as they approach you so the pitch sounds higher. The sound waves spread out as they pass you and the pitch sounds lower. The change in the pitch of the siren is known as the Doppler Effect, named after Christian Johann Doppler, an Austrian who developed the principle in 1842. Carschool mad scientist John McChesney offers this experiment to test the Doppler Effect.

Take your carschoolers on an outing. At some point out in the middle of nowhere make up a reason to drop off one parent and the kids at the side of the road and then drive away (maniacal laughter is optional). Drive down the road until you are out of sight, then turn around and head back toward the hapless, stranded family members at a high rate of speed (within the limit). When you can see them again, hold the horn down the whole time until they are way behind you. If you ever see them again, ask them what the horn sounded like. When the honking car went by them, they should have heard the sound change from a higher pitch to a lower pitch.

## Getting in Touch

Teach your carschoolers about their sense of touch on your next car trip. Get a large shopping bag and put into it 10 to 15 things that have a distinct texture, such as a cotton ball, steel wool, sandpaper, an eraser, a scrap of velvet, a safety pin, a sandwich baggie, a walnut, a quarter, a lemon, a rubber band, a ping pong ball, a screw, crumpled aluminum foil, jacks, golf tees, and a leaf or a flower. Write down all of the things that are in the bag on a piece of paper. Write each carschooler's name on the paper. Pass the bag around and count how many things each player can identify correctly by touching without looking. Set a time limit. (Give younger carschoolers more time to feel the objects than older children.) The person who identifies the most objects correctly wins!

### From the Information Highway

On a warm day the inside temperature of a closed car gets hot. If you get into the car, you may start to sweat. Your body sweats to cool itself down. Sweat glands in your skin release water. As the water evaporates, it absorbs heat from your skin and cools you down.

Don't stop there! Go down the list and talk about what each item felt like. Pull items out of the bag one at a time and let everyone touch them again. Compare and contrast the objects. What feels smooth, rough, prickly, sticky, soft, brittle, sharp, or slick? Discuss what it might be like to lose your sense of touch. What if you couldn't feel something hot? What if you couldn't feel something sharp? What could you do to remedy that? There is no "right" answer; just encourage carschoolers to think about the problem and try to find possible solutions.

# PHYSICAL SCIENCES

## Ever Hear a Rubber Band?

Carschool mad scientist John McChesney offers this sound experiment to try on the road. Buy a cheap bag of assorted sizes of rubber bands and let your carschoolers take turns holding different types out the window or sunroof while driving at freeway speeds if it is safe to do so. They will shortly discover that the stretched rubber band vibrates and can make a variety of sounds. Try cutting holes in some small boxes and stretching the rubber band over the opening and holding that in the wind as well. Tie a stout string to the box so it can't escape! Did the rubber band vibrate faster or slower the more it was stretched? Did fat ones sound the same as skinny ones? Did the box make any difference?

### Explanation

These rubber bands act just like your vocal chords; stretch them tight for a high pitch and loosen them for a lower pitch. Heavier rubber bands vibrate more slowly and have a lower pitch. The box acts like your mouth—it is a resonant cavity that can amplify and modify the sound.

## Making Mouth Sparklers

When driving at night (it must be dark) give your carschoolers each a pack of WintOGreen Lifesavers. Tell them to chew the candy with their mouth open and they will see sparks! Have the students suggest reasons for what causes the sparks.

### Explanation

This two-part phenomenon is called triboluminescence. When you crush sugar crystals with your teeth, they split apart with positive charges on one side and negative on the other, and emit an invisible ultraviolet light. It's very difficult to see the light with most sugar crystals. However, Wintergreen Lifesavers have another ingredient that makes the light brighter. Methyl salicylate, the flavor ingredient, absorbs the ultraviolet light and emits it as visible light.

## Sticky Science

Experimentation is a key component of the scientific method. Cars may not be the ideal place for beakers and Bunsen burners, but magnets will transform any car into a science lab for experimentation on what sticks and what doesn't. You can purchase magnets in all shapes and sizes at most hardware stores. Every magnet has a north pole and a south pole. Poles that are alike (for example, two south poles) repel one another. Poles that are different (one north, one south) attract each other. Different kinds of metals such as copper, iron, nickel, aluminum, steel, brass, zinc, gold, and silver will react differently to magnets.

Have your carschoolers experiment with their magnets to find the north and south poles. Tell them to push the ends of two magnets together. Do they repel or attract? Some items are very strongly attracted to magnets, and some things are just slightly attracted. Bring along a little bag of items for your carschoolers to test. Have them predict the results before they test each one. Here are some items to include: paper clips, coins, hairpins, a piece of aluminum foil, rocks with minerals, a spoon, nails, screws, and nuts and bolts.

Also, have them try the magnets on things in the car such as door handles, pens, jewelry, seat belt buckles, lipstick cases, belt buckles, shoe buckles, rivets on jeans, and clasps on purses or backpacks to see what affect the magnet has on them. Have carschoolers put a paper plate between an object and a magnet that attracts and see if they can make the object move "invisibly" on the top of the paper plate with the magnet hidden below it. If you ask your carschoolers to predict the results before doing the experiment, they learn two more elements of the scientific method: prediction (hypothesis) and experimentation.

*Note:* Keep small items (paper clips, screws, and so forth) out of the reach of small children to prevent choking hazards. Also, to avoid damage, do not put magnets on computer screens of any kind— whether a laptop computer, a GPS, or a handheld electronic game.

# 18-Wheeler Chemistry

Some truckers haul hazardous materials and chemicals, and hazardous material codes are posted on these trucks to alert emergency service crews to the type of chemical being hauled. In the event of an accidental spill, crews can then take the necessary steps to protect people and the environment. Your carschoolers can use a code chart to determine what chemicals the trucks they see on the road are hauling. Then, using a Periodic Table of Elements, they can look up the chemical to learn its symbol and atomic weight and number. Following is a list of some of the hazardous materials codes you might see on trucks (and the corresponding element).

There are thousands of codes for hazardous materials. Many of the substances are chemical compounds. If you have an *Emergency Response Guidebook*, your carschoolers can look up more common codes like 1202 which is diesel fuel and read about some of the chemical elements of their composition.

## Hazardous Materials Codes

| Element | ID Code # | Hazardous Material | Potential Hazard |
|---|---|---|---|
| Arsenic (As) | 2760 | Arsenical Pesticide | Toxic, may be fatal if inhaled, ingested, or absorbed through skin |
| Carbon (C) | 1013 | Carbon Dioxide | Vapors may cause dizziness/asphyxiation |
| Helium (He) | 1046 | Helium Gas | Vapors may cause dizziness/asphyxiation |
| Hydrogen (H) | 2015 | Hydrogen Peroxide | Toxic, inhalation, ingestion, contact (skin, eyes) with vapors, dust, may cause injury, burns, or death |
| Iron (Fe) | 2793 | Ferrous Metal Shavings | Potential fire and explosion and/or health hazard |
| Nitrogen (N) | 1977 | Liquid Nitrogen | Vapors may cause dizziness/asphyxiation |
| Oxygen (O) | 1073 | Liquid Oxygen | Vapors may cause dizziness/asphyxiation |
| Sulfur (S) | 1830 | Sulfuric Acid | Toxic, inhalation, ingestion, contact (skin, eyes) with vapors, dust, may cause injury, burns, or death |

## *Ready Resources*

★ Bar Charts, Inc. sells laminated charts for every subject, including the Periodic Table of Elements. You can order one directly from their Web site at www.barcharts.com.

★ A complete list of codes, a description of the materials, the harmful effects, and the recommended emergency procedures are included in the *Emergency Response Guidebook*. It is available in government bookstores located throughout the United States, or you can download the entire guide for free online at: www.tc.gc.ca/canutec/erg_gmu/erg2000 _menu.htm.

## 20 Questions with Famous Scientists

Lacey of Nebraska and her family play 20 Questions to guess the name of a famous scientist. One person thinks of the name of a scientist. The players then take turns asking questions that can be answered with a "yes" or "no." For example, a player might ask: "Is the scientist a woman?" "Was she a chemist?" "Did she discover radium?" (Marie Curie) "Is the scientist a man?" "Did he develop the Theory of Relativity?" (Albert Einstein) After 20 questions are asked, if the players have not already guessed the answer, each player gets a last chance to make a guess. Then a new player tries to stump the group. Lacey related that "the result of playing this game has been that my kids (ages 9, 13, and 15) have begun researching scientists in order to stump the other players. Both the encyclopedia and the *Usborne Book of Scientists from Archimedes to Einstein* have been useful."

## Road Cut Geology

A "road cut" is a place where highway construction workers blasted through hillsides to make the road. It shears away the hillside so that you can see a cross section of the sedimentary layers of the Earth's crust. You will see horizontal layers of sandstone and limestone, and depending on where you are, you might even see fossilized remains such as seashells and shark's teeth—remnant sediment of ancient seas that once covered the land. Carschoolers can use a field guide to identify the different layers. You can see road cuts along most highways, but you've got to keep your eyes open for them. It's a good game for the kids to see who can spot a road cut first. If it's safe, pull over and stop to investigate. It will lead to great discussions about how the Earth formed and maybe even to collections of rocks and minerals. Kids will spend hours inspecting rocks (and everything else) collected along the way.

### Ready Resources

A jeweler's loop (similar to a magnifying glass but with more powerful magnification) is an excellent tool to use to examine rocks and minerals to see the variegated formations. Jeweler's loops are available from Acorn Naturalists at 1-800-422-8886 or online at www.acornnaturalists.com.

*Roadside Geology* published by Mountain Press is a series of books written by professional geologists for people who want to learn something about the rocks and landforms they see as they travel down the road. There are 23 titles in the series focusing on individual states in the U.S. with more planned for publication. Each book includes a detailed discussion of landforms in particular state regions, a series of road guides so that you can find the landforms and investigate them, and maps, photographs, and illustrations. For more information visit: www.mountain-press.com.

# WEATHER SCIENCE

## Sunroof Observatory

Does your car have a sunroof? If so, you have a mobile sky observatory. Open the roof and see what's up! Even by just looking out the windows carschoolers can observe and identify cloud formations.

Clouds are made up of water droplets and/or ice crystals and come in some basic shapes that have scientific names. Here are the most common:

> *Cirrus clouds* received their name from a Latin word that means "curl of hair." The clouds are white, thin, and wispy looking, often with curly ends. They are located high in the sky and are mostly composed of ice particles.

> *Cumulus* comes from a Latin word that means "heap." The clouds look like a heap of cotton puffs or popcorn. They are closer to the Earth than cirrus clouds and are made up of water droplets and ice crystals.

> *Stratus* means "layer," and the clouds appear low and flat or thin and usually blanket the sky in sheets. They are closest to the Earth and are composed mainly of water droplets and are associated with rain.

> *Nimbus* refers to rain. These cloud formations in combination with others in multilayers and levels are usually dark and bring lots of precipitation. They are also responsible for lightning, thunder, hail, strong winds, tornadoes, and other severe climatic conditions.

> **From the Information Highway**
>
> Fog is a low stratus cloud that has made contact with the ground.

From their car observatory, challenge your carschoolers to name that cloud (1 point) and tell some facts about it (2 points for each fact).

## Capture the Cloud Game

The next time you drive through a fog bank, have your carschoolers roll down the windows for just a minute to see what a cloud feels

**From the
Information Highway**

Are you safe in the car
during a lightning
storm? The answer is
yes, but not for the rea-
son that many people
think. Do you think the
tires protect you from
electrical shock if the car
is struck by lightning?
The tires would have to be
solid rubber and almost
one mile thick to provide

*(continues opposite)*

like—cold, moist, and thin as air! Then tell the kids to roll the windows up fast to see if they can capture a part of the cloud in the car. Does it work? Try it and see!

## Clouds: The Ultimate Shape-Shifters

Almost everyone has gazed at cloud formations and seen the shapes of animals, mythical creatures, and other things. When carschooling, search for geometrical shapes (circles, squares, rectangles, hexagons, pentagons, pyramids, cones, cylinders, triangles, diamonds). When your carschoolers see a geometrical cloud shape, tell them to call it out. If the others agree, that person gets 2 points. *Bonus:* The first to find a patch of blue sky in a star shape peaking through the clouds gets 5 points. The first person to get 20 points wins.

## Weather Watchers

Weather is easily observed through car windows and prompts scientific discussion. Talk about how it impacts the natural environment. What do spring rains do to winter snow? Talk about the water cycle including concepts like *precipitation* and *evaporation*. Does your car have an outside temperature gauge in it? That can lead to an entire discussion about equipment that measures weather such as a barometer (measures atmospheric pressure), hygrometer (measures humidity), and a psychrometer (measures the amount of moisture in the air).

When having conversations with your kids, give them as much accurate information as you can. If you don't know the answer, admit it. Then ask the kids to write down the question in their Carschool Science Journals. When you get home, show your carschoolers how to find the answers to their questions on the Internet or at your local library.

*Ready Resources*

★ *The Kid's Book of Weather Forecasting*, by Breen and Friestad, teaches kids (ages 7–13) how to record their observations and predictions about clouds and wind patterns. They can even learn to graph weather trends and build their own rain gauge. Available at bookstores and libraries.

★ *Skywatching: A Video Guide to the Daytime Sky*, is a fascinating video with discussions about the sun, clouds, wind, rain, storms, hurricanes, and more. In forty minutes you will learn how to interpret what you see in the daytime sky. Geared for ages 9 to adult. It is available from Acorn Naturalists (1-800-422-8886).

★ An Internet search engine such as www.askjeeves.com or www.google.com is a quick way to find information; type in the key words "seasons" or "weather."

enough protection! So what does protect you? Believe it or not, it's the metal cage of the car that surrounds you. This is due to the Farrady or Skin Effect, which says that electricity (such as lightning) dissipates or travels only on the surface area of enclosed metal objects. So as long as you are inside the car, you should be safe.

# Guess the Wind Speed

Here is a good example of what one family learned because a carschooler asked a simple question about the wind:

We were driving in the car on a windy day. The trees were swaying, and as we drove across a bridge I complained that the wind was blowing the car all over the road. My son asked, "Do you think the wind is blowing at hurricane speed?" I assured him it was not. He persisted, "How fast is the wind blowing?" I had no clue. I turned the radio on and learned from the weather reporter that we could expect winds of up to 40 miles per hour that day. My son said, "That's pretty fast. How fast does the wind usually travel?" I suggested we look that up when we got home. We did, and to our amazement learned that in 1806 Admiral Sir Francis Beaufort (1774–1857) created a simple rating system to estimate wind speed at sea and its effect on the sailing rigs of the British Navy. His system was adapted to determine wind speed and its effects on land as well. His rating system is called the Beaufort Wind Scale and is used to this day. We found a copy of the scale compiled by the U.S. National Weather Service and used it when we were in the car to determine how fast the wind was blowing. In fact, we turned it into a game. We each took turns looking at the landscape to see the effect the wind was having on it. Then we tried to guess the wind speed.

Use the Beaufort Wind Scale shown here to play Guess the Wind Speed with your carschoolers when you're on the road.

## How Far Away Is the Lightning?

The car provides you with an opportunity to be out in the storm without getting wet. You can observe weather phenomena and use it as a teaching moment. If you see a flash of lightning, for example, explain to the kids that they can figure out how far away it is using this simple method: Watch for a flash of lightning in the distance. Then start counting the seconds until you hear the thunder (one Mississippi, two Mississippi, and so on). Each five seconds that you count is equal to one mile. If you count 25 seconds, the lightning flash was five miles away.

**Beaufort Wind Scale**

| Wind Speed (mph) | Wind Effects Observed on Land | Terms Used in NWS Forecasts |
|---|---|---|
| 0–1 | Calm; smoke rises vertically | Calm |
| 1–3 | Direction of wind shown by smoke drift, but not by wind vanes | Light |
| 4–7 | Wind felt on face, leaves rustle, ordinary vane moved by wind | Light |
| 8–12 | Leaves and small twigs in constant motion; wind extends light flag | Gentle |
| 13–18 | Raises dust and loose paper; small branches are moved | Moderate |
| 19–24 | Small trees in leaf begin to sway; fresh crested wavelets form on inland waters | Moderate |
| 25–31 | Large branches in motion; whistling heard in telephone wires; umbrellas used with difficulty | Strong |
| 32–38 | Whole trees in motion; inconvenience felt walking against the wind | Strong |
| 39–46 | Breaks twigs off trees; generally impedes progress | Gale |
| 47–54 | Slight structural damage occurs; chimney pots and stales removed | Gale |
| 55–63 | Seldom experienced inland; trees uprooted; considerable structural damage occurs | Whole gale |
| 64–72 | Very rarely experienced inland; accompanied by widespread damage | Whole gale |

# Just Married—A Test for Wind Resistance

Carschool mad scientist John McChesney came up with this idea to test for wind resistance. Get some poster paint and mix in a little detergent so it will come off easily, and decorate the car as though you just got married. Then tape dozens of short, medium-length, and long, red and white streamers of crepe paper all over the car. Drive through town honking the horn and waving at complete strangers. When you come to a quiet road, set up some chairs and a table with a red and white checkered tablecloth (candles optional), put out some snacks, and let the children settle down and watch the streamers as you drive by at different speeds. (This is especially cool if you have a convertible or a truck.) Did the streamers all get blown straight back? Did the red ones do anything different than the white ones? Did the length of the streamers make any difference?

### Explanation

Car designers use this technique to show if the air is flowing smoothly around the car so that there is less wind resistance. If your streamers were swirling backward, that means *suction* on the car was holding it back. Race car drivers call this area of suction a *slip stream* and try to get real close to the leading car so that they can take advantage of this free ride.

# THE SCIENCE OF EVERYDAY THINGS

Every moment spent in the car is an opportunity to learn. Never underestimate the science in everyday things. The next time you run out of ideas for science, look around and notice what is happening and think of explanations to share with your carschoolers. For example: Did someone in the car yawn? What causes that? It can be the result of being sleepy or bored, or it may indicate a lack of oxygen. Yawning helps us breathe in a large amount of air. Yawning is involuntary—and contagious! If you see someone else yawn, you will probably yawn, too.

You see? Science is everywhere!

# Carschooling MATH

# CHAPTER 4

**K**IDS ARE eager to learn, from the minute they wake up in the morning until they hop into bed at night. Some kids may resist schooling, but they rarely resist learning—especially if they can see the relevance of a subject to their own lives. A discussion about how math is used every day can help them to see that it is worth their while to learn. As you are driving, ask your carschoolers to spot ways math is used for road signs, mileage markers, in advertisements on billboards, at fast-food restaurants, at gas stations, and so forth. These observations help kids to see that math is everywhere and that everyone needs or uses it at some point in their lives. Make it as fun as possible and learn together by playing games. Math really lends itself to this idea.

As you drive from place to place, encourage your kids to look around and find numbers—they are everywhere! You will find them on houses, buildings, street signs, buses, trucks, taxis, license plates, speedometers, clocks, outdoor thermometers, and so many more places. Encourage your kids to count, add, subtract, multiply, and divide the numbers they see. Not only is this a practical way to learn and practice math skills, but it reinforces the message that learning math is useful and fun.

In this chapter you will find all kinds of math activities to do in the car. Sing subtraction drills to the tune of "100 Bottles of Juice on the Wall" or rock 'n' roll your way through the multiplication tables. Discover the drive-by math games Marnie Ridgway, a physicist and professional math tutor, uses when she and her daughters go on road trips. You've heard of counting sheep? Try estimating the number of cows on a hillside, or how many bugs will be stuck in the radiator grill of the car by the end of the trip. Use the license plate numbers of other cars to practice math facts. Explore "E-Car-Nomics," using money as a math manipulative. Measurement, fractions, percentages, and dashboard decimal drills are all included—start your engines and enjoy miles of math!

# MATH TOOLS

Many of the math activities and games in this chapter don't require any tools at all. There are, however, a few that do. Get into the habit of stocking up on the tools you will need to play games and conduct activities *before* you go on a trip. That way, you will always be prepared to play and learn when the opportunity comes along. Here is a list of tools you will need for carschool math:

Analog (not digital) wrist-
    watch or clock
Ball of string or yarn
Calculator
Cellophane tape
Cloth measuring tape

Coins, a miscellaneous assortment
    (pennies, nickels, dimes, quar-
    ters, half dollars, and dollars)
Currency, including at least one
    of each of these bills: $1, $5,
    $10, $20

Deck of regular playing cards

Dimes (at least a roll, perhaps more)

Flash cards (numbers, addition, subtraction, multiplication, and division)

Magnifying glass

Odometer (mileage counter/ tracker)

Paper or notepads and graph paper

Pencils with erasers

Plastic containers (two small ones)

Red marker pen and green marker pen

Scissors

Treats for prizes (for example, raisins, M&Ms, peanuts, pennies)

# DRIVE-BY NUMBERS

Marnie Ridgway is a physicist, math tutor, and carschool mom who lives and works on the San Francisco peninsula. Here are some of her tips for playing math games in the car: "Do you play any math games with your family requiring a random number generator— like dice or a spinner? Use car license plates or roadway signs to generate those numbers. An example is passing a car and adding all the numbers on its license plate, or adding and subtracting alternate numbers, or multiplying all the numbers, or making a number out of the digits and factoring it and so on." Here are some other math games that use license plates to generate numbers.

## Count Me In!

Use numbers found on car license plates and roadway signs to find numbers in chronological order. It's pretty easy for 0 to 9. Finding double-digit numbers gets harder because of the rule that both digits must be on the same license plate or sign, even though they don't have to be in the right order. Triple-digit numbers don't have to have all the digits on the same sign, but you do have to find the digits in the proper order. Here are some variations on the counting game:

**Odds and Evens:** One person counts only odd numbers (1, 3, 5, 7, . . .) and the other person counts even numbers (2, 4, 6, 8, . . .).

**Count Number Families:** One person counts multiples of 2 (2, 4, 6, 8, . . .) and another counts multiples of 3 (3, 6, 9, 12, . . .) or multiples of 5 (5, 10, 15, 20, . . .).

**Count Backward:** Count backward from 20 (20, 19, 18, . . .). Now try it with odds or evens or by number family.

## Play "21"

Each player looks for license plates with numbers that add up to 21 or more. License plates with three or more numbers are the only ones that will work for this game. For example, license number 4VJD875 would add up to 24. When players find a license that adds up to 21 or more, they call it out and earn a point. First player to get 10 points wins.

## My Number Is "Greater Than" Your Number

Here's a quick game to help kids understand the math concepts of "greater than," "less than," and "equal to." Everyone finds one license plate on a passing car and copies it down on a piece of paper. Remove the letters in the license plate, leaving just the numbers. Each person takes a turn reading his or her license plate number. For example, if the license is 1JLR297, the number would be 1,297. Compare your number with the numbers of the other players. Whose is the largest? Whose is the smallest? Are any numbers the same or equal? Are the other numbers greater than, less than, or equal to your number? Now, write the other players' numbers down on your paper. Using the mathematical symbols for "greater than" (>), "less than" (<), and "equal to" (=), write down the results.

## *Ready Resources*

One of the greatest carschooling resources is the *Guinness Book of World Records*. It has many practical uses for math in it that help kids see how math is used in the real world. It includes statistics, facts, and figures on the greatest speed achieved by a human being; circumnavigations by balloonists, ships, and airplanes; the highest mountain; the deepest ocean; survival records; the biggest galaxy; the longest jump; the largest bubble gum bubble; the longest fingernails; the most petted dog; the biggest Barbie doll collection; the richest person; the oldest tightrope walker; the highest hotel; the fastest tap dancer, and much, much more. It will often inspire kids to measure, calculate, and estimate their own feats while trying to set records of their personal bests. It's a great read in the car and a wonderful conversation stimulator, not to mention a really fun and practical example of the ever-present world of numbers.

# Rounding Up License Plates

Leslie Pitts of California suggests using license plates in learning to round numbers. She said, "As we see a car go by, I challenge my son to 'Round that number to the nearest ten (hundred, and so on).' He enjoys this form of practice because it's like a game, and a speedy response is required because the cars drive away so quickly."

Ask your carschoolers to pick a license plate on a passing car and write down the number. Remind them to eliminate the letters; for example, a license plate that reads 4HGB980 would become 4,980. Once they have their own special number, have carschoolers estimate the difference between their own number and a license plate number on a passing car. Sometimes it is easier to round up or down when estimating. Try rounding to the nearest 10, 100, or 1,000.

# License Plate Equations

All of the players in the car pick a license plate number together, for example, 9MBR318. Eliminate the letters, which leaves the numbers 9, 3, 1, and 8. Using only the numbers from the license plate and the processes of addition, subtraction, and multiplication, each player tries to create as many new numbers as possible from 1 to 10 in a designated time frame. Here are some new equations using the numbers in our example:

$$9 - 8 = 1$$
$$9 - 8 + 1 = 2$$
$$3 \times 1 = 3$$
$$9 - 8 + 3 = 4$$
$$8 - 3 = 5$$

$$9 - 3 = 6$$
$$9 - 3 + 1 = 7$$
$$8 \times 1 = 8$$
$$9 \times 1 = 9$$
$$9 \times 1 + 1 = 10$$

The first carschooler to make equations that represent all 10 numbers wins. If no one can make all the numbers from 1 to 10, the person who made the most numbers from 1 to 10 wins. Carschoolers can create some very complicated equations to get the numbers they need, but remind them that they can only use the numbers in their license plate.

## Ready Resources

Learning Wrap-Ups are a great tool to use in the car. They consist of bookmark-sized plastic game cards that are notched. The player uses a precut piece of string/yarn that is supplied to wrap around the board while following a number sequence and pattern of math facts. The back of the board is etched with the correct pattern that the wound string should ultimately resemble if the player knows his or her math facts. Learning Wrap-Ups are available in addition, subtraction, multiplication, division, fractions, and pre-algebra. They also have Wrap-Up Rap CDs that you can use to drill math facts in the car, while using Learning Wrap-Ups. Go to their Web site (www.learningwrapups.com) to order their products and even download lesson plans.

## Where Is My Place?

To start the game, select one person to be the impartial "Caller" to randomly call out the cars that are to be used. That person assigns a passing car to each player in each round of the game, to avoid duplication or arguments. For example: The first set of cars that drive by is for the ones place. The Caller says, "Player one gets the green Volvo on the left. Player two gets the brown Toyota on the right." Each player then chooses the largest number from the license plate of the car he or she was assigned and writes it down in the ones place. The object of the game is to learn about place value, and each player uses car license plates to collect the numbers needed to create the largest number in any given place value. The next set of cars that drive by is for the tens place—each player chooses a number from a newly assigned car license plate and puts it in the tens place. Play continues in this manner through the highest place value that has been predetermined by the players. The person with the largest number when all place values have been filled wins! You can change this game by trying to get the *lowest score* in each place value, or let your carschoolers decide if they are going "high" or "low"—they must declare before play begins. This variation will produce two winners and is fun to try when you have a car full of road scholars.

> **From the Information Highway**
>
> The average speed of cars traveling on highways during commute times is 35 mph.

## You Can Count on It

Tired of looking at license plates and road signs for math games? Try these alternatives.

**Count Cows:** Two players, one sitting on each side of the car, count the cows on their side of the road. Carschoolers must count fast and add that number to their old number. When carschoolers pass a fast-food hamburger restaurant on their side of the road, all their cows are left there and they start back at zero. First one to count to 100 wins.

**Count Bugs:** Carschool mom Sher says her family counts Volkswagen Bugs. As players spot VW Bugs, they call out the color of the car they spot (to prevent two players from calling the same one) and score one point for each Bug. Players keep a running total of the number of Bugs they count. If a player spots a VW Van, it counts as 4 Bugs. The player with the most points at the end of the game wins. Carolyn's family counts real bugs as they drive in the car. She says, "I know this sounds gross, but we guess how many real bugs will get smooshed on the windshield. We count them as we drive along. The person who comes the closest to an exact guess wins. The person who had the worst guess gets to clean the windshield."

**Count Cars:** This is a combined sorting and counting game. One player is the Caller. As you drive down the road, the Caller calls out a category of car. Each player then has five minutes or five miles (whichever comes first) to find as many in that category as possible. As soon as the time or mileage are up for a particular category, the Caller calls out another car category and the next round begins. The player with the most cars in any category wins a round. The player with the most cars spotted overall at the end of the ride wins the game. Here are some possible car categories:

Antique or vintage cars          Sedan

Convertible                      Sports car

Hatchback                        Sports utility vehicle (SUV)

Racing car                       Vans and mini-vans

**Count Bumper Stickers:** For this game each player will need a paper and pencil. Each player picks a category that bumper stickers usually represent. Here are some useful categories to get you started:

Political slogans or campaign         Radio station advertisements
  ads                                   or call letters

Sports events/teams/slogans          Stickers with slogans (for ex-

Education/schooling (for ex-           ample, "I'd rather be ____")
  ample, "I'm proud of my           Funny/comical stickers
  honor student")                   Stickers with "attitude"

                                    Warnings (real or silly)

Once everyone chooses a category, look for bumper stickers on passing vehicles. When players see one in their category, they read it aloud and give themselves one point. Add up the total at the end of the car ride—the person who spotted the most bumper stickers in their category wins.

## Just for Road Scholars

Graph the results of the bumper sticker game to determine the category of bumper sticker most often seen on the road.

**More Things to Count:** Young children enjoy counting items they see along the road. Here are some things they can practice counting: Sheep, horses, dogs, bridges, barns, schools, gas stations, telephone poles, fast-food restaurants, boats, flags, telephone booths, and so on. Have your carschoolers use their imagination to make up more counting games as you ride along.

# MATH FACTS THAT GO ROUND AND ROUND

## 100 Bottles of Juice on the Wall

A teacher in Santa Cruz, California, came up with this way to help her own kids (ages 5 and 8) do mental math with addition and subtraction. She revamped the old song "100 Bottles of Beer on the Wall" in the following way:

5 bottles of juice on the wall

5 bottles of juice

You go to the store and buy 3 more

How many bottles of juice on the wall?

*(Pause and let the kids figure out that the answer is 8; then continue the song)*

8 bottles of juice on the wall

8 bottles of juice

You take 2 down and pass them around

How many bottles of juice on the wall?

*(Again, pause to let kids figure it out by subtracting 2 from 8 to get the answer of 6; then continue with addition and subtraction.)*

## Roman Numeral Hunt

Look for Roman numerals in signs and on billboards along the way. This is a cooperative

### From the Information Highway

If you add up the numbers from 1 to 100 consecutively (1 + 2 + 3 + 4 + 5, . . .) the total is 5,050!

game. All of the players look for Roman numerals and tell what the value is in Arabic numerals, the numbers we usually use. (*Hint:* Look for clocks, movie copyright dates on billboards, Super Bowl ads, and so on.)

An easier version of this game is to look for Arabic numbers on license plates, street signs, and billboards and translate them to Roman numerals. See if your carschoolers can use these Roman numerals with ease:

| | |
|---|---|
| I = 1 | X = 10 |
| II = 2 | XV = 15 |
| III = 3 | XX = 20 |
| IV = 4 | XXX = 30 |
| V = 5 | XXXX = 40 |
| VI = 6 | L = 50 |
| VII = 7 | C = 100 |
| VIII = 8 | D = 500 |
| IX = 9 | M = 1,000 |

*Ready Resources*

You can find a complete list of Roman numerals and their equivalent Arabic numerals to print out (for easy access in the car) at this Web site: www.deadline.demon.co.uk/roman /num1.htm.

# Driving in Circles

Every car has at least five circles, and probably six. Can you find them? Answer: 1 steering wheel, 4 tires on the car, 1 spare tire. (You might find more on knobs, handles, speedometers, and so on.) When looking for circles, tell your carschoolers about parts of circles, and see if they can find any of the ones listed here:

**From the Information Highway**

To convert miles to kilometers, multiply the miles by 1.61. To convert kilometers to miles, multiply the total number of kilometers by 0.62.

**Arc:** A curved line that is part of the circumference of a circle.

**Circumference:** The distance around a circle.

**Diameter:** The longest distance across a circle.

**Radius:** The distance from the center of the circle to any point on its circumference.

**Pi:** The ratio of the circumference and diameter of any circle (3.14).

## Ring Around the Circle

Trace your finger around the outside of the round steering wheel and explain that this is the circumference of a circle. Get a ball of yarn or string and have each carschooler cut off a piece based on their estimate of what will be necessary to go around the steering wheel. Place a piece of tape on the end of their string and attach it to the steering wheel. Then, let them wrap their string around the circumference of the steering wheel. The person who has cut a piece of string that comes closest to the actual circumference wins! Afterward, let everyone guess the exact number of inches in the circumference. Measure the steering wheel circumference with a cloth tape measure. The person who comes closest to guessing the correct number wins. Don't forget to use the steering wheel to demonstrate concepts like diameter and radius, too.

## Pi in My Eye

Pi is what mathematicians call the ratio of the circumference and diameter of any circle. In numeric terms, Pi is 3.14159265358979323846264333832795502 . . . (the numbers go on forever and never repeat). To play the Pi game, players try to find the first eight numbers of Pi on passing car license plates. Players can use only one number from each passing license plate, and they must find the numbers in sequential order. Players call out the number and identify the car they saw it on, then no one else can use that car's license numbers. The first one to get all eight numbers in a row gets treated to a piece of pie at the next drive-in restaurant you go to.

Pi and numbers like it are called irrational numbers. Because the numbers go on forever, most people just refer to it as 3.14. If you want to remember a bigger portion of Pi, just remember this sentence, "May I have a large container of coffee?" and count the letters in each word in the sentence: "May(3) I(1) have(4) a(1) large(5) container(9) of(2) coffee(6)?"

> **From the Information Highway**
>
> National Pi Day is March 14, at 1:59. (3/14 1:59). Celebrate with a piece of pie at 1:59 P.M. on March 14.

## Round and Round We Go

Players try to find all of the circles in passing scenery as they look out of the car windows. They have to call the object out to gain a point—the first to call it gets the point. If it's a tie, both get a point. (*Hint:* You might want to eliminate tires and steering wheels to make the game more challenging.) The person who finds the most circles in five miles or five minutes wins.

# E-CAR-NOMICS

Money is the best way to demonstrate to kids that math has meaning and usefulness in their lives. It is the one "math manipulative" that children consistently look forward to using to improve their math skills. A carschool mom had this to say:

> We practice lots of money math on the road. We count money, and we are training the kids to bargain and to do some comparison pricing. For example, whenever we are on vacation, I pay a nickel for every white horse the kids see. Much time is spent figuring how many white horses they need to get a dollar or more. My

kids begin to bargain for a higher payout by suggesting higher fees for other animals or objects. ("Mom, can we get a nickel for every tree we see?" "If I see a white unicorn, will you give me $500 dollars?") The older kids were assigned the job of keeping track of mileage and figuring out how long the gas would last—estimating the mileage to the next fill-up stop. As the gas gauge got low, they kept an eye out for the cheapest gas.

Here are some activities to help kids see the relevance of math through money.

## Math on the Menu

Carschoolers eat on the road. Fast food drive-ins and sit-down restaurants provide many opportunities to learn math skills with money. When you go to a fast food restaurant, give the kids a budget amount to spend and then have them look over the menu and choose the items that stay within their budget. Let the kids estimate the total amount you will spend for all the meals. The person who comes closest gets an extra french fry from the others.

When you eat at a restaurant, let the kids calculate the tip: 10 percent, 15 percent, 20 percent. Explain what a tip is, how you determine what percentage to use based on quality of service, and then have them calculate the amount of money you will leave based on a percentage of the total food bill. Kids really enjoy discussing the service and how much tip they think is warranted. It also gives them practice in calculating percentages for use in the real world.

## Time Is Money

This simple activity helps kids understand how long a car trip will take, while teaching them about time, money, and math. You will need two clear, small, plastic containers labeled "Before" and "After," a roll of dimes, and a clock (analog, not digital, preferred).

Before your trip begins, estimate the total amount of minutes you think the trip will take. Then divide the total minutes into 10-minute segments. (For example, a 60-minute trip will have six 10-minute segments.) Allow one dime to represent each 10-minute segment of the trip. Put the number of dimes needed to represent the total time the trip will take in the container marked "Before." Then give the containers to your carschoolers. Tell them that every time 10 minutes passes on your trip, they are to move one dime from the "Before" container to the "After" container. As you complete each 10-minute segment of the trip, children will be able to better understand the passing of time. At the end of the trip, all of the dimes should be in the "After" container. The kids may want to count the dimes, or skip-count by 10s to count the total amount of money in the container. Tell them that they can use their dimes to buy a treat!

## Just for Road Scholars

You can use a digital clock (your car probably has one) to tell the time in this activity. However, to extend the learning, you might want to consider bringing along a battery-operated analog clock or wristwatch. Kids can watch the minute hand move, and see minutes that have passed, and the minutes left to go on the trip. This helps conceptualize the ideas of past, present, and future, too. Additionally, you can begin to help your kids understand fractions. Each 10-minute segment, is $1/6$ of an hour. This game can be altered by using nickels to count 5-minute increments. To introduce a bit more abstract concept, use quarters to count 15-minute increments or $1/4$ of an hour.

# What's on a Coin?

Test your carschoolers' memory about money—and also provide an opportunity to learn about social studies. In addition to a selection of coins, you will need a paper and pencil to keep score. One person is the banker. The banker keeps the coins—ideally one of each kind: penny, nickel, dime, quarter, half-dollar, and dollar. The banker takes one coin, say, a penny, and asks the first player what is on the heads side. If the player cannot answer the question correctly, no points are awarded and play moves to the next person. If the player identifies it correctly as Abraham Lincoln, then that player gets 2 points. If the player can tell you a historical fact about Abraham Lincoln (he was the sixteenth U.S. president, or he wrote the Gettysburg Address), an extra 3 points is awarded, for a total of 5 points. Play moves to the next player, who is asked "What is on the tails side of a penny?" If the player answers correctly (the Lincoln Memorial), 5 points are awarded. Each time players are finished with one coin, pass it around so all of the players can examine it—so they will remember it next time they play. Play continues in this manner with each different coin until the banker runs out of coins. The player with the most points wins all of the *coins*!

Here's a guide to what's on standard U.S. coins:

| Coin | Heads | Tails |
| --- | --- | --- |
| Penny | Abraham Lincoln | Lincoln Memorial |
| Nickel | Thomas Jefferson | Monticello |
| Dime | Franklin Roosevelt | Torch and Olive Branch |
| Quarter | George Washington | American Eagle |
| Half-Dollar | John F. Kennedy | Great Seal of the U.S. |
| Dollar | Sacagawea | Soaring American Eagle |

# Coin Toss–Testing the Theory of Probability

This is a simple way to teach carschoolers about chance and probability. First of all, designate one person as the official coin "Tosser." Each player starts the game with 10 points and a coin. The Tosser flips a coin and watches to see if it lands heads up or tails up. Then each person in turn flips his or her coin and tries to match the way the Tosser's coin landed. If the coin matches, the player scores a point.

Carschoolers can play the odds to try to improve their score by betting some or all of their points on the next toss. For example, let's say the Tosser's coin lands heads up. A player may say, "I'll wager 3 points that my coin will land heads up, too." If the coin lands heads up, the player keeps the 3 points bet and adds 3 more for a total of 6 points (in other words, double the points that were wagered). But if the coin lands tails up, the player loses all of the points bet (in this case 3 points). Keep a tally of each person's points. The player with the most points after 50 coin tosses wins.

To extend this activity a bit, have the kids keep track of the total number of times the coin lands heads up and tails up out of 50 flips. Ask whether they think it is possible to accurately predict which way the coin will land. The mathematical theory of probability says that the chance of getting heads is 50:50, or once in every two tosses, or half of the time. But a coin won't come up heads exactly half of the time in 50 tosses. See how close your carschoolers' results come to matching the theory of probability.

# Stock Car Average

If you listen to news broadcasts in the car, you will hear the broadcaster mention the Dow Jones Industrial Average—and whether it is up or down. That is a perfect opportunity to introduce the concept of the stock market to carschoolers with this simplified explanation: The Dow Jones Industrial Average is a method for measuring how 30 different companies' stocks perform each day. By tracking how these big companies are doing, we can get an idea for how well the whole economy is doing. When the average goes up, it means businesses are making a profit; when it goes down, it means businesses are not making as much money. One carschool mom reported that her kids got interested in the idea of owning stock and becoming shareholders in a company. To try this out, they invented the stock car game. Each player started with an imaginary $500 to invest in the stock of his or her choice and picked a publicly held company inspired by companies seen along the road. For example, carschoolers might pick McDonalds, Chrysler, or Texaco. As you drive to your destinations, bring the newspaper along or stop and purchase one. Have each player look up his or her stock in the business section of the newspaper and discuss any changes in its value. Have carschoolers graph their stock's price on a daily or weekly basis. After one month, the person whose stock has increased in value the most wins the game.

## The Dollar Bill Detective

When you run out of things to do in the car, a one-dollar bill and a magnifying glass can provide an interesting way to pass the time. The dollar bill is called "paper money," but it is really material made from a blend of 75 percent cotton and 25 percent linen fibers. Red and blue synthetic fibers are distributed throughout the bill. (Prior to World War I these fibers were made of silk.) It is printed and then starched to make it crisp and water resistant. Your children can be detectives, magnifying glass in hand, to find out what is printed on the bill.

Challenge your carschool detectives to find these clues on the front of a one-dollar bill:

1. A portrait of George Washington, the first president of the United States.

2. To the right of the portrait, find a circle that is the United States Treasury Seal. Inside the seal, find the balanced scales representing a balanced budget. Below the scales is a carpenter's T-square, a tool used for an even cut. Underneath the carpenter's tool is the key to the United States Treasury.

3. To the left of the portrait, find a circle that is the Federal Reserve Seal with the Federal Reserve Code Letter in the center of the Seal. The code is one of 12 letters from A to L that designate where the bill was printed:

| | |
|---|---|
| A = Boston | G = Chicago |
| B = New York | H = St. Louis |
| C = Philadelphia | I = Minneapolis |
| D = Cleveland | J = Kansas City |
| E = Richmond | K = Dallas |
| F = Atlanta | L = San Francisco |

4. In the upper right-hand section of the bill, and in the lower left-hand section, find identical Serial Numbers. The serial number identifies that particular bill. It can be traced in the event it is stolen. The first letter in the serial number matches the Federal Reserve Code, identifying where the money was printed.

5. Find two signatures located on either side of the portrait of Washington. The signature of the Treasurer of the United

States is on the left, and the Secretary of the Treasury is on the right.

6.  Find the Series/Year. This shows the year of the most recent design change in the bill. This date does not change annually; it only changes when there is a major revision in the basic design. If there is a capital letter following the series year, it indicates that a minor design change was made in that series. For example, after the appointment of a new Secretary of the Treasury or Treasurer of the United States, the signature must be changed. A change in only one signature is considered a minor revision.

**From the Information Highway**

There are 293 ways to make change for a dollar.

On the back of a one-dollar bill, carschool detectives will find two circles that represent the front and back of the Great Seal of the United States. The front of the Great Seal has a bald eagle, our national bird. The back has a pyramid. The Great Seal was adopted in 1782 as a symbol of the United States government. When you see it on money, it means it is the official currency of the United States. There are many groups of 13 items in the Great Seal, and all of them represent the 13 original colonies or states.

Challenge your carschool detectives to find these clues on the back side of the Great Seal (the pyramid side):

1.  The "All-Seeing-Eye" above the pyramid, which refers to the divine guidance of God in America. (Notice the words "In God We Trust" printed above the word "one" between the front and back seal.)
2.  There are 13 layers of bricks in the unfinished pyramid. The pyramid is a symbol of strength and endurance. The fact that it is unfinished means the United States will always grow, build, and improve.

3. There are 13 letters in the Latin words "Annuit Coeptis" above the pyramid. The words mean "He [God] has favored our undertakings."

4. The Roman numerals below the pyramid are the date of the Declaration of Independence, 1776.

5. The Latin words "Novos Ordo Seclorum" mean "a new order of the ages" and represent the beginning of a new era in America.

Challenge your carschool detectives to find these clues on the front side of the Great Seal (the eagle side):

1. There are 13 stars shining through a cloud above the eagle's head. This represents 13 "United States" taking their place among the sovereign nations of the world, as the clouds of disagreement part.

2. The bald eagle was selected to symbolize the United States because it is strong and smart. The eagle was seen as courageous, unafraid of storms, but also smart enough to soar above them. The eagle's head is turned toward the olive branch that he is grasping in his talons, signifying a desire for peace.

3. The motto of the United States is on the banner in the eagle's beak. The Latin motto is "E Pluribus Unum" and means "out of many, one." Notice that the motto has 13 letters.

**From the Information Highway**

To prevent the illegal production of fake currency, the Bureau of Engraving and Printing began distributing a new series of currency in 1996. There are two counterfeit deterrents in the bill: (1) An embedded polyester thread that denotes the amount of the currency that is visible to the naked eye when held up to a light source, and (2) microprinting around the face in the portrait that is only discernible with a magnifying glass. Neither of these things can be photocopied, which is the method used by most counterfeiters.

4.  There is a shield in front of the eagle, with 13 stripes representing the 13 original states (colonies). The bar above the stripes symbolizes the unifying power of Congress. The shield is unsupported—it stands on its own, which is representative of the fact that the United States is independent.

5.  The olive branch, a symbol of peace, held in the eagle's right talon, has 13 leaves and 13 berries.

6.  There are 13 arrows (a symbol of war) in the eagle's left talon.

## Ready Resources

Information about currency is a matter of public record, and many interesting facts about it can be found at the U.S. Treasury's Bureau of Engraving and Printing Web site at www.bep.treas.gov/document .cfm/18/120.

### Just for Road Scholars

Five-Dollar Bill Facts: On the front of this bill is a portrait of Abraham Lincoln, the sixteenth president of the United States. On the back of this bill is the Lincoln Memorial. The actual memorial has the names of the 48 states that existed in 1922 when the monument was dedicated engraved on the front and back. This picture of the front of the Memorial shows only 26 states. Challenge your road scholars to find all 26. The upper portion of the Memorial bears the states of Arkansas, Michigan, Florida, Texas, Iowa, Wisconsin, California, Minnesota, Oregon, Kansas, West Virginia, Nevada, Nebraska, Colorado, and North Dakota. The lower portion lists the states of Delaware, Pennsylvania, New Jersey, Georgia, Connecticut, Massachusetts, Maryland, Virginia, and New York. In addition, New Hampshire was abbreviated as "Hampshire" and South Carolina as "Carolina."

*(continues)*

Ten-Dollar Bill Facts: On the front of the bill is a portrait of Alexander Hamilton, the first Secretary of the Treasury. Four cars are represented on the reverse of the ten-dollar bill; see if your road scholars can find them. There are no specific makes or models of cars represented. All of the automobiles are a composite of the type of automobiles that were manufactured in the early 1920s.

Other U.S. Currency Facts: The individuals pictured on the other currencies that are currently circulated are as follows: $20 bill is Andrew Jackson, $50 bill is Ulysses S. Grant, $100 bill is Benjamin Franklin.

# IMAGINE THESE MATH FACTS

## The Grate-Googol Game

Kids are fascinated by big numbers—a million, a billion, a trillion, and so on. One carschool family invented a game based on their fascination with large numbers. As the mom explained, "One of our favorite books was *How Much Is a Million?* by David M. Schwartz, and as we rode in the car the kids passed the time considering the sheer size of a million tires, or telephone poles, or cars, or other things they saw along the way. Sometimes they would even try to count one million of these objects, although they never got past 1,578. When they learned about a googol, they were truly amazed. It's a 1 with 100 zeros after it. It is so big, in fact, that mathematicians don't have time to write a googol out, so they created a shortcut. It's $10^{100}$. In the *I Hate Mathematics Book,* author Marilyn Burns explains that 'A googol is more than the number of grains of sand in the entire

**From the
Information Highway**

The only denominations
of currency that are
presently printed are
$1, $2, $5, $10, $20,
$50, and $100. Denom-
inations in the amount
of $500, $1,000,
$5,000 and $10,000
were distributed until
1969. Then more secure

*(continues opposite)*

world.' She reports that in the book *Mathematics in Everyday Things* the author, William C. Vergana, explains that all of the grains of sand needed to fill a sphere the size of the Earth would be only a 1 with 32 zeros after it or $10^{32}$. That little piece of information helped my kids realize that the chances of counting to a googol were slim to none, but they did think it was fun to write the number googol out, as opposed to using the shortcut. On one of our car trips boredom resulted in the discovery that there are many sewer grates in the streets. They invented The Grate-Googol Game. Each player will need a pencil and paper. Put a 1 on the paper. One player looks out the window on one side of the car, and the other player looks out the opposite window. Then every time you pass by a sewer grate, call it out and write a zero after the number. You need to spot 100 grates to get 100 zeros to make a googol. The first one to write a googol (with all of the commas in the right place) wins."

## 20 Math Questions

Marnie Ridgway, a carschool mathematician, suggests this game of 20 Math Questions to practice factoring numbers and thinking logically. Marnie says, "When teaching this game to younger students, it is important to go through the reasoning you use to pick your choices. They learn a whole lot about factoring numbers into families, but they have to learn the logic you go through first. You can't imagine how quiet the car gets when they are going through all the factors in their heads for 6,357,498." Here's an example using a smaller number (63):

> I'm thinking of a number between
>    1 and 100.
> Is it even?
> No. (Okay, then it must be odd.)
> Is it a multiple of 3?
> Yes. (Okay, then it must be 3, 9, 15, 21, 27,
>    33, 39, 45, and so on.)
> Is it a multiple of 5?
> No. (Okay, then that eliminates 15, 45,
>    and so on.)
> Is it a multiple of 7?
> Yes. (Great! Let's try 3 × 7.)
> Is it 21?
> No. (Hmmm, it wouldn't be 6 × 7 because
>    that would be even, so let's try 9 × 7.)
> Is it 63?
> Yes!!!

methods to transfer large sums of money were developed. The largest denomination of currency ever printed was the $100,000 Gold Certificate of 1934. It had a portrait of President Wilson on it and was only used for official monetary transactions in Federal Reserve banks. It wasn't circulated outside of the Federal Reserve.

If your carschoolers are young, try these simpler variations recommended by carschool mom Sue (from Chico, California) who said, "I played the following games in the car with a 6- and 7-year-old for about an hour."

**Discover a Number I:** One person mentally chooses a number in some range, say, between 1 and 10 or 1 and 100. The "guesser" asks questions such as "Is the number 50?" The person who knows the number gives either "too high" or "too low" as an answer. The "guesser," by process of elimination, eventually discovers the number.

**Discover a Number II:** This game works on math concepts and vocabulary as well as deductive reasoning. One person chooses a number in a range, say, between 1 and 10 or 1 and 100. The "guessers" may ask questions about the number that require a yes or no answer, such as these:

Is the number even?

Is the number less than 40?

Is the number a two-digit number?

Is the number a perfect square?

Is the number divisible by 3?

Are the digits in the number the same?

Is the first digit a 3?

Does the number end in a zero?

Is the sum of the digits 10?

As numbers are eliminated through the question and answer process, the actual number chosen should be easy to discover.

**From the Information Highway**

There is a number larger than a googol—it's called a googolplex. It's a 1 with a googol number of zeros after it. You won't be able to find that many sewer grates!

## Ready Resources

There *is* a way to make repetitious memorization of math facts fun and relatively painless. It is often easier to memorize math facts when they are set to music, as these companies have done:

★ School House Rock carries *Multiplication Rock*, which sets the multiplication tables to rock music. To purchase the tapes visit their Web site at www.schoolhouserock.com.

★ Rock 'N Learn has addition, subtraction, and multiplication facts set to your choice of rock, rap, or country music. To order the math tapes or CDs, visit their Web site at www.rocknlearn.com.

★ Wrap-Up Raps are random math facts (addition, subtraction, multiplication, and division) set to rap music by the same company that makes the math manipulatives called Learning Wrap-Ups. For more information visit: www.learning-wrapups.com.

---

## Just for Road Scholars

Here's a challenging variation of "20 Math Questions." In this version, no question type can be repeated. For example, if one player should ask "Is the number greater than 40," no other question can be asked using the "greater than" concept.

---

# TRUCK MATH

Trucks are a preferred method of transportation for commerce. They come in many shapes, sizes, and varieties. Use them to play sorting and counting games with your road scholars.

## Keep on Truckin'

Here is a list of types of trucks to watch for on the road. Pick a category and tell the kids to count them. The person who finds the most after 10 miles or 10 minutes wins the game!

**Flatbed Truck** (A truck cab with a flat, open trailer attached to it.)
**Semitrailer** (A truck cab with an enclosed trailer attached to it.)

**Tanker** (A truck cab with large, cylindrical containers on an attached trailer. They usually carry liquids or gases and may have "Hazardous Materials" warning signs on them.)

**Dump Truck** (A truck cab with a dumpster attached that moves up and down to dump its contents of gravel, sand, and so on.)

**Car Transporter** (A truck cab with a trailer hauling new or demolished cars. Sometimes the cars are stacked on double-decker trailer beds.)

**Tow Truck** (A truck that tows individual cars.)

**Lowboy** (A truck with a trailer low to the ground that carries heavy things like a tractor.)

**Fire Truck**

**Snow Plow** (A truck that removes snow from the road.)

**Concrete Mixer** (A truck cab with a large cylindrical container attached that moves in a circular motion, often while the truck is moving, to mix the concrete it contains.)

**Street Cleaner**

**Garbage Truck**

**Moving Van**

## Designer Label Trucks

There are lots of different truck manufacturers. The name of the truck manufacturer is usually prominently displayed, although sometimes it is less obvious in a logo or emblem on the truck. In this game, have carschoolers make a few columns on grid paper and write out the names of different truck manufacturers above each column. Set a time or mileage limit and tell the carschoolers to search for as many as they can of each manufacturer to win the game. Which is the most common type of truck on the road? Here is a list of some truck manufacturers:

| | |
|---|---|
| Diamond Reo | Mack |
| Freightliner | Marmon |
| Ford | Oshkosh |
| International | Peterbilt |
| Kenworth (KW) | WHITEGM |

## The Wheels Go 'Round and 'Round

Big rigs, also referred to as "semis," are the largest trucks on the road. They have two parts: a tractor and semitrailer. The tractor includes the cab (where the driver sits) and the engine. The tractor has two wheels in front and two axles with a double set of wheels for a total of eight wheels in back. That's a total of 10 wheels on the tractor. The semitrailer is attached to the tractor, behind the cab. It's called a semitrailer because only the back end of it has wheels. The front end is supported by the tractor, and the back end trails behind on a double set of eight wheels. The combination of the tractor with 10 wheels and the trailer with 8 wheels is the reason these big rigs are called 18-wheelers. Kids love to count the wheels on trucks to determine if they are the biggest rigs on the road.

**From the Information Highway**

The widest road in the world is Brazil's Monumental Axis—160 cars can drive alongside one another on the gigantic road.

## Truck Talk

Lots of kids are really fascinated with trucks. If you see a truck stop with a restaurant, pull in and have lunch. Talk to the truckers, and let the kids ask them questions about their jobs, what they haul, how many miles they travel in a day, how many hours they are on the road each day, how much fuel they use, how much the truck weighs, how much the goods they are delivering weigh, and so on. Some friendly truckers might offer to give the kids a tour of their truck—or let them toot the truck horn.

### Just for Road Scholars

A nonprofit organization called Trucker Buddy helps establish pen pal or e-mail pal relationships with real truckers for kids in school classrooms (grades 2 to 8). The students use their math skills to map the trucker's course and follow his trail as he delivers goods throughout the country. The truckers in the program comment on the places they see, giving kids a glimpse of the geography of faraway places. This service is only available to public and private school classes with a minimum of 15 students. Homeschoolers might want to visit the Web site to read interesting and funny sample messages from trucker buddies and their trucker pets. There are also links to other trucker buddies (who maintain their own Web sites) that you can visit to learn more about truckers and the trucking industry. For more information contact www.truckerbuddy.org.

# DRILL AND PRACTICE WORK

Reciting math facts can be sheer drudgery for some kids. Turning drill work into a game helps to improve math skills in a fun way. Try these drills with your carschoolers. You will be amazed at how much fun they will have!

## Skip-Counting Game

Bev in New York taught her children to skip-count by 2s, 3s, 4s, 5s, and so on in the car. She said, "It really helped with multiplication.

We would start at different numbers, not always 2. We'd count backwards and forwards and had lots of fun. One person would start by saying '4,' and the next person would say '8,' the next '12,' and so on. When someone missed, they were out until the next number round."

## Skip-Counting to Rhymes

Sharon S. discovered that her children learned to skip-count more easily (in preparation for multiplication tables) when they set the counting into a rhyme. Here are some samples:

> 2, 4, 6, 8, who do we appreciate?
> 3, 6, 9, 12, take the numbers from the shelf
> 15, 18, 21, 24, take them all we'll need lots more
> 27, 30, 33, 36, keep the numbers pick up sticks
> 39, 42, 45, 48, number fun sure is great.

Sharon said, "You can make up your own rhymes. My son was in third grade and struggling with counting by threes, and this helped him tremendously. We learned it all together in the car!"

## Mileage Sign Math Drills

Practice math skills by asking your road scholars to convert mileage signs into decimals, percentages, and fractions. First, they have to imagine that every mileage sign number has a decimal point in front of it. For example, if they see a sign that reads 25 mph they should imagine it as a decimal number with a decimal point in front of the 25. So they would imagine and call out .25. Then they need to convert that decimal to a percentage or 25 percent and then to a fraction that would be $25/100$ or $1/4$. Here are some common mileage signs to look for and their conversions:

10 mph = 0.10 = 10 percent = $10/100$ = $1/10$
25 mph = 0.25 = 25 percent = $25/100$ = $1/4$
35 mph = 0.35 = 35 percent = $35/100$ = $7/20$
45 mph = 0.45 = 45 percent = $45/100$ = $9/20$
55 mph = 0.55 = 55 percent = $55/100$ = $11/20$
65 mph = 0.65 = 65 percent = $65/100$ = $13/20$

# IT'S IN THE CAR-DS

Here are a few math games that can be played in the car using flash cards and regular playing cards.

## Flash Card Games

Divide a deck of number flash cards evenly among the players in the car. Players try to find their numbers on road signs. Each time a player finds one of his or her numbers, the player throws the card it matches into a discard pile. The first person to get rid of all their cards wins!

### Just for Road Scholars

Use addition, subtraction, multiplication, and division flash cards. Players must read the math problem on the flash card out loud. Then they must find the answer to the problem on their flash card on a road sign before they discard. The first person to get rid of all their cards wins!

## Deal the Cards, Jack!

Practicing number and word recognition is easy in this game. Deal out all the cards in a regular deck of playing cards among the players in the car. Players look out of the car window and try to spot the number that is on each of their cards in signs, license plates, and so on along the road. When players find a number on the road that matches a number of a card in their hand, they discard that card. An ace is equivalent to the number 1. The face cards don't represent numbers—they represent the words "jack," "queen," and "king." If players see those words in a sign, they discard the corresponding card. (If you drive by a Jack-in-the-Box, Dairy Queen, and Burger King, the game may end quickly!) The first player to discard all cards is the winner.

# MATH-LISH

When we combine mathematics with English language arts, we get "math-lish," and lots of fun new games to try.

## Letters to Numbers

Each player in the car finds a license plate on a passing car and writes down the number. Cross out all of the numbers, retaining only the letters. Give each letter on your license plate the number value of its position in the alphabet (for example, A = 1, B = 2, C = 3, and so on until Z = 26). If your license number is 24J5KZE, you eliminate the numbers 2, 4, and 5 and are left with the letters J, K, Z, and E (J = 10, K = 11, Z = 26, and E = 5). Add up the value of your letters. In this case, 10 + 11 + 26 + 5, for a grand total of 52. The person with the highest score wins.

## Number Homophones

Here's a quick activity that will plunge your road scholars into deep thought for a few minutes. Have you ever heard of a homophone?

It's a word that sounds the same as another word, but it has a different meaning and is spelled differently. How many homophones are there in the numbers from 1 to 10? (*Answer:* There are three homophones: 4 = four, for, fore; 2 = two, to, too; and 8 = eight, ate).

# Palindrome License Plates

A palindrome is a number that looks the same forward or backward; 747 is a palindrome. In this game, players try to find palindromes in license plate numbers (street addresses or house numbers can also be used). Each player needs a paper and pencil and writes down as many palindromes as he or she can find in license plates or street numbers in 10 minutes or 10 miles, whichever comes first.

## Just for Road Scholars

You can turn any number into a palindrome with this math trick. Pick a number; for example, the number 142. It's not a palindrome. But reverse it, to create a new number 241. Now add the two numbers together. 142 + 241 = 383. As you can see, the result is 383—a palindrome! Some numbers will require a few extra steps to create a palindrome. For example, let's use the number 48. Reverse it and you get 84. Add the two together (48 + 84) and you get 132. That's not a palindrome. But reverse 132 and you get 231. Now, add those two numbers together (132 + 231) and you get 363—a palindrome! Some numbers will take much longer to get to a palindrome—but just keep reversing and adding and eventually you'll get there. If you are taking a really long car ride and have lots of paper, try your hand at turning 98 into a palindrome.

# Math Vo-car-bulary

You will need an odometer (mileage tracker) or a watch, and a paper and pencil for each player. Players have five miles or five minutes to write down as many math words or terms as they can think of: for example, arithmetic, cube, decimal, fraction, geometry, calculus, sum, dividend, quadratic equation, and so on. (Have younger children spell out the number names such as five, seven, one-half, and so on.) Players score one point for every correct word and subtract 5 points for every word that isn't a math vocabulary word. A more challenging version is to think of a math term for every letter of the alphabet. For example: A = addition, B = base ten, C = centimeter, D = dividend, and so on. The first one to complete all 26 wins!

### Variation

Find math vocabulary words on road signs, passing cars and trucks, billboards, and so on. With paper and pencil, players write down as many math words as they can find, and at the end of the trip the person with the most words wins! (*Hint:* Gas stations have prices per "gallon," store windows touting sales may say "half off," and so on.)

# Number Words

Players write down as many number words as they can find on road signs, passing cars, billboards, shop windows, and so on within a given time or mileage frame. Look for signs such as these:

| | |
|---|---|
| open twenty-four hours | five for one dollar |
| one-stop shopping | buy one, get one free |
| two days only | thirty-day guarantee |
| one-hour martinizing (cleaning) | open seven days a week |

# THE ROAD RULES

## Give Me a Brake–A Lesson in Math and Physics

When your teenager acquires his or her driver's permit, use your driving lesson time to demonstrate how long it takes to stop a car at different speeds—counting seconds and/or car lengths till you come to a complete stop. Explain that when a driver presses on the brake pedal, the brake pads press against the brake discs that are attached to the wheels. This increases the friction and slows the car. A number of conditions can affect the braking distance. The condition of the tires is important; worn tires have smooth tread, which provides less friction, so it takes longer to slow the car down. The larger a car is or the more mass it has, and the longer it will take to slow it down. Road conditions also must be considered. Icy roads mean smooth surfaces and less friction, so it takes longer to slow the car down. Gravel roads have rough surfaces and provide more friction, so it takes less time to slow the car down. The reaction time of the driver is a factor, too—and tiredness, certain medications, age, and alcohol or drugs can increase the time it takes a driver to react and apply the brakes.

One factor taught in driver education classes is that the faster the speed of the car, the longer it will take to stop the car. The braking or stopping distance is proportional to the square of the speed of the car. So, for example, a car traveling 10 mph under normal road conditions may require 4 feet to come to an abrupt stop, but a car going twice as fast (20 mph) would require four times the distance or 16 feet to brake to a stop. If you *double* the speed, you *quadruple* the required stopping distance. If you triple the speed of the car, you automatically increase the stopping distance by a factor of 9. And if you quadruple the speed, you increase the stopping distance by a factor of 16. That is an important safety concept for new drivers to understand—stopping distance is proportional to the square of the speed of the vehicle.

## Are We There Yet?

The odometer on the dashboard can help kids learn to estimate how long it takes to travel one mile in the car. Of course, traveling at different speeds will vary the length of time it takes. This game is easiest to play if you will be traveling at a consistent speed for a while without having to stop for traffic lights and so on. Highway travel is a good time for this game. Have one person watch the odometer go from one mile to the next. Odometers generally track miles and tenths of miles. Wait until the tenths of miles slot is at zero, and then shout "Go!" The Guessers close their eyes when they hear the word "Go" and open them when they think the car has traveled one mile. Whoever comes closest to estimating exactly one mile wins.

## Guess How Far?

One person points to an object in the distance (in the direction the car is traveling), and everyone guesses how far away the object is from them. Then, use the odometer to measure the distance to see whose guess is most accurate. The person who comes the closest to being exact wins.

## Curves Ahead—Geometry on the Road

Traffic signs are great tools for teaching kids the names of different shapes. Stop signs are octagons, yield signs are triangles, the car pool sign is a diamond, and street signs are rectangles. When you

## From the Information Highway

Look for interstate highway signs along your route. Notice the numbers. The numbers on the signs mean something. The higher the number is on the sign, the farther north or east your location. The lower the numbers, the farther south and west your location. If a highway sign number can be divided evenly by 5 or 10, the highway is most likely a main route that stretches for a very long distance.

point out a sign, talk about what makes a particular shape: for example, a triangle is a three-sided figure, a square has four sides of equal length and four corners with four right angles. Carschool mom Pat not only used street signs for teaching geometric concepts but discovered circles, squares, pentagons, pyramids, cubes, spheres, and more on buildings, windows, signs, cars, in lawn ornaments, and even in shrubbery that had been groomed and shaped by gardeners.

Point out to the kids that these different shapes (circles, squares, triangles) can be grouped into "sets," such as a set of circles or a set of cubes. Use geometry terminology—polygons (multisided figures), right angles, acute or obtuse angles, and so on—when describing the scenery around you. The more your carschoolers hear these terms and see samples of what you mean, the easier the concepts are to grasp. Reinforce this learning with the geometry game. Here's how to play: One player calls out a shape, say, a triangle. The person who spots the most things of that shape in five minutes or five miles gets a point. Then everyone searches for another shape. Play continues in each round until someone has 10 points.

## Red Light, Green Light Graphs

Kristine of Pennsylvania taught her children to keep track of how many red lights they had to stop for and how many green lights they passed along the road by graphing. She got the idea from an Internet discussion list and provided these directions. Try this out on your carschoolers:

> I gave each of the kids a piece of graph paper divided into two columns—one for red lights and the other for green lights. They were each given a red pen and a green pen. I told them to fill in a red square in the red column every time we stopped at a red light, and a green square in the green column when we went through an intersection with a green light. Each time they recorded a red light or green light, they entered the information directly underneath the previous information, forming a neat column or row. At the end of the trip, I had them compare the columns and tell me if we had experienced more red lights or green lights, or an equal amount of each. In this way, I taught them how to record information and use it to make a graph. We expanded this exercise by searching for other things on our trips: fast food restaurants (how many Burger Kings, McDonalds, Kentucky Fried Chickens, Taco Bells, and so on). We also kept graphs of out-of-state license plates. The kids had fun creating and using graphs to essentially journalize information about our car trips.

## Visit Number Families Along the Way

Here's a clever idea for teaching the concepts of number families and factoring from Marnie Ridgway, a carschool math tutor extraordinaire. "Every town you pass is an opportunity to teach your children about number families. For example, I live on the San Francisco peninsula. As we drive to a field trip, we pass through several different towns. To my girls, Sunnyvale will always be Sevenstown. We have to yell 'Hi!' to all the members of the 7 multiplication table before we get through Sunnyvale or someone in the Seven family will have his or her feelings hurt. Redwood City is

Ninestown, and so on. If you drive across country, you can assign number families to the various towns on the map. (Don't put them too close together though because you don't want a math mutiny on the trip.) We have been known to receive gifts from some of the number families we visited; when we drove through Foster City on our way to a destination in the East San Francisco Bay area, the Six family had little offerings for us like M&Ms in groups of six. Of course, these treats from the number families depended on how much time I had to put it together before we left on a road trip, but the gifts came often enough that the kids were willing to play the game on the gamble that they would get a treat instead of just having to shout out those factors within a time limit of how fast I drove through the town!"

## I Spy Math

This version of the classic game has a math twist. One player is the "Spy." The player says, "I spy, with my little eye, something with (fill in the number) (fill in name of thing)." For example: four wheels, two doors, three letters, six words, and so on. Of course, the thing chosen by the Spy must be an item everyone in the car can plainly see. Players have five miles or five minutes to guess the correct item.

## DASHBOARD DECIMALS

The odometer on your dashboard has spaces for whole numbers or miles and for tenths of miles, so the odometer might say 10358.5. The number that comes after the decimal point represents tenths of a mile—in this case, five tenths of a mile. Read the odometer and ask your carschoolers to convert the decimal number into a percentage. In this case 0.5 is equivalent to 50 percent. Here are all of the percentages the different tenths of miles represent:

0.1 = 10 percent          0.6 = 60 percent
0.2 = 20 percent          0.7 = 70 percent
0.3 = 30 percent          0.8 = 80 percent
0.4 = 40 percent          0.9 = 90 percent
0.5 = 50 percent

## Fast Lane Fractions

The odometer on your dashboard really moves quickly when you are traveling 55 mph or more in the fast lane. Use the frequently turning tenths of miles space on the odometer to help the kids practice fractions. Read the odometer (for example, 10358.5) and ask your carschoolers to convert the decimal number into a fraction. In this case 0.5 is equivalent to $^5/10$ and that can be further reduced to $^1/2$. Here are all of the fractions the different tenths of miles represent:

$0.1 = ^1/10$                $0.6 = ^6/10 = ^3/5$
$0.2 = ^2/10 = ^1/5$         $0.7 = ^7/10$
$0.3 = ^3/10$                $0.8 = ^8/10 = ^4/5$
$0.4 = ^4/10 = ^2/5$         $0.9 = ^9/10$
$0.5 = ^5/10 = ^1/2$

## Fill 'er Up

Here's an easy way to test addition and multiplication skills. If a gallon of gas costs $2.17, what will 2 gallons cost? 5 gallons? 10 gallons? 20 gallons? Test your carschoolers' skills each time you gas up!

## Freeway Math

The speed limit is posted as 65 mph on the freeway. If you drive at the speed limit, how far will you travel in 1 hour? 2 hours? 3 hours?

30 minutes? Now that you know how many miles you will travel in an hour, how long will it take to go 300 miles? 20 miles?

## Just for Road Scholars

The speed limit is posted as 65 mph. If there are 1,760 yards in a mile, how many yards will you travel in one hour? If there are 5,280 feet in a mile, how many feet will you travel in one hour?

## Can You Tell Me How to Get to Symmetry Street?

There are lots of patterns in the things around us—and you can see them as you drive down the street. Most are symmetrical, or balanced. For example, look at the face of the road scholar next to you. Imagine a line drawn down the middle of that person's face from hairline to chin. Looking at both sides of the face, you can't help but notice that there is an eye on one side and an eye on the other; a cheek on one side and one on the other; the same goes for nostrils, teeth, lips, and ears. Everything is even or balanced on each side. That's symmetry—and it's everywhere. You can see symmetry in nature in leaf patterns, snowflakes, flower petals, insect wings, seashells, trees, and fruit. Most man-made things are symmetrical as well—cars, houses, fences, and so on. Some things have *mirror symmetry*—they are exactly the same on both sides. Other things have *rotational symmetry*—they look the same no matter which way you turn them. Some examples of this are a snowflake and some flower petals. Help your carschoolers discover symmetry with this game. Each player will need a pencil and paper. One player looks on one side of the street, and the other player looks on the other. As you drive down the street, challenge your carschoolers to write down as many examples of symmetry as they can find on their side of the street in five minutes or five miles. Make the game a bit more challenging by limiting the items to those having only mirror symmetry or rotational symmetry.

## Meet You There!

Each player needs a road map, pencil, and paper. Someone picks a beginning and ending destination: for example, Palm Beach, Florida, and Olympia, Washington. All of the players figure out the shortest route between the two cities using the highways and roads on the map. Then they use the map key and their math addition skills to determine the mileage of the route they chose. The player with the route that is the shortest distance between the two points wins.

Carschooling
LANGUAGE
ARTS

CHAPTER

5

**Y**OU CAN improve your child's overall literacy by learning to weave imagination, critical thinking, and creative writing skills into storytelling games in the car. In this chapter, carschooling parents show you how. You will also discover how to use road signs and license plates to help your carschoolers practice their ABCs and spelling. Take magnetic letters, words, and poetry off of your refrigerator and bring them along in the car to improve vocabulary and polish prose. Play car games to learn parts of speech. Use one carschooler's technique for learning Greek and Latin root words. Sing your way to good grammar. Use audiotapes to improve your vocabulary to ace those SATs! Carschoolers are huge fans of audiobooks, and you will find favorite family listening titles here. Many of the activities are not only excellent for use in the car but can be used to help pass the time at stops along the road. For example, play the games in restaurants while waiting for the food to arrive, or while waiting in long lines at the bank or post office. You'll be surprised at how quickly and pleasantly the time passes.

# LANGUAGE ARTS TOOLS

Most of the activities in this chapter can be done without any tools at all, although a paper and pencil will always come in handy for keeping track of scores in games. If you stock your carschool with items from the following list, you will be able to enjoy all the activities without having to scramble to find an item or two to play a spur-of-the-moment game. Skim through the chapter before you take a trip to make sure you have what you need to play the games your family will enjoy.

| | |
|---|---|
| Alphabet flash cards | Magnetic poetry |
| Bubble gum | Dictionary |
| Cardboard tubes (toilet paper rolls) | Stopwatch or clock with second hand |
| Crayons or markers | Thesaurus |
| Flannel board* | Paper |
| Paper bag | Plain brown paper lunch bags |
| Tape recorder | Pencil/pen |

# CRACKING THE ALPHABET CODE

When it comes to language arts, carschoolers start at the beginning with the alphabet. These games are easy to play and fun for all ages.

---

*A flannel board is a great storytelling tool to bring along in the car. Your kids can use it to create wonderful pictures and characters to help act out an original or favorite tale. Here's how to make a flannel board that you can take with you on car trips. You will need flannel, felt, sturdy cardboard, stapler, and scissors. Cover the cardboard in flannel, using staples to hold it in place. Cut out shapes of characters for your stories using felt. When you put the shapes on the flannel board, they will stick! Carschoolers can move the shapes on the board to illustrate a story, poem, rhyme, or song. (*Note:* Cut out numbers to use for math drills and letters to practice the alphabet or spelling words, too.)

## Searching for ABCs

While riding in the car, try to find the letters of the alphabet in order from A to Z on passing billboards and road signs. You can only use one letter from each sign that you see. The first person to complete the alphabet wins.

## License Plate A to Z

The object of the game is to find all the letters of the alphabet in order (A to Z) using only the large letters on the license plates—not the letters in the state mottos or on vanity frames. Letters must be called out in alphabetical order, and you can use more than one letter on a license plate—as long as you are using them in order. The first player to get to Z is the winner.

    For a complicated twist, try playing this game backwards from Z to A. This method levels the playing field when you have younger and older kids in the car. By the way, learning to sing the alphabet backwards is a cool trick. Most people can't do it (without practicing) and are amazed by those who can. Learning the alphabet backwards is a fun way to spend time in the car. You sing it to the same tune as the traditional alphabet song.

> "Z, Y, X, W, V, U, T, S, R, Q, P, O, N, M, L, K, J, I, H, G, F, E, D, C, B, A
> Now I've sung by Z, Y, X—I think you should sing it next."

## I'm Going to a Tailgate Party

This game starts simply but gets more difficult with each player's turn. The first player starts by saying, "I'm going to a tailgate party, and I'm bringing _____." The object the player picks must start with the letter A (for example, apples). The second player then says, "I'm going to a tailgate party and I'm bringing _____ (whatever the first player said) and _____ (an object that starts with the letter B)." Play continues with each player repeating what the previous players said, then adding a new object beginning with the next letter of the alphabet. A player who needs to use the letter F might say, "I'm going to a tailgate party, and I'm bringing apples, bread, carrots, dishes, eggs, and forks." If a player forgets to list an item mentioned by other players, that player drops out of the game. Play continues until only one player who can remember the entire list without any mistakes is left—that's the winner!

## Alphabet Count Down

Christy, a carschooling mom in Canada, says that her young children enjoy playing Alphabet Count Down. You start with the letter A and work your way through the alphabet. The first player looks out of the car window and spots something that begins with the letter A and says (for example), "I see an airplane." The next player looks for something that begins with the letter B and says, "I see a billboard." Play continues through the alphabet. (*Hint:* J and Q are the hardest letters to find.)

## Flash Card Letter Hunt

Carschooling dad Duane G. uses alphabet flash cards to play a letter identification game with his kids. Shuffle the cards and put them in a stack. Each player then draws a card and has to find that letter on a road sign. Once players find their letter, they can draw another card. Play continues until all of the cards have been drawn. The one with the most cards at the end of the game wins! (*Note:* This game can also be played with number flash cards to practice number identification with young children.)

## Alphabet Jump Rope

Kathleen borrowed a jump rope jingle to create an alphabet word game in which her carschoolers try to construct several sentences that include words that start with a specific letter of the alphabet. Here is an example using the letter A:

A my name is _____(Annie)
My best friend's name is_____(Art)
We live in_____(Arizona)
And we sell_____(Apples)

The next person uses the letter B and play continues through the alphabet. Kathleen says that her kids think it's really fun even though certain letters are very challenging!

> **From the Information Highway**
>
> What sentence uses every letter in the alphabet? "The quick brown fox jumps over a lazy dog." It was developed by Western Union to test telex communications.

# HOW DO YOU SPELL THAT?

Car rides are the perfect setting for practicing spelling and phonics with these easy and fun activities, games, and tools.

## If C-A-R Spells "Car" . . .

Here's an activity that Gretchen M. played with her beginning readers that reinforced spelling and phonics as they rode in the car. As she explains it, "When they were learning to read and spell, I would say things like 'If h-o-p says hop, what would p-o-p say? If c-a-r spells car, what does b-a-r spell?' We would do this for long periods of time. Just think of words that rhyme and you will have a long list in no time. For example: bee–see, cat–hat, dog–fog, freeze–breeze, nut–hut, and so on."

*Ready Resources*

At this Web site (www.rhymezone.com) you can type in any word and a list of words that rhyme with it will appear on the screen.

# Rhyming Signs

Ask your carschoolers to pick one word from a billboard or road sign. Then tell them to try to find all of the words that sound alike or that rhyme. For example, let's say they pick the word "free" from a billboard. Now think of all the words that rhyme, such as "tree," "bee," "see," "me," "he," and "she." For a more challenging version, ask your carschoolers to find a word on one sign and then find a word that rhymes with it on another road sign or billboard.

# Read Your Palm

This game requires two players. One player closes his eyes and holds his hand out, palm up. Another player uses her finger as a pen to write a letter on the person's palm. The first player opens his eyes and tries to guess the letter that was traced on his palm. If he guesses correctly, he gets to write a letter on the other player's palm. You can also make the game more challenging by writing entire spelling words on the other person's palm.

# Highway Hangman

This is a twist on the classic spelling game Hangman, and it is easy to play in the car. The object is for players to guess a word or phrase before the player who thought of it can complete a drawing of a stick figure in a hangman's noose. One player draws a hangman's noose on a piece of paper. Then that player thinks of a secret word—but it has to be something seen out of the car window. The player draws a blank line for every letter in the secret word on a piece of paper so other players know how many letters are in the word. The other players take turns guessing the letters of the secret word. When a player guesses a correct letter, the player who chose the secret word writes that letter on the corresponding blank line, and the person who guessed the letter gets to try and guess the word. If a player guesses a letter not in the word, the letter is written down underneath the blank lines to show that it has been used but is not one of the letters in the secret word. For each incorrect guess, a stick-figure body part is drawn in the hangman's noose as follows: head, body, arms, and then legs, and if you need more guesses add hands, feet, eyes, nose, and mouth. To win, a player must guess the word before the hangman figure is complete. (*Hint:* When playing Hangman, remember that the most frequently used letters are T, S, R, L, and N. The letters used least are Q, Z, K, X, and J. The most frequently used vowels are E, A, and O.)

> **From the Information Highway**
>
> What is the longest English word according to standard dictionaries? "Pneumonoultramicroscopicsilicovolcanokoniosis"—this 45-letter word is the name of a lung disease suffered by miners.

## Backseat Spelling Bee

Donna W. discovered that there are fewer distractions in the car, so concentrating on learning spelling words is easier. She said, "I bring the children's spelling list and review it in the car with my kids. It's a practical way to use time in the car after school while I run errands. The kids enjoy it, too, because they get their spelling homework done before we even get home!"

## Spelling Themes

One carschooling mom said that her children were more receptive to learning spelling words when the words on their spelling list had a single theme. For example, here is a list of words that describe parts of cars and things used in cars. Use them for spelling words or try to make a complete sentence using each word—it can be silly or sane.

| | |
|---|---|
| Battery | Mirror |
| Brake | Muffler |
| Bumper | Oil |
| Dashboard | Seat belt |
| Engine | Speedometer |
| Gas | Tire |
| Glove compartment | Transmission |
| Hubcap | Turn signals |
| Lights | Windshield |

## Disassembling Road Signs

Use words on road signs and billboards to help your carschoolers learn to identify words with certain letter blends, suffixes, or prefixes. Tell them to find all of the words that begin with the letter blend *th*, or all of the words with the prefix *pro*, or all of the words with the suffix *ing*. Here are some more to look for:

**Letter Blends:** ch, ea, qu, sh, th
**Prefixes:** dis, pre, pro, sub, trans
**Suffixes:** ed, ould, ough, tion, ing, ary

## Ghost

This game is an oldie but a goodie! It is more complex than other word games, so players need to have good spelling skills. One person thinks of a letter, perhaps T. The next person thinks of a word that begins with T such as "table" and says the second letter in that word: A. The next person thinks of a word that is spelled with a T followed by an A, such as tack and says C. The next player thinks of a word that begins with the spelling T-A-C such as "tachometer" and says H. The play continues in this way until a player cannot think of anymore words that fit the spellings and completes a word or passes (if you pass, you lose your turn until the next round begins with a new word). The players never reveal the words they are thinking of when they add another letter to the word-in-progress. However, they must be thinking of a real word that is spelled in the way they are reciting the letters. If a player says a letter that doesn't make spelling sense, the other players can challenge and the player must say a real word. If the player can't come up with a word, the player is out for that round. Play continues until there is only one player left— the winner.

Now here's where the GHOST comes in. The first time a player loses a round, they get a G. Each time a player loses, they get another letter in the word "ghost." After losing five rounds, players acquire all of the letters in the word, becoming the GHOST and dropping out of the game. You can see that this can take quite a while to play, especially if there are more than two or three players, which is why it's a great game for long car trips.

## Ready Resources

Here are two more ideas for happy carschool spelling:

**Franklin Spelling Ace:** One of the great products on the market for carschoolers is the Franklin Spelling Ace. This little hand-held, battery-operated device offers lots of ways to reinforce language arts. It was designed to help check and correct spelling. Carschoolers can key in a word to see how to spell it. The speller also provides definitions of words and gives synonyms and antonyms. But that is just the beginning of this useful little device. It also contains eight word games including Hangman, Anagrams, Word Jumble, Word Flash Cards, and a Spelling Bee. The Franklin Spelling Ace is available at many retail stores or visit their Web site at www.franklin.com.

**Leap Frog's Turbo Twist Spelling:** Many carschoolers sing the praises of the portable, electronic Leap Frog spelling toy. Designed for elementary school ages, it can also be used (with dignity) for remedial work by high school students and adults. Davina's comments were echoed by many: "We bought our daughter Leap Frog's Turbo Twist Spelling to use whenever we ride in the car. It was an answer to a prayer. She went from an F to a B+ in spelling. We have the optional component that allows us to download spelling lists from Leap Frog's Web site, so we always have new material. It was well worth the money we paid for it. Her teacher thinks it was a good buy, too." Leap Frog toys are available at most toy stores or call them direct at 1-800-701-LEAP (5327).

# TALL TALES RISING

Storytelling is a unique educational tool that is often overlooked in our hectic world. In the car, with a captive audience, you can take the time to tell stories orally or use storyteller tapes and CDs to help instill values such as honesty, courage, responsibility, and concern for others while establishing a foundation for reading by helping your children develop listening skills and a rich vocabulary. Listening to and understanding the components of a good story will improve your kids' creative writing skills, too. Children who listen to storytellers often become good storytellers themselves—a skill that will serve them well when it comes time for public speaking.

If you are not sure how to begin, consider telling a fairy tale; you probably know one or two by heart. Fables and folktales in which animals take on human characteristics (good and bad) infuse morals and provide inspiration. Legends about real people (for example, Davy Crockett, Johnny Appleseed, and Sojourner Truth) can lead to wonderful discussions about history. Multicultural myths of ancient people that explain the origin of the universe or describe gods and goddesses with super powers will stimulate your child's imagination.

Don't underestimate the value of family stories about unusual relatives or funny or poignant circumstances. Use these tales to pass down information about family history. Telling personal stories gives your kids a glimpse of who you are and how you learned the things you know about life. You may find that your children want to hear your escapades over and over again. Tell them. Learning more about you, their grandparents, cousins, aunts, and uncles will help your children know and appreciate the incomparable feeling of belonging to a family.

> **From the Information Highway**
>
> The longest word in the English language with only one vowel is "strengths" which is only nine letters long.

Your kids will inevitably see storytelling as playful. Encourage your kids to retell the stories they have heard. If they get stuck, ask them questions to stimulate their memory. Applaud your kids' efforts to tell their own unique stories. If you are a patient and eager listener, they will happily comply.

# Paper Bag Story Starters

Here is a great story starter from Elise B. of Utah: "My sister-in-law took a brown paper bag and wrote the words 'Once Upon A Time . . .' on the outside of it. Inside the bag, she put little scraps of paper with a story-starting idea written on each. For example, 'there was a cat who loved to swim.' She had many story-starter ideas in the bag. When her family took a long car ride, she would pull out the bag and say, 'Once Upon A Time . . .' and then let one of the kids pull a story-starter scrap of paper from the bag and read what it said. Each person in the car added one sentence that made sense to create a simple story. Sometimes the stories would be very short. But most of the time the story would go on and on with carschoolers adding storylines each time it was their turn. Some of the family stories they developed were really funny and interesting. She got into the habit of recording the stories as they developed and then editing them so that they could listen to them over and over again on subsequent car rides."

## Literature Lessons

If you are able to plan ahead for a trip, here is Georgia carschooler Ellen's way of getting her carschoolers involved in storytelling: "When we planned our family vacations, I would ask everyone to learn one poem, story, fairy tale, or folk legend by heart to share with everyone in the car while we were driving to our destination. It was really fun to see what each person chose and to listen to their interpretation. Even our 3-year-old was able to recite a simple nursery rhyme. Competition among older family members to tell the best story took hold, and that led to lots of advance research and reading to come up with a winner!"

### Ready Resources

To get a good introduction to the art of storytelling, look for these audiotapes. They are available at some bookstores and libraries or can be purchased directly from the Web sites indicated.

A *Storytelling Treasury* features 37 tellers who performed at the 20th Anniversary of the National Storytelling Festival. It

includes tales from the Orient, Africa, and Europe, and legends from the Appalachian, Native American, and African
American traditions. The boxed set of five audiocassettes has
about five hours of vibrant storytelling. Available at the National Storytelling Web site at www.storynet.org.

*Best Loved Stories Told at the National Storytelling Festival* is a
selection of stories told by popular storytellers on audiocassette. It includes work by Donald Davis, Elizabeth Ellis,
and others. Available at the National Storytelling Web site at
www.storynet.org.

Jay O'Callahan is a storyteller extraordinaire with titles for all ages
from *Earth Stories* to *The Gouda*. To see the selection of titles,
visit the Web site at www.ocallahan.com or call 1-800-626-5356.

Jim Weiss offers a huge selection of fairy tales, myths, mysteries,
Shakespeare, and condensed literature on tape. He is a master storyteller who appeals to every age—including adults!
Call for a catalog (1-800-477-6234) or visit his Web site
(www.greathall.com) where you can preview recordings prior
to ordering them.

Odds Bodkin, a superb storyteller with titles for all ages from *Little Proto's T Rex Adventure* to *The Hidden Grail: Sir Percival
and the Fisher King* to *The Odyssey*. To preview the titles prior
to purchasing, visit the Web site (www.oddsbodkin.com) or
call for a catalog (1-800-554-1333).

Rabbit Ears produces award-winning folk tales and fairy tales on
tape that are narrated by celebrities such as Robin Williams,
Denzel Washington, and Meryl Streep. Preview the tapes before purchasing them at www.rabitears.com.

# Let's Have a "Tellabration"

On the weekend before American Thanksgiving, storytelling groups
all over the world host "Tellabrations" to celebrate storytelling! For

more information, ask your local librarian, or visit the Tellabration Web site at www.tellabration.org. Many cities throughout the country sponsor local storytelling festivals. Check with your local library or bookstore for information.

## Auto-Biographies

Carschool parents recognize the benefit of sharing the stories of their lives with their children. Candace of New York says, "Because of his work schedule, my husband doesn't have many opportunities to read to our children. But whenever we go on a car ride he tells the kids a story about his childhood. They love to hear about his boyhood adventures, the descriptions of his zany friends, and some of the wild pranks they pulled on one another. They particularly enjoyed a story he called "Smelly in the Dark" about a game of tag played in the dark with smelly socks! This is a terrific way to pass down a little family history and give your kids some insight on the people and events that shaped your life."

Kathy H. of California suggests some further ideas for initiating your own auto-biographies: "Telling stories to your kids about your childhood, or about your father and mother (their grandparents), or about things that happened when you were a kid fascinates them. I told my kids a story about a friend who said I was stupid and what it made me feel like. They came up with all kinds of advice for how I should have handled that situation. If you don't remember any stories, make something up. You can always tell a good story that belongs to a friend of yours and make it your own." To encourage family members to share things that happen in their lives while riding in the car, take turns telling each other about events that were embarrassing, funny, happy, sad, or scary.

## Tell Me My Story!

Gina of Iowa discovered that children love to hear about themselves—maybe even more than hearing about anyone else! "My kids love to hear the story of the day they were born, especially on long rides in the car. They like all of the details about the labor, how we drove to the birthing room at the hospital, the midwife and doctor, the people who were there, the first moment we saw them, what they did, what everyone said, and how we felt about them. This is such a simple storytelling device because it's easy for adults to remember, and kids love hearing about their debut in the world. The only problem is that you need to make sure you will have time to tell everyone's story. All of the kids want to hear about their birth day in turn, so make sure you plan your time to include everyone or pouting is guaranteed."

## Car Puppetry

Canadian carschooling mom Christy wrote, "Puppets are great tools to use to enhance storytelling in the car. You can use store-bought puppets or make some finger puppets before you go on a trip with the appropriate characters from the most recent book you are reading *(The Three Little Pigs, The Billy Goats Gruff)*. My kids love this!"

Simple finger puppets are easy to make; try these cardboard tube puppets made with toilet paper tubes. Don't discard toilet paper tubes; place them in a bag and keep them in the car. Turn them into instant finger puppets to facilitate storytelling when you're on the road. The upright tube can be fashioned into story characters including people and animals. Just decorate the tubes with marker pens or crayons to create a unique cast to act out your favorite fairy tales and stories. Then slip them over your fingers as you tell your story. To make a snake, truck, or other long object, turn the tube on its side and poke a hole in the bottom so you can slip the tube over your finger.

## Bubble Gum Blowout!

Give each player a piece of bubble gum. Then assign each player the name of an auto part (for example: hood, wheel, door ). Choose one player to be the "Storyteller." The Storyteller tells a story about a car trip—it can be silly or serious. While telling the story, the story-teller must mention the auto parts chosen by the other players in the story. As players hear their auto part mentioned, they put their bubble gum in their mouth and start to chew it. When the Story-teller yells "Blowout," players must immediately blow a large bub-ble, get approval from the Storyteller that the bubble passes muster, and pop their bubbles. The last player to blow and pop a bubble loses. Each time a new round begins, the role of Storyteller passes to another player. A fresh stick of bubble gum is needed for each round. Play continues as long as everyone wants to chew.

## Fortunately, Unfortunately

Carschooling mom Dorothy Flynn shared this classic storytelling game that her five kids enjoy playing in the car. One player begins a story by saying something like this: "We went on a field trip to the zoo last week." The next player must say something beginning with the word "unfortunately." For example, "Unfortunately, we forgot to bring money to pay the admission." The next player continues the story by beginning with the word "fortunately." For example, "Fortu-nately, it was the monthly free admission day." This continues around the group, alternating between fortunately and unfortu-nately. The stories can be serious or silly; it's up to the players mak-ing the next statements. For example, if the play in this example continued, players might say, "Unfortunately, no sooner did we walk in the gate than my brother ran up a hill to see the giraffes and fell off a cliff." "Fortunately, there was a pillow factory at the bottom of the cliff, and he fell safely onto a truckload of pillows." The imagination each player brings to the story is great fun for everyone.

## The Thing Is the Thing

This is a fun activity to stimulate storytelling. Give each player an object to hold (a purse, a doll, a whistle, a cookie, a tissue, or whatever else you have in the car). The first player begins to make up and tell a story that includes the object that player is holding. At any time the player may choose any other player to continue the story, and that player must include the object he or she is holding in the story. Play continues until every player has had a turn. Then the player who started the story must finish it by including his or her object in the story once again.

> **From the Information Highway**
>
> The most commonly used word in *written* English is "the." The most commonly used word in *spoken* English is "I," followed by "you," "the," and "a."

## You're on the Air

Katy Hunt suggests turning your car into a recording studio: "We use a tape recorder in many ways in our car travels. We tape stories as we read them, with lots of dramatic interpretation. We tell a portion of a story from memory and record it on tape. We use the tape recorder when we play progressive storytelling games. Interestingly, when the tape recorder is on, the kids are less likely to bicker about whether or not you could say something that didn't make sense in the middle of a progressive story. We turn the tape off if someone needs time to think before adding to the story. In addition to storytelling, we recite poetry, play around with alliteration and limericks, try creating haiku (usually inspired by the weather that day), and invent our own poems in the car. We listen to our renditions of stories and poems on tape, and then talk about them and make corrections. We talk about what didn't work, or what else could be added or changed to make it better. It is a great way to teach kids editing skills."

# AUDIOBOOKS LISTENING GUIDE

Carschoolers will tell you that the most important resource to have in the car is audiobooks. Most parents recognize the value of reading out loud to their children. Books help carschoolers develop literacy skills; they are windows on the world and introduce us to people, places, and ideas that stimulate our minds and provide a springboard to further learning adventures.

For some families, it can be difficult to find the time to sit down and read a good book out loud. When our schedules became too busy to incorporate reading into our days and evenings at home, I resorted to using audiobooks in the car. The subjects in the stories led to many wonderful discussions and a productive and positive use of our time as we drove from one destination to another.

## Real World Adventures

Audiobooks have enhanced my sons' education. When they were young, a game described in a story suddenly took shape in our car. A character in a book we listened to talked about going to the art museum, so we stopped at one on our way home. Another book character was interested in rock collecting, and as a result we discovered precious gems and minerals that the boys collected on our car travels. The Hardy Boys mystery series introduced us to metal detectors, so we borrowed one and spent hours sifting sand along the Pacific Ocean in search of our own clues to unsolved mysteries. An audiotape about the solar system led to an exploration of astronomy coupled with frequent car trips to the planetarium. A story about dinosaurs led to the discovery of archaeology and spawned field trips to see robotic dinosaurs. We learned about many foreign countries as we listened to stories on CDs. I kept an inflatable world globe in the car and made a habit of encouraging the kids to locate countries as we read about them. We extended our reading experiences by seeing plays and occasionally movies based on books we had listened to on tape. As you can see, audiobooks can play an enormous role in your children's education.

## Ready Resources

Audiobooks are available from many sources. Here is a small list of top sources (recommended by carschooling parents):

**Audio Bookshelf:** The production quality of Audio Bookshelf's unabridged versions of popular books is superb. The tapes come in attractive and sturdy storage cases that are especially effective for use in the car. (If you've ever seen the result of a plastic jewel case that gets caught underfoot in the car, you will appreciate this feature.) Audio Bookshelf's Web site (www.audiobookshelf.com) has a unique educational tool called "Curricular Connections" located on the title page of each book that they offer. It contains a biography of the author, ideas and activities for enhancing learning, and suggestions for further reading and resources. It can be printed out for use in the car or at home.

**Audiobook Central:** This company sells and rents audiobooks. It is the rental aspect of this business that makes it so unique. The rental procedure is simple, and customer service is superbly delivered by the family-owned company. Visit their Web site (www.audiobookcentral.com) to see the titles they offer and to read instructions for how their rental program works.

**Audiobooks.com:** This online bookstore sells used audiobooks at reasonable prices, available through their Web site at www.audiobooks.com.

**Storytapes.com:** This site carries a wide selection of audiobooks to buy or rent; visit them at www.storytapes.com.

**The British Broadcasting Company:** The BBC produces audiobooks that are read with dramatic interpretation. To view the many titles they offer, visit their Web site (www.bbcworldwide.com /spokenword/default.htm). Some libraries also carry BBC tapes and CDs.

**Audible.com:** This Web site lets you download audiobooks into digital files that can be delivered to your PC or laptop over the Internet. You can then transfer them to an AudibleReady player, such as a PocketPC or Rio MP3 player, and listen anywhere. They have a huge selection of book titles to choose from; many can be downloaded for free, others for a fee. For more information visit their Web site at www.audible.com.

**Cracker Barrel Country Stores:** This chain of family restaurants located throughout the United States has a Books-On-Audio program that is rather unique. When you finish listening to one of their 200 titles on cassette or CD, return it to a Cracker Barrel restaurant. They will refund the purchase price less $3.00 for each week the tape or CD was in your possession. For more information, visit their Web site at www.cracker barrel.com.

**Scholastic, Inc.:** This is the largest publisher of children's books in the world. It has reading programs and products for every age, grade, and ability level. Many of the early reading programs include kits that contain a book with cassette. Young children can look at the book while listening to the story. For a catalog or more information call 1-800-SCHOLASTIC or visit their Web site at www.scholastic.com.

# Let's Hear a Story

Manuela G. of New Mexico suggests making your own audiobooks: "I read my kids' favorite stories and record them as I read them. Then they can listen to me 'read' a story as we ride in the car." Older children can make a book into a play-on-tape by choosing different parts and reading into the tape recorder whenever their character speaks.

## Ready Resources

Listed below are many audiobooks that were recommended by carschooling parents. You will find recommendations for historical fiction audiobooks in the Carschooling Social Sciences chapter of this book as well. One homeschool mom sent this tip along with her recommendations: "Keep a pocket dictionary handy to look up the words your children hear but don't understand. People comment on how articulate my children are, and I credit listening to audiobooks for their vocabulary development." This list barely scratches the surface of the quality titles available:

> *Bambi* by Felix Salten as adapted by Janet Schulman, published in 1923; this is the original tale (not the Disney version) of the life of a deer in a forest glade (cassette: ISBN 1-88333-78-8; CD: ISBN 1-88-333-82-6; Audio Bookshelf).
>
> *Cheaper by the Dozen* by Frank B. Gilbreth Jr. and Ernestine Gilbreth Carey; the hilarious antics of a very large family.

Appeals to all ages 5 and up (available on cassette at bookstores and libraries).

*Chronicles of Narnia* by C. S. Lewis is a classic. This beloved collection of seven fantasy books includes *The Magician's Nephew; The Lion, The Witch and the Wardrobe; The Horse and His Boy; Prince Caspian; The Voyage of the Dawn Treader; The Silver Chair;* and *The Last Battle.* Available in several audio versions, one of the best renditions is a recent unabridged release (October 2000) that brings the tales to life. Listeners of all ages will fall under the spell of the mystical land of Narnia, where good and evil battle among mythical creatures (ISBN: 0694524662; HarperCollins Children's Books).

*Charlotte's Web* and *The Trumpet of the Swan* by E. B. White are classic children's books available on tape and CD from bookstores and libraries.

*Hank the Cow Dog* by John Erickson; some of the best family listening you will ever experience is this series of tales about Hank the Cow Dog's adventures as the head of security on a Texas ranch. These stories of dogs, owners, ranch life, and animals are pure fun for the kids, and the subtle social commentary will have parents in stitches as well (available from Maverick Books, 1-806-435-761; www.hankthecowdog.com).

*Harry Potter* series by J. K. Rowling; the unabridged audio versions of this massively popular series are available at bookstores and libraries. The titles include *Harry Potter and the Sorcerer's Stone, Harry Potter and the Chamber of Secrets, Harry Potter and the Prisoner of Azkaban,* and *Harry Potter and the Goblet of Fire.*

*Indian in the Cupboard* series by Lynn Reid Banks is a popular series of books about a boy who discovers that his plastic toy Indian comes to life when locked in a medicine cabinet. The unabridged tapes, read by the author, are great listening (available in bookstores, libraries, and at the author's Web site at www.lynnreidbanks.com).

*All Creatures Great and Small, All Things Bright and Beautiful, All Things Wise and Wonderful, The Lord God Made Them All, It Shouldn't Happen to a Vet, Only One Woof,* and *The Christmas Day Kitten* by James Herriot are autobiographical accounts of the life of a country veterinarian in England beginning in the 1940s. His descriptions of his patients and the people he meets in the course of his work are funny, sad, and full of a sense of wonder about life and nature. The unabridged audiobooks are the best and are available at some bookstores and your local library.

*Lost On a Mountain in Maine* by Donn Fendler is the true story of a 12-year-old boy's harrowing ordeal and triumphant survival (cassette: ISBN 1-883332-04-4; CD: ISBN 1-883332-65-6; Audio Bookshelf).

*My Side of the Mountain* by Jean Craighead George is the tale of one boy's wilderness survival experience (available on audio-cassette at bookstores and libraries).

*Where the Red Fern Grows* by Wilson Rawls is the touching story of a boy and his dogs. Be prepared to pull over at the end of the tape to have a good cry (available on audiocassette from bookstores and libraries).

*Whirligig* by Paul Fleischman is the story of a young boy whose deadly error in judgment takes him on a journey of atone-ment through which he discovers the preciousness of life (cassette: ISBN 1-883332-38-9; CD: ISBN 1-883332-69-9; Audio Bookshelf).

# VO-CAR-BULARY

Building vocabulary helps your children succeed with their studies and with life in general. It will improve their reading capability, writing, and how they articulate thoughts and communicate with others. Carschoolers can even improve their scores on SATs by improving their vocabulary. Learning to have fun with words helps kids to realize what great tools they are for expression. Keep a dictionary and a thesaurus handy in the car so you can look up new words you see on signs along the road, or that come up in conversations, or that are narrated in audiobooks. Here are some activities you can do to expand your vocabulary and have fun with words while on the road.

## The Car Mechanic's Cat

Here is an old parlor game we renamed "The Car Mechanic's Cat." One player begins by saying, "The car mechanic's cat is an adorable cat." The second player has to come up with another A word to describe the cat and might say, "The car mechanic's cat is an aggressive cat." Play continues until someone can't think of another A word. That person is "out" and play continues with B words. Play continues through each letter of the alphabet or until one player is left. This game works really well in a large group. A small family can adapt the game so players don't have to drop out. Simply offer a jelly bean or a penny or some other treat to the players that make it through each letter of the alphabet round. The player that couldn't think of a word in any given round wouldn't get the treat at the end of that particular round.

## How Many Words Per Minute?

Here's a game that tests a player's vocabulary. Use a stack of alphabet flash cards or write down each letter of the alphabet on a separate piece of paper and put them all into a bag. Shake them up until they are thoroughly shuffled. In addition to the bag with alphabet letters, you will need a stopwatch or a clock with a second hand and a paper and pencil. One player is the Timekeeper. The Timekeeper draws an alphabet letter from the bag. The other player must say all of the words he or she can think of that begin with that letter in one minute. As the player calls off words, the Timekeeper keeps track of them with tally marks. When the minute is up, the Timekeeper totals up the tally marks to find the score. Then the players switch roles and repeat the process. The person with the highest score wins. (*Note:* Certain letters will present more difficulty than others. To be fair, players might want to eliminate Q, J, K, X, and Z from the game.)

### Ready Resources

*Word Smart Junior-Living Language: Build a Straight 'A' Vocabulary*, published by Random House (ISBN: 0609600141), contains two 60-minute audiotapes based on the popular paperback book. This thoroughly entertaining vocabulary booster has funny examples of word usage that your carschoolers are sure to remember so they can ace those SATs! It is available through bookstores and at www.amazon.com.

## Pave the Way with Palindromes

A palindrome is a word that is spelled the same forward or backward. Examples include "dad," "mom," "wow," "radar," "kayak." There are even palindrome names, titles, phrases, and sentences (some that make sense, and some that don't) in which the series of words that make up the sentence or phrase are spelled the same forward and backward. For example, if you were traveling in northern California in the city of Yreka, you might visit the "Yreka Bakery"—it's spelled the same forward or backward. Another popular palindrome is "A man, a plan, a canal—Panama!" Challenge your carschoolers to find palindromes on billboards and advertisements or make up their own! Award one point for each word palindrome, two points for each name or title, three points for each phrase, and five points for each sentence. The person who gets the most points wins!

*Ready Resources*

Would you like to have more palindromes to peruse in the car? You can print out a free list of palindrome words, phrases, sentences, and even riddles (where the answer to a question is a palindrome) at the Kids' Pages Web site for the National Institute of Environmental Health Sciences (www.niehs.nih.gov/kids/palindromes.htm).

# Getting to the Root of It

My kids are fascinated with learning how our language (English) developed. We have studied the Greek and Latin roots of English words, and it has improved their vocabulary as well as their spelling. We use a book called *English From the Roots Up* by Joegil Lundquist and flash cards designed to use with the book (available from Excellence In Education 1-626-821-0025 or www.excellenceineducation .com). It's fun to find root words on billboards and buildings as you travel along your route. Have carschoolers call out as many words as they can find that have Greek and Latin roots, scoring one point for every word and two more points if the carschooler can correctly identify the root and its meaning. Here are some of the most common Greek and Latin roots that we have found along our route:

> *Autos* from the Greek word for self. The Greek word for move
>     is *mobilis*. So "automobile" translates to self-moving.
> *Corpus* from the Latin word for body. Many companies are
>     in*cor*porated, so that's an easy one to find on buildings
>     and billboards.

*Centum* from the Latin word for hundred. We look for ads in store
windows that say, "Twenty per*cent* off" to find this one.

*Dens* from the Latin word for tooth. We've seen this word on *den*-
tist's office signs.

*Inter* from the Latin word for between. In Silicon Valley, California (where we live), this root word is readily apparent in
products involving the *Inter*net.

*Photos* from the Greek word for light. We
find this in *photo*graphy advertisements
for cameras and film.

*Phone* from the Greek word for sound. We
have found this on tele*phone* booths.

*Polis* from a Greek word for city. Every time
we see a *pol*itical slogan or see a *pol*ice
car we call out this root word.

*Techne* from the Greek word for art or skill.
*Techno*logy is a word we see frequently
on signs.

*Tele* from the Greek word for faraway or distant. We find this in ads for *tele*vision
and *tele*phones.

## Word Chains

To improve vocabulary skills and an understanding of how words go together to create
phrases, create a chain of words. The first
player begins by saying a short, intelligible
phrase made up of two to four words such as "rest stop." The next
player says a phrase that beings with the last word of the first
player's phrase, for example, "stop on a dime." Play continues with
each player creating a phrase using the last word of the previous

> **From the
> Information Highway**
>
> In English, the letter
> combination "ough" can
> be pronounced nine dif-
> ferent ways as demon-
> strated in this sentence:
> "A rough-coated, dough-
> faced, thoughtful plough-
> man strode through the
> streets of Scarborough;
> after falling into a
> slough, he coughed and
> hiccoughed."

player's phrase. In this example, the next phrase might be "dime store" and the play would continue as follows: store closed, closed for lunch, lunch box, box matches. Eventually someone will not be able to think of a phrase, and that player is out. Play continues until only one player remains—the winner.

# Crack the License Plate Code

Text messaging or "texting," as it is sometimes called, refers to the abbreviated method of writing people use to send messages in e-mail and on cellular phones. It was originally a shorthand method for writing messages that could be read on a tiny pager or mobile phone screen. To save time and space, the sender uses abbreviations for words and phrases. For example, instead of writing out the entire phrase, "For Your Information," the letters FYI were substituted. Instead of "Be Right Back," you simply write the letters BRB. Many kids who use e-mail like the "secret language" aspect of texting. With the ever-increasing popularity of e-mail communication and cell phones, it looks as if text messaging is here to stay. As a matter of fact, the *Concise Oxford Dictionary* now considers it an integral part of the English language and includes an appendix listing many of the abbreviations and their meanings. Here is a list of some of the more popular text message shortcuts.

### MINI TEXT MESSAGE DIRECTORY

| | |
|---|---|
| B = be | EZ = easy |
| BCNU = be seeing you | FX = fix |
| BRB = be right back | GTG = got to go |
| BTW = by the way | HAND = have a nice day |
| C = see or sea | HS = house |
| COZ = because | K = okay |
| CU = see you | LOL = laughing out loud |

LV = love

M = am

NE = any

NE1 = anyone

NO1 = no one

O = oh

OIC = oh, I see

PLS = please

R = are

RU = are you

THX = thanks

U = you

UR = you are

WKND = weekend

XLNT = excellent

Y = why

YR = your or you are

Some numbers, such as these, have several meanings in text messages :

2 = two, or to, or too

4 = four or for

8 = eight, or ate, or it can be substituted in any word that has the "ate" sound such as GR8 for "great," L8 for "late," or W8 for "wait" or "weight."

Also look for letter-number combinations such as these:

2DAY = today

2NITE = tonight

CUL8ER = see you later

4EVR = forever

URGR8 = You are great.

Use the Mini Text Message Directory and your imagination to create personalized license plates for various occupations. (The license plates cannot contain more than seven spaces in any combination of letters and numbers.) For example:

2THDOC = Tooth Doctor (Dentist)
PNO2NR = Piano Tuner
HS4U = House For You (Real Estate Agent)

## Create a Text Message

The object of this game is to come up with your own text message using the letters on passing cars' license plates. So, if you spot a license such as BMV 432, you would eliminate the numbers and call out, "BMV stands for Be My Valentine." You score a point for each reasonable one you make. The person with the most points in five miles or five minutes wins!

### Just for Road Scholars

Try to create phrases, poems, or sayings using text messaging and your imagination. Here is a clever poem using text messaging that has been circulated on the Internet. The author is unknown:

2YSUR (Too Wise You Are)
2YSUB (Too Wise You Be)
ICUR (I See You Are)
2YS4ME (Too Wise For Me)

# CAR-RESPONDING

Writing in the car can be a difficult proposition as you dodge potholes and make sharp turns. A lap desk designed for use in the car (see Chapter 2) can provide a steady surface so that the future

Pulitzer Prize–winners in the backseat can write without interruption. Clipboards also provide a convenient writing surface in the car. Try some of these activities with your carschoolers.

## Thanking You

Laura L. of North Dakota has found a surefire way to teach her carschoolers the art of saying "Thank you." "When we travel long distances (usually during the holidays), I bring along stationery and envelopes for the ride home. The kids write (or draw) thank-you notes while their enthusiasm for the gift is still fresh. I bring along an address book, too, and we mail our thank-you notes at post offices we pass along the way."

## Silly Sign Sentences

Give a paper and pencil to each player. Designate one person to be the Caller, and for a period of three minutes have the Caller call out words on passing road signs. Players write the words down and have five minutes to use all the words in one complete sentence containing a subject, verb, and object. The person who uses the most words to create a complete sentence that makes sense wins that round.

## It's Magnetic

Carschoolers like to play with magnetic manipulatives, which are great tools to reinforce spelling and writing skills. Even the most reluctant spellers and writers will begin to fashion new words, phrases, sentences, and even poetry while riding in the backseat. Carschooling mom Kimberly had this to say:

Why leave the magnetic letters, words, and poetry on the fridge? Some cars have places where the magnetic words will stick. If you can't find a place in your car, try using an upside down cookie baking sheet. It's fun to create words and poems with letter and word magnets while you're tooling down the highway.

Have carschoolers choose seven or eight magnetic words each and stick them in any order to a magnetic surface. Have the first player read out loud what her words say, as if reading a sentence. It will probably make no sense at all, but everyone will have a good laugh. Then ask the player to rearrange the magnets to see if she can create a phrase or sentence that makes sense and read it aloud again. If the player can't make any sense of the words she chose, take turns giving other players an opportunity to add one word from their magnetic tiles to help make sense of the player's string of words. This game can be lots of fun with everyone cooperating to create a coherent sentence. This activity can be altered for almost any ability range from new readers to old pros.

### Ready Resources

Most toy stores carry magnetic letters. Here are two Web sites where you can purchase magnetic words, poetry, and more:

www.abcstuff.com/html/magnetic-letters.html
www.magneticpoetry.com

The Magnetic Poetry Company also carries portable magnetic journals and boards that are especially convenient for car travel. You can order a catalog at 1-800-370-7697.

## Making Words Stick

This is a fun activity to reinforce reading and writing skills. Have carschoolers pick out words that they know how to read and stick them to a magnetic surface. Suggest that your carschoolers copy the words on to a piece of paper to create a personal journal of words they can read. Here is another way to save their work. Donna B. says, "We use cookie sheets as a surface to play with our magnetic letters and words in the car. Sometimes the kids are especially proud of a poem or sentences they create and don't want to lose their work. We simply mount their cookie sheet on their bedroom wall so they can admire their work for as long as they want. We also used a cookie sheet to display the magnets we collect as souvenirs from places we visited in our carschool travels."

> **From the Information Highway**
>
> What is the shortest complete sentence in the English language? "I am."

## Car Bumper Poets

Your kids can have fun creating messages to inspire other drivers on the road! The Magnetic Poetry Company has large magnetic words for your car bumper and blank magnetic strips and stencils so carschoolers can create their own words for your car bumper too. Have your carschoolers refine their ideas on paper first, then let them tell the world what they are thinking (available at www .magneticpoetry.com/shopper/carbumper.html).

### Ready Resources

Magna Doodle is a terrific tool to keep in the car. They come in two sizes, one of which is a small, travel version. It reminds me of an Etch-A-Sketch, but it is much easier and less frustrating to use. The Magna Doodle consists of a magnetic drawing board and an attached wand-type writing/drawing device. Put the wand on the screen and create words, sentences, poetry, numbers, pictures, and more. Magna Doodles are available wherever toys are sold.

# SPEAKING GRAMMATI-CAR-LY

Learning grammar and parts of speech can be an interminable bore for many kids. The only way to make learning grammar as painless as possible is to do it with a sense of humor. Carschoolers definitely don't recommend diagramming sentences in the car, but they do have some neat ideas for making grammar fun.

## What Part Is That?

A simple way to help kids identify parts of speech is to have them search for words that are examples on road signs and billboards. Have carschoolers find words representing each of these parts of speech:

**Nouns** are words that describe a person, place, thing, or idea.

**Pronouns** substitute for nouns such as *we, I, he, us, she, them*.

**Verbs** express action or a state of being such as *run, jump, fly,* and *is* or *was*.

**Adjectives** describe nouns; for example, *big, blue, cold, thin*.

**Adverbs** modify or describe a verb and often end in "ly"; for example, *happily, slowly, really*.

**Prepositions** give a noun's relation in place, direction, or time to another word in a sentence. Words that are prepositions include *to, at, behind, under, in, from, by, on, in,* and *after*.

**Conjunctions** join other words such as *and, but, or, although*.

**Interjections** add emphasis, are usually used alone, and are frequently followed by an exclamation point: *Wow! Oh! Cool! Yikes!*

*Ready Resources*

If you need to brush up on your own grammar, here are some good places to start:

*The Princeton Review Grammar Smart Junior: Good Grammar Made Easy* by Liz Buffa, published by Random House. This Parents' Choice award-winning book (also available on CD) provides fun and simple exercises for learning good grammar. Available at bookstores and online at www.randomhouse.com.

*Basic Skills for Homeschooling: Reading, Writing, and Math for the Middle School Years,* by Lee Wherry Brainerd, Jessika Soban- ski, and Ricki Winegardner published by Learning Express (ISBN: 1576853950).

## Can You *Automobile?*

This is a fun verb-search game. The first player, the Guesser, covers his or her ears while the rest of the players think of a verb. (Remem- ber, a verb is an action word like "jump," "laugh," "run," or "cook.") Then the Guesser tries to guess what the verb is by asking questions with the word "automobile" substituted for the verb. For example, if the verb is "cry," the Guesser might ask, "Do cats automobile? Do you need a ball to automobile? Do you automobile with your hands?" The other players answer "yes" or "no." When the first player correctly guesses the verb, the play passes to the next person. The game is over when everyone has had a chance to be the Guesser.

## Miles of Metaphors and Similes

Metaphors and similes are figures of speech used to make comparisons. There is a slight difference between the two forms of comparison. When making a metaphor, you take one thing or noun and literally describe it as something else. For ex- ample, "The clouds were cotton balls dotting the sky" or "The leaves were fluttering butterflies as they fell to the ground." When making a simile, you compare two things by linking them with the words "like" or "as." For example, "The road curved like a snake through the mountain pass" or "He was cold as a snowman."

Have each carschooler pick a noun from a billboard or sign. Challenge them to create a metaphor and a simile using the word. For example, you might see the word "computer." An example of a metaphor would be, "His brain is a computer." An example of a simile would be, "His brain works *like* a computer."

## Mission Onomatopoeia

Onomatopoeia is a figure of speech for a word that imitates the sound of what it describes. For example *buzz, clang, hiss, moan, purr,* and *splash.* Tell the kids that their mission is to find examples of onomatopoeia on billboards and road signs.

## Impersonating a Person

Personification is a term used to describe a figure of speech that gives an inanimate or nonhuman object human qualities. For example, "The *cars crawled* along the highway" or "The *monkeys laughed* at the zoo visitors." Have your carschoolers pick a word that describes an inanimate object from a roadside sign (such as airplane). Then find a verb (an action word) commonly associated with human behavior from a sign (such as played). Challenge them to use the two words to make a sentence that is an example of personification. For example, "The airplane played in the clouds."

## Alliteration with Tongue Twisters

Alliteration is a technique used in writing or speaking in which several words in a row (in a phrase or sentence) begin with the same consonant. Tongue twisters are notorious for using alliteration, such as "Peter Piper picked a peck of pickled peppers." You will discover alliteration in prose, too; for example, "The cunning cat crouched carefully before capturing the mouse," or "Little Lucy's lizard lay in her lap." Reciting tongue twisters is one way to encourage the use of alliteration.

Tongue twisters are fun for everyone. Pick a tongue twister and have every passenger take a turn repeating it three times in a row—as fast as they can go. The player who can do it without making a mistake wins. To level the playing field, you may want to give young children easier and shorter phrases and give older children the longer versions. Here are some tongue twisters to get you started:

The big black bug bled blue blood on the bare barn floor.

Clean clams crammed in clean cans.

Green glass globes glow greenly.

Peter Piper picked a peck of pickled peppers. If Peter Piper picked a peck of pickled peppers, how many pickled peppers did Peter Piper pick?

Real rock wall.

She sells seashells down by the seashore.

Six thick thistle sticks.

Throw three free throws.

Toy boat.

Unique New York.

I wish to wash my Irish wristwatch.

How much wood would a woodchuck chuck if a woodchuck could chuck wood? He'd chuck all the wood that a woodchuck could if a woodchuck could chuck wood.

## Ready Resources

For more ways to turn grammar drudgery into "grammati-car" fun, check out these resources:

*Mad Libs,* by Roger Price and Leonard Stern, is a simple and fun
game that can be played with two or more players. Purchase
a Mad Lib tablet at your local book or toy store. In it you will
find stories containing blank spaces where words are left out.
One player, the Reader, selects one of the stories. The Reader
doesn't tell anyone what the story is about. Instead, the
Reader asks the other players, the Writers, to provide words.
These words are used to fill in the blank spaces in the story.
To play, the Reader asks each Writer to call out a word that is
an adjective, verb, noun, or whatever part of speech the blank
space in the story needs. The Reader writes the words in the
blank spaces in the story. After all the spaces are filled in, the
Reader reads the story out loud—usually with very funny results (published by Price Stern Sloan, Inc.).

*Grammar Rock* is awesome! Diane B. says, "My kids are addicted.
These catchy songs are perfect to help with the boring rote
learning involved with grammar rules. School House Rock
has been around since I was a kid and has proved itself with
its longevity. Now owned by Disney, you can get them at
many record stores or online at www.barnesandnoble.com.
My daughter has the CDs for her room and we keep the audiocassette tape in the van."

*Grammar Songs* by Audio Memory Publishing sets all of the parts
of speech (except conjunctions) along with the rules of punc-
tuation to music. Available on CD or cassette, Grammar
Songs includes a 72-page workbook with song lyrics, illustrations, drills, and writing exercises (available at 1-800-365-
SING or www.audiomemory.com).

*Funky Phonics* by Sara Jordan teaches reading readiness skills
with phonics and whole language. The songs about vowels
are lively and upbeat. There is also an "Animal Song" that introduces letters of the alphabet and includes interesting facts
about animals. There are other interesting songs about

telling time and learning the days of the week, and even an environmental tune (available in cassette/book: ISBN 1-895523-08-7; and CD/book: ISBN 1-894262-20-4; call to order at 1-800-567-7733 or go online at www.sara-jordan.com).

# THE RHYTHM OF THE ROAD

## Bumper Sticker Poetry

This is a really fun game that will appeal to all of the backseat poets in the family. Every player will need a pencil and paper. Designate one person to be the Word Collector for each round. As you drive by cars with bumper stickers, the Collector chooses one word from each of four different bumper stickers. Then the Collector tells the other players the four words he or she selected. The players have five minutes or five miles to create a four-line, rhyming poem using one word in each line. At the end of five minutes everyone reads their poems out loud. Play continues as long as you like. At the end of the game, collect all of the poems and make a bumper sticker po-etry booklet. Each time you play the game, add the poetry to the booklet. Have a car poetry reading from time to time to remind everyone of the creative, silly, fun, and interesting poems they have made.

## Poetry in Motion

K. O'Hara of Illinois reports, "Poetry was always in mo-tion in our car. Even though most of the poetry available on audio-tapes is designed for adults, we'd listen and talk about the poem and what the poet was trying to say while we were driving along in the car. Sometimes I would introduce a poet at home and then in the car we'd extend that lesson to memorizing poetry verses and trying to recite them. We'd help each other out by reminding each other of a part that was left out. Usually the kids' memories were very accurate—and it was a great way to let them show off. I'd initiate poetry recitations by saying, 'Do you remember a poem about a flower or a dog?' Or I'd say, 'Do you remember a poem by Emily Dickinson, Shel Silversteen, or Daniel Pinkwater?' The kids loved funny poems and enjoyed those recitations most of all."

## Road Rhymes

Rhyming and reciting words with the same sounds give children metaphonological awareness or sound-symbol awareness that is crucial for reading. Rhyming can also help with spelling as children learn to recognize words with similar sounds in which portions of the words are spelled the same way. Bill and Christy of Canada carschool their children and enjoy playing this rhyming game.

Each player takes a turn saying the rhyme and filling in the blanks with words that rhyme. Play continues in rounds. At the end of each round, if all the players made successful rhymes, everyone gets a treat—a penny, a peanut, a raisin, whatever. If someone doesn't make a rhyme, they skip the treat and sit out one round. Play continues as long as everyone is enjoying the game. Here is a sample round of the rhyming game:

*I can make a rhyme any old time.*
*To rhyme with _____ I say _____.*

Here is a sample of a completed rhyme:

*I can make a rhyme any old time.*
*To rhyme with <u>car</u> I say <u>star</u>.*

**From the Information Highway**

Hyperbole is an exaggeration. For example, "I'm so hungry I could eat a horse," "I've got a ton of homework to do," and "I'm so tired I could fall asleep with my eyes open."

(*Note:* If you are playing the game with very young children, simply fill in the first blank and let the kids fill in the next one.)

## Just for Road Scholars

In this game players use a clue word to figure out the Rhyme Riddle. One player is designated as the "Rhyme Riddler." The Rhyme Riddler thinks of two words that rhyme. The first word is the riddle or mystery word, and the second word is the clue. The Rhyme Riddler says, "I'm thinking of a word that rhymes with (<u>the clue</u>)." The other players try to guess what the rhyme word is by asking questions that describe a word that rhymes with the clue word. The Rhyme Riddler may answer, "Yes" or "No, it isn't a (<u>the word that the other players described</u>)." For example, the Rhyme Riddler thinks of "car" and "far." He or she says, "I'm thinking of a word that rhymes with far." Another player says, "Does it twinkle in the night sky?" The Rhyme Riddler responds, "No, it isn't a star." The first player to guess the mystery word wins and becomes the Rhyme Riddler. If a player asks a question that stumps the Rhyme Riddler, that player wins and gets to be the next Rhyme Riddler. For example, if a player asks, "Is it a glass container?" and the Rhyme Riddler can't think of "jar," then the player who asked the question that stumped the Rhyme Riddler wins.

# LAST WORD

All of the games and ideas suggested in this chapter can help create a lifelong love of language arts. Storytelling and audiobooks will improve listening, memory, and comprehension skills as well as develop vocabulary. Playing games with grammar and parts of speech will help your children to express themselves well both orally and in writing. These activities are not meant to be used as a rigid curriculum, but as a fun method for cultivating the development of your children's literacy skills. By providing opportunities to play with language, your kids will learn volumes about the art of communication.

CHAP
6
Carschooling
**SOCIAL
SCIENCES**

ARSCHOOLERS ENGAGE in drive-by history. In this chapter you will discover how to use roadside textbooks called "historical markers" to learn the history of your town, county, state, and country. Join the carschool tradition of passing down family stories to your children to preserve family history and promote understanding of previous generations and bygone eras. Turn lunchtime into learning time with Brown Bag History. Play the Tour Guide game and comment on the houses, people, and landscapes you see to raise awareness of social and cultural differences. Learn how listening to historical fiction can increase your family's knowledge of important historical events. I have included carschoolers' favorite activities, historical trivia games, and their recommendations for the latest portable tools to expand your knowledge of the history of the world.

## SOCIAL SCIENCE TOOLS

Here is a list of the basic items that are needed to do most of the activities in this chapter. Always take an inventory of the tools you keep stocked in your carschool before each trip to make sure you have what you need to play the games your family will enjoy.

Aluminum foil

Audiocassette and/or CD
  player

Camera and film (Polaroid
  preferred)

Clothesline

Clothespins

Dry cloth

Flat, black crayons or a lumber
  crayon

Masking tape

Paper bag

Paper for notes, butcher
  paper, newsprint paper

Pen

Soft-bristle brush

Spray bottle of water

Sponge

Scissors

Shoebox (or a box with a lid)

Tape recorder

# ROADSIDE HISTORY

My kids used to think of history as irrelevant because it happened long ago to people with whom they had no connection. That misconception stopped during our carschooling travels as historical highway markers shouted at us, "Something important happened right here!" As I hit the brakes and pulled over to read the marker, it gave my kids a *place* in their own world that they could connect to the history that had occurred there. Highway historical markers exist along interstates and byways in America and on the roads of other countries as well. They offer an informative trip back in time to the era and events they commemorate. Your carschoolers can learn a lot by reading these roadside history textbooks. If your family enjoys this activity, it might be helpful to get a bumper sticker that says, "Caution: I Brake for Historical Markers!"

# Roadside Markers As Springboards to History

Historical markers often contain just a few short sentences about the person or event they commemorate. If your kids seem interested, encourage them to look up more information about the people, places, or events described on the marker using the Internet, an encyclopedia, or by contacting your local historical society or library. When I noticed that my children were particularly interested in a person or event, I tried to find audiobooks about them. The kids really enjoyed knowing they had walked right on the spot that an explorer had walked on, and it enriched their understanding of that aspect of history. In fact, they frequently asked to revisit a site after hearing a fictional or biographical account that included a person or event they had read about on a historical marker. Other parents have had similar experiences, as Robin explains:

> We stop at historical markers along the way. I just pull over and quickly read them. Rarely do we bother to get out of the car. There's so much local history in these markers that go unnoticed to the traveler who just heads for the famous spots. Other times I simply comment as we are driving by a marker, "Oh, we're on the same road as the Oregon Trail," or "That exit takes you to the site of the Battle of Little Bighorn." Usually conversations continue for miles about the events the markers commemorate.

## *Ready Resources*

You don't have to drive aimlessly around searching for historical markers. Many are indicated on maps provided by historical societies, automobile clubs, and in some cases, various government departments of transportation. I also maintain a directory at www .Carschooling.com that includes Web sites and guide books for each state where you can find information on the location of historical markers.

# Historical Marker Countdown

Carschoolers in Georgia decided to visit every historical marker in their county. Their mother, Michelle, reported that they spent an hour or two every day over a two-week period traveling to different marker locations. The kids took close-up photographs of every marker so that they could read the text on the developed photograph. Then they put the photos in an album along with written comments about the site and what they thought about it. Sometimes the kids commented on the history, other times they wrote about a game they played nearby, or mentioned something that they found close to the site that was of interest. The written comments helped the family to remember each site and what it designated. Michelle says, "They still like to flip through the album and talk about local history."

## Just for Road Scholars

Did you know that not all historical markers are accurate? Just as in history textbooks, mistakes are sometimes made in what is written in stone along the highway. Some markers have incomplete information, others are misleading, and still others are downright wrong. Encourage your road scholars to be roadside researchers. What is the topic of the marker? What do they already know about that person or event? Is some information missing that would give a more accurate depiction of the event or person? If your carschoolers discover mistakes, look on the marker to see who erected it. Contact the organization to report the discrepancy and find out how to go about correcting the information. Many historical societies and government agencies that are responsible for marker placement and maintenance rely on individuals just like you to help them. You can get involved in some historical marker projects and help to get old markers corrected or repaired and get new markers placed.

*Ready Resources*

*Lies Across America: What Our Historic Sites Get Wrong*, by James W. Loewen, identifies historical markers, monuments, and sites in every state that have historical interpretations that are either misleading or wrong. Loewen is the author of the award-winning bestseller *Lies My Teacher Told Me*, a book that discredits 12 leading high school history textbooks for erroneous content.

# Rubbing Up History

Carschoolers can do wax rubbings of historical markers as an artistic record of the sites they visit. Rubbings result from placing paper over a raised surface (like the marker) and then rubbing wax crayons over the paper to imprint the patterns. It provides a method for your carschoolers to preserve a little bit of roadside history. (*Note:* Before beginning, always check with the proper authorities to get permission to make the rubbing.)

You will need a soft-bristle brush, small spray bottle of water, sponge, dry cloth, plain white paper, butcher paper, or newsprint paper, scissors, masking tape, and flat black crayons (available from school or art supply stores) or a lumber crayon (available at hardware stores), to rub over the design. Use the soft brush or rag to gently remove dirt from the surface. Spray the marker lightly with the water and use the sponge to clean it. Dry it completely with the cloth. Cut a piece of paper slightly larger than the marker itself and write the name of the marker, its location, and the date of your rubbing on the back. Fasten the paper securely to the marker with tape so that it doesn't move. Glide the rubbing crayon evenly in long strokes along the outside edges of the marker, creating an outline or frame. Then fill in the middle with strokes that follow in the same direction, applying even pressure. You may need to experiment a bit with the amount of pressure to use to get the desired look. The harder you rub, the darker the rubbing will be. You will start to see the designs and words from the marker emerge on your paper. When finished, remove the paper from the marker. Remove the tape and trim the rubbing to the desired size.

For an easy alternative to crayon rubbings, try using aluminum foil and a damp sponge. Place the foil (shiny side down) on the marker. Press the damp sponge gently across the foil to create an instant impression of the marker.

### How to Make Your Own Rubbing Crayons

Collect all of the broken crayons in the house, or purchase used crayons at garage sales. Remove the paper. Place them in an empty, clean can (a coffee can, for example). Put the can in a saucepan with just a few inches of water and bring the water to a simmer. The crayons will melt. Use a wooden paint stirrer to blend the colors. When they are completely melted and a uniform color, pour the wax into an old muffin tin (lined with paper cups). Let the crayons cool completely in the tins until they are solid again. You now have crayon blocks for making rubbings.

### *Ready Resources*

Historical marker rubbings are just like the popular hobby of gravestone rubbing. Gravestone Artwear (1-800-564-4310 or www.gravestoneartwear.com) offers a beginner's "Gravestone Rubbing Kit" that will work for historical markers as well. It contains two cupcake-shaped rubbing waxes, five sheets of rubbing paper (24 × 36 inches), a natural bristle brush, masking tape, and instructions. All are packaged in a heavy-duty black paper tube. Keep it handy in the car to preserve your memories of roadside history.

## Brown Bag History

Use bagged lunches to introduce a morsel of history. In addition to sandwiches, fruit, and chips, include a note in each lunch bag that tells about some historical event that occurred on that day or the name of an important person in history who was born on that day. Have your carschoolers read their note out loud and let your lunchtime conversations revolve around the people who were born and the events that occurred on that day in history. Create your own historical calendar as a reference for Brown Bag History, selecting events that may have more meaning or be more interesting to your carschoolers.

## Ready Resources

Here are some resources for finding out about historical events that occurred on any given day of the year.

### WEB SITES

**Carschooling Web site:** At www.Carschooling .com you can access a calendar with historical information about each day of the year and print it out for free.

**Library of Congress Web site:** American Memory at http://lcweb2.loc .gov/ammem/today/ offers "Today in History," which lists events that took place in American history on any given date. It provides a brief description and contains links for further information from the archives of the Library of Congress.

**History Channel Web site:** "This Day in History" at www.history channel.com/thisday/ offers a listing in all of the following categories: Automotive History, Civil War History, Cold War History, Crime History, Entertainment History, Literary History, Old West History, Technology History, Vietnam War History, WWII History, and Wall Street History. You can search all of the categories by date.

> **From the Information Highway**
>
> The Lincoln Highway was the first interstate highway and was built in 1915. It went from New York to San Francisco. Today, Interstate 80 follows much of the original highway.

*New York Times* **Web site:** Try "On This Day" at www.nytimes.com
/learning/general/onthisday/ for a story of historical signifi-
cance that corresponds with the day's date. Stories are from
the *New York Times'* archive, are worldwide in scope, and include original photographs and illustrations.

**BOOKS**

*On This Day in History* by Leonard Spinrad et al. This book offers
a day-by-day historical collection of significant world events.

*A Dictionary of Dates (Oxford Paperback Reference)* by Cyril Leslie
Beeching. A comprehensive compendium of birth dates of
historical figures and anniversaries of historical events. From
famous cultural icons to scientific developments, this chroni-
cle of world history will keep you informed about what happened on any given day in history.

# PERSONAL HISTORY

The fact that several generations are represented in most families at
any given time makes it a natural starting place for a discussion of history. Helping your children to understand that the story of their own
lives is a part of history can make the subject much more meaningful.
Here are some ideas and activities carschooling parents use to reinforce the idea that history is very much a part of our everyday lives.

## Clothesline History

Katy Hunt is a homeschooling mom and history buff. She spends a
lot of time in the car with her family. For a variety of reasons they
commute three-and-a-half hours one way between two homes in
California; one is located on the Mendocino coast, and the other is

just south of San Francisco. Knowing that many children don't like history, Katy and her husband, Stephen, determined to make it relevant to their children, Huckleberry and Hallie. Clothesline History is one of the ingenious ideas they used to "turn their kids on" to history. To play Clothesline History, you will need a Polaroid camera and film, some clothesline and clothespins, and paper and a pen. Explain to your children that you are going to keep a pictorial history of your car trip using a clothesline and pictures you take along the way. Since the starting point for your trip is home, instruct one of the kids to take a Polaroid picture of the family at home. Get a piece of clothesline and attach the new picture of your family to the beginning end of the clothesline to represent the start of your trip. Now string this clothesline across the car, in a not-too-inconvenient spot. (The Hunts strung the line between the two hooks in the car that are for clothes or jackets.)

Each time you stop along the way, take a picture of where you stop or purchase picture postcards of places you visit. When you get back in the car, attach the new picture to the clothesline in the order in which it was taken, creating a history of your road trip. You can hang other things besides photographs from the clothesline as reminders of the trip. (Katy's kids started to save their candy wrappers when they stopped to buy a snack and hung them from the history line.)

When you stay at a motel or in a campground, remove the clothesline from the car, hang it in a conspicuous place, and talk about what you have done. Encourage conversation by asking the kids what they like most about the trip, or ask them to recall what they have seen along the way. Listen to their comments and select one or more to write down and hang next to that day's pictures. (For example, let's say you visited a redwood tree grove and took a picture of a redwood tree. Your child comments, "The redwood tree was really tall." Write down that comment—or have your child do it—and hang it on the line next to the picture.) Your children can also draw a picture of what they saw or did to be hung on the line. Never force your children to journalize; simply ask for a comment, record it, and hang it on the line in the right chronological order, thereby demonstrating history as it happens.

Your children will begin to understand that history is really just the story of people's lives—an account of what happened in their day and time. Talk to your children and help them make the connection that ancient history is about the people who lived during a certain period of time and what their days were like—just as current history is about your children's days and their lives.

At some point, your history line may become too full. If that happens, simply store the full line carefully and cut a new piece of line to record subsequent events. (Katy and Stephen explained to their kids as they stored the line that it represented their *past* history and would eventually become their *ancient* history.)

When your trip is over and you arrive home, take all of the pieces of history lines, tie them together in chronological order, and string it through the house. Then walk along your history timeline and recall the highlights of your trip.

During this recollection, pick up the starting place on your history line and point out to the kids that your family history doesn't just begin with the start of your trip and go forward into the future—it also goes into the past. Ask, "What came before that first Polaroid picture on our trip?" Your kids may shout out, "Our whole lives!" Help them to really understand the concept of past history by explaining that part of their life history did come before the trip. Explain that before their history began, their parents were little kids taking trips with Grandma and Grandpa. Before that, Grandma and Grandpa were kids taking trips with Great Grandma and Great Grandpa. By demonstrating how their personal history is connected to the history of other relevant people in their lives (living or deceased), they can begin to see what history is really all about.

## What's in a Name?

Did you ever wonder who thinks up the names for cars? Where did the names Honda, Jaguar, and Volkswagen come from? Many are named after the people who designed or manufactured them; others have more unique origins. Ask your carschoolers to spot different makes of cars along the way and guess how they got their names. Here is a list of car names and a little history behind the names to share with your carschoolers:

**BMW:** I thought this was an acronym for British Motor Works, but it really stands for "Bayrische Motorenwerke," German for "Bavarian Motor Works."

**Buick:** Named after David Dunbar Buick (1854–1929), a Scottish immigrant who sold his plumbing business to build cars and establish the Buick Motor Company.

**Cadillac:** Named after LeSieur Antoine de la Mothe Cadillac (1656–1750), a French explorer who colonized land in America near Lake Erie and called it "Ville d'Etroit," which became Detroit, the car capital of the world.

**Chevrolet:** Named after Louis Chevrolet, a race car driver hired to help design a line of automobiles that would bear his name.

**Chrysler:** Named after Walter Percy Chrysler (1871–1940), a master mechanic who founded the Chrysler Corporation and designed the first Chrysler automobile. Chrylser said: "I feel sorry for the person who can't get genuinely excited about his work. Not only will he never be satisfied, but he will never achieve anything worthwhile."

**Datsun:** DAT is an acronym created from the initials of the last names of the Japanese builders of the car: Den, Aoyama, and

Takeuchi. The word "sun" was added to subsequent car models to indicate they were descended from the original.

**Ferrari:** Named after Enzo Ferarri (1898–1988), Italian race car driver and designer. Ferrari said: "Bad luck does not exist."

**Ford:** Named after Henry Ford (1863–1947), inventor of the Model T Ford and the person who introduced moving assembly lines in manufacturing. Ford said: "Any customer can have a car painted any color that he wants so long as it is black."

**Honda:** Named after Soichiro Honda (1906–1991), Japanese manufacturer of motorcycles and cars. He said: "Looking back on my work, I feel that I have made nothing but mistakes, a series of failures, a series of regrets. But I also am proud of one accomplishment. Although I made one mistake after another, my mistakes or failures were never due to the same reason."

**Jaguar:** This name was selected by the car manufacturers from among several submitted by an advertising agency. They proposed jaguar to represent elegant lines, strength, and endurance, much like the jungle cat.

**Mercedes:** Named after the daughter of French car importer Emil Jellinek, upon his strong suggestion to the car manufacturer Gottlieb Daimler.

**Pontiac:** The car was named after the town of Pontiac, Michigan. The town was named after the Ottawa Indian, Chief Pontiac, of the Great Lakes region, who fought to limit British dominance in the 1700s.

**Porsche:** The car was named after Ferdinand Porsche Jr. (1875–1951), who designed airplane engines before turning his attention to car engines and starting his own car company.

**Rolls-Royce:** This car was named after Charles Rolls, an engineer, and Henry Royce, a marketing specialist, who together owned a successful airplane engine manufacturing company.

They eventually branched out and developed the Rolls-Royce automobile.

**Toyota:** Named after Sakichi Toyoda (the spelling is correct), a textile manufacturer who invented Japan's first power loom. His son Kiichiro applied the industrial techniques from manufacturing textiles to manufacturing cars.

**Volkswagen:** A German word for "people wagon," a term that was to represent a reliable car that all people could afford.

**Volvo:** A Latin word that means "I roll."

## Family History in Seven Questions

On a cross-country carschooling trip to visit relatives, the Hunt family composed seven questions to ask grandparents that would reveal their personal history. When they arrived, they tape-recorded the answers to create an audio version of their family history.

The Hunts said that one of the most stunning answers came from the children's grandfather who was born in 1906. He said that he had not traveled more than six miles from his home until he was 18 years old and went away to college! On their car trip home, the children began to count distance in six-mile increments and marveled at the small space in which 18 years of their grandfather's life and history had unfolded. When they arrived home, they used a compass to draw a circle on a map representing a six-mile radius from their home. Then

**From the Information Highway**

In 1920, police officer William Potts adapted red, amber, and green railroad lights to make the world's first automatic traffic light for use on the streets of Detroit, Michigan. At about the same time, Garrett Morgan, reportedly the first African American to own an automobile in Cleveland, Ohio, invented the electric automatic traffic light on which modern four-way traffic lights are based.

they got in the car and drove six miles in four directions from their home: north, south, east, and west. The children were amazed to think that if they had been like Grandpa they would never have seen anything beyond that distance until they were 18 years old. For the Hunts, that exploration into family history through seven questions led to an interesting lesson in geography as well.

Have your carschoolers try these seven questions out on your next family trip:

1. When you were little, did you live in a town or the country?
2. When you were little, did you travel by car, by public transportation, by horse, or by foot?
3. When you were little, what kinds of games did you play and what toys did you own?
4. When you were little, what kind of food did you eat?
5. When you were little, what kind of work or chores did you have to do at your house?
6. When you were little, did you go to preschool, elementary school, high school, or were you homeschooled? What was it like for you?
7. When you were little, did any major event in history take place that you remember? What was it, and what did you think about it?

## A Day in the Life of . . .

Share your personal history with your kids while driving in the car. Chris of Portola Valley, California, succumbs to her children's pleas to hear stories from her childhood and adulthood. She says, "This passing on of my personal history has been an important way of educating my children about their own roots and helping them to see me as a whole person. Hearing about my interesting experiences makes them believe that their lives will be interesting and meaningful, too, and work to make it so."

Dawn of Alabama said that her children (ages 6 and 10) love to hear stories from when she and her husband were little or when their parents dated. Telling personal stories has been a family tradition. Dawn's mother lived four hours away, so she recorded stories about her life on audiocassettes for her grandchildren. Dawn said, "The kids really enjoyed listening to their grandmother tell their favorite stories over and over again. She recently passed away, and now those audiocassettes with her voice will be a treasured keepsake forever. My dad is now continuing the tradition by writing stories  about when he and Mother dated and when I was growing up. Many of the stories provide an opportunity to instill and encourage such qualities as honesty, perseverance, cooperation, and other values our family feels are important."

## Memory Boxes

Here is a terrific idea from the Hunt family of California for encouraging a love of history. On a six-week-long car trip, they used a Memory Box to help the kids record a history of their trip and to instill an understanding of historical *artifacts*. You will need a shoebox, plain adhesive stickers, pen, and things collected and gathered along the way.

Give each child a Memory Box (a shoebox) and tell them to collect things that will not only be reminders of their trip but *artifacts* that record the *history* of their trip. At each stop along the way, encourage them to find an item to put into their Memory Box, such as rocks or feathers found on the ground, or a postcard purchased from a souvenir store. Use the stickers and pen to label the items with the date and location they were found. Each Memory Box will be a mishmash of collections that have relevance to that child and will trigger reminiscences of the trip.

Katy and Stephen Hunt discovered that even though their children knew what was in the boxes they were fascinated by them and spent hours reviewing the contents and talking about them, which made the time on the road pass quickly and painlessly. Katy felt the project was successful because "at the end of the trip the kids considered burying the boxes and their contents, imagining a futuristic archaeologist excavating our yard and discovering these priceless artifacts."

# SOCIAL STUDIES

Learning about different cultures and people in the world, and how they live and work, opens our minds and broadens our point of view. Carschoolers have come up with some unique ways to include social studies on the road.

## The Tour Guide

Here's an interesting suggestion from a carschooling family in Pennsylvania for broadening your children's understanding of the world and the diversity of people in it.

During a lull in a long car trip, look out the car window and explain to your children that history is literally going by them. Tell them that they are traveling through time and passing towns and cities that they have never heard of before, and may never see again. Encourage them to really observe them and lock them into their memories. Instruct them to pretend they are tour guides and describe what they're seeing. Ask, "Is there anything unusual about this particular place that will help us all to remember it?"

If you are traveling through an ethnically diverse area, the kids may start to notice the different cultural influences from one town or neighborhood to the next. One place might be filled with storefronts bearing Chinese names, writing, and architecture, whereas another might be filled with the sights, smells, and sounds of Italy or Mexico or India. Discuss these different cultures and (if time permits) stop to have a meal or snack, ordering a food item that reflects the flavors of that region of the world. Allow your carschoolers to look for souvenirs in little shops as a keepsake of the culture they are experiencing. Keep a world atlas in the car and ask your children to locate the region of the world they have just sampled in miniature.

## Take to the Field

Many cities have neighborhoods with distinct ethnic or cultural influences. To locate them, call the chamber of commerce or visitors bureau. Ask if audiotours of these areas are available that allow you to listen to information about their history and learn about points of interest while touring in your car. If audiotours do not exist, ask for a map with the points of interest highlighted for a self-directed tour. Another way carschoolers can learn about other cultures is by attending cultural festivals. Check to see when these events are nearby and be sure to take your carschoolers out into the field of rich diversity that is represented in our land.

### Ready Resources
Festivals throughout the United States that celebrate the food, music, dance, and customs of other cultures are listed at this Web site: www.festivals.com/.

Museums and historical societies sponsor living history events such as Pioneer Days, Victorian Days, and Civil War Reenactments. You can find listings of living history events at www.livinghistory-online.com and at www.alhfam.org.

Magazines from Cobblestone Publishing (available either by subscription, at bookstores, or at your local library) can be used in the car to explore different people, cultures, and societies. To order or for more information, call (1-800-821-0115) or visit the Web site (www.cobblestonepub.com/pages/callmain.htm). Here is a list of magazines available for carschoolers of various ages:

*Apple Seeds*, general social studies for young readers ages 7 to 9 (9 issues per year).

*Calliope*, world history magazine for readers ages 9 to 14 (9 issues per year).

*Cobblestone*, American history for readers ages 9 to 14 (9 issues per year).

*Dig*, archaeology for readers ages 9 to 14 (6 issues per year).

*Faces*, world culture for ages 9 to 14 (9 issues per year).

*Footsteps*, African American history for ages 9 to 14 (5 issues per year).

Weekly Reader Corporation can be contacted at 1-800-446-3355, or visit their Web site at www.weeklyreader.com. They offer a variety of age-appropriate news publications for classroom and in-dividual use, including these two publications:

*Weekly Reader*. A timely, elementary-grade newsmagazine that en-hances social studies curriculum. A different version of the magazine is published for each grade, taking into account typ-ical reading and interest levels. (25 issues, weekly delivery)

*Current Events*. A weekly newsmagazine covering current world-wide news stories that are written exclusively for students in grades 6 to 10. (25 issues, weekly delivery)

# How Do They Make That?

Learning how the economy works and what jobs and careers people choose can easily be accomplished by visiting businesses. Many offer tours of their facilities for curious students. Have you ever wondered how jelly beans, chocolate, and ice cream are made? How do you make a crayon or a car? Your carschoolers can discover these things and more by taking factory tours. Next time you take a car trip, see if factories in the area you will be visiting offer tours. Not only will your carschoolers learn how different products are made, but they will learn the history behind these products and gain insight into the American economy.

> **From the Information Highway**
>
> The official name of the Statue of Liberty is "Liberty Enlightening the World." Designed by Frederic Auguste Bartholdi, it was a gift from France. The statue was dedicated in New York Harbor in 1886.

*Ready Resources*
*Watch It Made in the U.S.A.: A Visitor's Guide to the Companies that Make Your Favorite Products* by Bruce Brumberg and Karen Axelrod is available at the library, in bookstores, or by calling 617-734-6184. This is an excellent resource for finding factories that offer tours all around the country.

An online source that lists some factory tours as well is www.howstuffworks.com/factory-tour.htm.

# AUDIOHISTORY

CDs and cassettes that have historical music, narratives, biographies, and historical fiction provide good listening experiences for seat-belted learners. Here are some suggestions your family may enjoy.

# Making History Sing

Bluestocking Press specializes in products that encourage interest and understanding in history, government, and economics and features good historical fiction, hands-on activities, coloring books, historical craft kits, historical paper dolls, historical movies, reprints of historical documents, and an unusual and excellent selection of historical music and narratives on audiocassettes and CDs. Jane Williams, owner of the company, homeschooled her own daughters who helped with the family business by sampling the products in their travels to various education conferences to sell their wares.

Background music can set the stage and the mood for studying a specific event or era in history or provide a nice ambiance in the car while doing some historical sightseeing. As you carschool, Jane suggests that you choose tapes that fit in with the respective geographical part of the country you are traveling through and the historical time period it most notably addresses. For example, if you are traveling through states where Civil War battles were fought, carschoolers could benefit from listening to some authentic Civil War songs. Here are Jane's suggestions for historical music for a variety of time periods.

## Ready Resources

All of the CDs and audiocassettes Jane Williams recommends are available or may be special-ordered from Bluestocking Press. For information, prices, a catalog, or to order, call 1-800-959-8586. You can also visit the Web site at www.bluestockingpress.com or e-mail uncleric@jps.net.

### PILGRIMS

*Penny Merriment: English Songs From the Time of the Pilgrims.* A Plimoth Plantation product, the musical selections on this CD reflect the lives of sailors, farmers, soldiers, craftsmen, courtiers, country lads and lasses, and more.

## COLONIAL TIMES

*The Good Old Colony Days: 18th Century Folk Music* by Linda
Russell. You really get a sense of what family entertainment
was like on this cassette, which includes a collection of political broadsides, marches, love songs, laments, and dance
tunes (including George Washington's favorite). Includes a
booklet of lyrics and the history behind the
songs (ages 9 and up).

*Echoes of Revolution: The Fifes and Drums of Colo-
nial Williamsburg.* Until the 1780s, American
military music was performed with the fife and
drum. All the music on this CD has been re-
searched and documented as authentic to the period.

*The World Turned Upside Down,* by Barry Phillips and friends.
Instrumental arrangements of music from the time of the
American Revolution are featured on this CD, including the
song played at Yorktown when Cornwallis surrendered.

## COLONIAL TO RECONSTRUCTION PERIOD

*America 1750–1890: The Heart of a New Land,* by Hear and Learn.
This historical music cassette is well performed and fun to
listen to, providing a chronological overview of America
through 16 songs, including "Oh Susanna," "The Star Span-
gled Banner," and "Yankee Doodle." This cassette comes
with a book that includes the history behind the songs, photographs, song lyrics, and more (especially good for ages
5 to 12).

## CIVIL WAR

Bobby Horton's series of Civil War CDs are excellent. He tries to
use authentic instrumentation from the time period, and his
voice is reminiscent of the singular soldier sitting around the
campfire singing of good times and bad. My favorites are

*Songs of the Union Army* Volumes 1 and 2, and *Songs of the Confederate States of America* Volumes 2 and 4.

*Hues of Blues and Greys,* performed by After Class. If you want instrumental background music while students are doing other work relative to this time period, this CD has the best selection I've reviewed. Instruments include hammered dulcimer, guitar, mandolin, violin, and cello (all ages).

### WESTWARD MIGRATION, EXPLORERS, AND PIONEERS

*Westward Ho,* by Hear and Learn. Travel West with the settlers, cowboys, and California gold diggers of 1849. Songs include "Home on the Range," "Oh California," "Chisholm Trail," and more. A book is included with the cassette, providing the history behind the songs, photographs, sheet music, and lyrics (especially good for kids 5 to 12).

*Trail's End,* by the Trail Band. The Trail Band applies their enormous talent to these songs, including "Down in the Valley," "Polly Wolly," "Wait for the Wagon," "Little Liza Jane," and more. This is a fun CD.

*Lewis and Clark,* by the Trail Band. This CD features instrumental and vocal music from and about the era of the 1803–06 expedition. Early American folk songs, French Canadian fiddle tunes, classical works, Irish ballads, marches, chanteys, and Native American songs are included.

*Rolling Uphill from Texas,* by Buck Ramsey. This musician makes the listener feel what the cowboy of the old West was feeling. A National Cowboy Hall of Fame award-winner, this CD includes "Git Along Little Dogies," "Cowboy Soliloquy," and "Santa Fe Trail."

For fans of the *Little House* series by Laura Ingalls Wilder, or if you will be carschooling through "Laura Country" in Wisconsin, Missouri, Kansas, Minnesota, and Iowa, you may enjoy these audiocassettes: *Musical Memories of Laura Ingalls Wilder,* a group of 13 songs from the *Little House* books and stories behind the songs in a booklet that accompanies the cassette; *Songs from Home,* a lovely recording of music played on "Pa's" actual fiddle and Mary's actual pump organ plus a vocal rendition of a song written by Laura; and *Laura Speaks,* listen to Laura in her 80s tell about her family and her books in the only known recording of Laura's voice.

# Decade or Dare?

A carschooling family (with three kids ages 9 to 16) changed the old Truth or Dare game into a history challenge. To play, first think of a list of silly consequences; when someone loses the challenge, they must do one of several preselected penalties: for example, singing a difficult song, stating the multiplication facts for a particular number, sitting in an uncomfortable position for five minutes of the car ride, or having to clean the windshields when you stop for gas. The game goes like this.

One person picks a decade (for example, 1490–1500, 1770–1780, 1860–1870, 1910–1920, 1990–2000) and challenges each person in the car to come up with one historical event or fact that occurred during that decade. Play continues from one person to another until someone can't think of a fact (or you can set a limit of 10 or 20 facts and move on to another decade if everyone passes the challenge). If a player fails to come up with a fact, the player must repeat all the facts just heard about that decade or perform a consequence. If the player successfully repeats all the facts, the player gets to restart the game with a new decade of his or her choice.

It is okay to bluff if you don't know. If no one calls your bluff, play continues. If someone calls your bluff, you must repeat all the facts you just heard about that decade or perform one of the preselected consequences. After someone performs a consequence, a new decade is selected and play begins again. Take turns choosing decades. It is also helpful to designate a "bluff-buster" who corrects any bluffs that weren't challenged after the game is over so that no one leaves the game with erroneous information. If the bluff-buster didn't catch your bluff, you must confess your bluff at the end of the game to set the record straight.

## Ready Resources

Here are some terrific resources your carschoolers can use to discover more facts for whatever decade they are interested in:

Boomerang! The Children's Audiomagazine (available at 1-800-333-7858 or www.boomkids.com). When you subscribe to Boomerang, you receive an audiotape in the mail every six weeks that features kid reporters traveling back in time to interview famous people from history, relaying the news, explaining current events, and much more. This is great listening!

Brain Quest for the Car contains more than 1,100 questions and answers all about America (available at most bookstores or visit their Web site at www.brainquest.com). Questions are geared for ages 7 to 12, but all ages could play or participate in some aspect of the game. Brain Quest has many versions, including math, history, and science for just about every age/grade range imaginable.

Fandex are information cards on U.S. presidents, scientists, the Civil War, explorers, state capitals, and more. The cards are all hinged together and fan out for easy use, don't get lost, and don't wind up all over the floor of the car (available at many bookstores and from Rainbow Resources at 1-888-841-3456 or www.rainbowresource.com).

*Lives of Extraordinary Women: Rulers, Rebels (And What the Neighbors Thought)*, by Kathleen Krull. Twenty biographies of powerful women in history complete with triumphs, failures, virtues, and flaws. Some of the women featured are Cleopatra, Joan of Arc, Marie Antoinette, Harriet Tubman, Eleanor Roosevelt, Golda Meir, Indira Gandhi, Eva Peron, and Aung San Suu Kyi. Available on unabridged audiocassette (ISBN: 1-883332-46-X) and CD (ISBN: 1-883332-73-7) from Audio Bookshelf (1-800-234-1713 or www.audiobook shelf.com), and at some libraries.

*Lives of the Presidents—Fame, Shame (And What the Neighbors Thought)*, by Kathleen Krull. American history comes alive as you listen to the tell-all accounts about the interesting and sometimes shocking conduct and behavior of presidents and first ladies. Available on unabridged audiocassette (ISBN: 1-883332-34-6) and CD (ISBN: 1-883332-62-1) from Audio Bookshelf (1-800-234-1713 or www.audiobookshelf.com), and at some libraries.

If you want a medium for imparting audiohistory to students that includes informative narration with music, here are some excellent choices recommended by Jane Williams that are especially good for middle school–aged students. All of the CDs and audiocassettes Jane Williams recommends are available or may be special-ordered from Bluestocking Press. For information, prices, a catalog, or to order, call 1-800-959-8586. You can also visit the Web site at www .bluestockingpress.com or e-mail uncleric@jps.net.

**Oregon Trail:** *Voices from the Oregon Trail,* by the Trail Band. From the theatre production of "Voices from the Trail,"this CD includes songs, narrative accounts, and music that represent the experiences on the trail, from hymns and Native American music to brass band marches. Outstanding!

**California History:** *McNeil's California Songs.* These CDs are chronologically arranged and include historical narration among their vocal and instrumental songs by Keith and Rusty McNeil. They are best suited for ages 10 to adult. *Volume 1—19th Century,* includes Spanish, Native American, and Gold Rush songs. *Volume 2—20th Century,* includes songs about farms, movies, immigration, and more.

**New England (Industrial Revolution):** *McNeil's Working and Union Songs.* These CDs include narration, 36 songs, and one poem that depict the changes in the human condition as America evolved from an agrarian nation to an industrial nation.

**Native American:** *Songs of Earth, Fire, Water and Sky: Music of the American Indian.* Features on-location recordings of Native Americans including the Cherokee, Seneca, Navajo, and Arapaho. There is commentary on the music and explanations of the Butterfly Dance, Alligator Dance, Eagle Dance, Women's Brush Dance, Ribbon Dance, Stomp Dance, and the Oklahoma Two-Step.

**World War II:** *Words and Music of World War Two.* The producers of this CD package have recaptured the mood of the period via broadcasts and popular music of the time linked to-gether by commentary. Includes broadcasts by Edward R. Murrow, the Pearl Harbor Attack broadcast, FDR declaring war, Account of American Forces Landing on Iwo Jima, Truman Announcing Dropping the Atomic Bomb, and Tokyo Rose Broadcasts to the American Troops in the Pacific.

## Just for Road Scholars

Knowledge Products audiocassettes are Bluestocking Press's first choice for studying history, as they include economic, legal, and philosophical history. Older students, ages 14 and up, who are ready and able to use critical thinking while listening will get more from this series. The only drawback to this thought-provoking series is that carschool drivers who want to listen and learn may not want to attempt it in heavy traffic when their concentration is distracted.

## *Ready Resources*

For the study of American history, the two best Knowledge Products series are *The United States at War* narrated by George C. Scott and *The Constitution* narrated by Walter Cronkite. *The United States at War* series is not just about battles; it also includes economic and political history as well as the philosophies behind the wars. *The American Revolution—Part 1* begins 200 years prior to Lexington and Concord and discusses the politics, economics, and ideology that led to the Battle of Lexington and Concord and the desire for separation from England. This particular series is narrated by George C. Scott with character actors delivering primary source material. It is outstanding!

For your study of world history, try Knowledge Products' *The World's Political Hot Spots* narrated by Harry Reasoner, Peter Hackes, and Richard C. Hottelet. Other titles in the series include *Giants of Political Thought*, *Giants of Philosophy*, *The World of Philosophy*, *Great Economic Thinkers*, *Constitutions of the World*, *Religions of the World*, and *Science and Discovery*. All of these resources are available from Bluestocking Press (800-959-8586).

# Facts Wrapped Up in Fiction

Historical fiction is one of the easiest ways to painlessly introduce children to history. The story itself is fictional (although sometimes based on a true story), but it is set in a particular era of history and includes accurate information about the people, culture, politics, and events that took place at that time. Many carschooling families listen to historical fiction while tooling down the highway. Try some of these stories out on your carschoolers.

## Ready Resources

These titles on audiocassette (and in some cases on CD) are among the favorites of carschooling families. I have provided some age-grade range guidelines, but flexibility is the key as children's listening and comprehension skills vary tremendously. All of these books are available in hard or soft cover from bookstores and/or your local library. I have provided ISBN numbers for those recordings that are available for purchase. Those that are out of print may be available at your local audiobook rental store or at your library (ask your librarian about interlibrary loans, if your branch doesn't carry a particular title). For convenience, I have grouped the titles under the historical era they address.

### MIDDLE AGES

*Catherine, Called Birdie,* by Karen Cushman. Gain insight into life in the Middle Ages through the diary of a young woman. Ages 9 and up. (Unabridged audiocassette available from Bantam Books; ISBN: 0553476696.)

### 1600S: PURITANS IN THE UNITED STATES

*The Witch of Blackbird Pond,* by Elizabeth George Speare. A young girl is accused of witchcraft when she tries to help a friend reputed to be a witch. An accurate portrayal of life in Puritan New England. Ages 10 and up. (Unabridged audiocassette available from Listening Library; ISBN: 0807207489.)

## AMERICAN REVOLUTION

*Johnny Tremain: A Story of Boston in Revolt,* by Ester Forbes. A young silversmith's apprentice becomes involved in Revolutionary intrigue that includes the Boston Tea Party and the Battle of Lexington. Ages 8 and up. (Available on audiocassette from your public library or audio rental bookstore.)

*My Brother Sam Is Dead,* by James L. Collier. The heartbreak of war for one family during the American Revolution. Ages 9 and up. (Unabridged audiocassette, ISBN: 1883332192 and CD ISBN: 1883332559 available from Audio Bookshelf.)

## PRAIRIE LIFE IN THE UNITED STATES

*Little House in the Big Woods,* by Laura Ingalls Wilder. Life on the prairie as seen through the eyes of a young girl. Ages 7 and up. (Unabridged audiocassette available from Harper Audio; ISBN: 0060012412.)

*Caddie Woodlawn,* by Carol R. Brink. The adventures of an 11-year-old pioneer tomboy are interspersed with the story of

> **From the Information Highway**
>
> The United States purchased 900,000 square miles of land from France on April 30, 1803, for $15 million (about 4 cents per acre). The Louisiana Purchase Territory became the states of Louisiana, Arkansas, Missouri, Iowa, North Dakota, South Dakota, Nebraska, Kansas, Wyoming, Minnesota, Oklahoma, Colorado, and Montana. The United States bought Alaska from Russia in 1867 for 2 cents an acre or $7.2 million.

her father's reasons for bringing the family to America from England and how he wrestles with a decision to return. Ages 9 and up. (Audiocassette available from your local library or audio rental bookstore.)

*Sarah, Plain and Tall,* by Patricia MacLachlan. A mail-order bride arrives on the Nebraska prairie and must contend with the harsh life while learning to be a stepmother. Glenn Close narrates. Ages 7 and up. (Unabridged audiocassette ISBN: 0898456355 available from Caedmon Audio Cassette; unabridged CD ISBN: 0694526029 available from Harper Audio.)

### THE U.S. CIVIL WAR 1861–1865

*Bull Run,* by Paul Fleischman. This is the story of the Civil War told from the point of view of 16 different people—some from the North and some from the South. The contrasts in perspective bring some understanding to the controversy that led to the war. Ages 10 and up. (Unabridged audiocassette ISBN: 1-883332-37-0 and CD ISBN: 1-883332-58-3 available from Audio Bookshelf.)

*The Red Badge of Courage,* by Stephen Crane. A young boy discovers what it's like to be on the battlefield and wrestles with fear, courage, death, and honor during the Civil War. Ages 12 and up. (Unabridged audiocassette ISBN: 1561004855 and CD ISBN: 9626342080 available from Naxos Audio Books.)

*Across Five Aprils,* by Irene Hunt. A farm boy comes of age during the five years of the U.S. Civil War. Ages 10 and up. (Unabridged audiocassette ISBN: 1883332486 and CD ISBN: 1883332753 available from Audio Bookshelf.)

### EARLY 1800–1900 SEAFARING ADVENTURES

*The True Confessions of Charlotte Doyle,* by Avi. A 13-year-old girl boards a ship in 1832 as a passenger but soon finds herself a member of a mutinous crew. Her seafaring adventure changes her forever. Ages 9 and up. (Unabridged audio-cassette available from your local library or audiobook rental store.)

*Shipwreck at the Bottom of the World—The Extraordinary True Story of Shackleton and the Endurance,* by Jennifer Armstrong. This amazing true story recounts the adventures of Ernest Shackleton and his crew, who set sail in 1914 in an attempt to cross Antarctica. What followed over the next two years is the most amazing human survival story ever told. Ages 10 and up. (Unabridged audiocassette ISBN: 1-883332-39-7 and CD ISBN: 1-883332-54-0 available from Audio Bookshelf.)

## WORLD WAR II AND THE HOLOCAUST

*Anne Frank: The Diary of a Young Girl,* by Anne Frank. This book is a classic and tells the story of a young Jewish girl hiding from the Nazi's with her family. Ages 12 and up. (Unabridged audiocassette available from Bantam Doubleday Dell; ISBN: 0553473476.)

*Number the Stars,* by Lois Lowry. Two girls' lives are changed forever when Nazi soldiers occupy Copenhagen. Ages 11 and up. (Unabridged audiocassette available from Recorded Books; ISBN: 1556908563.)

*Night,* by Elie Wiesel. A heart-wrenching, real, first-person account of the horrors of Nazi death camps told from the point of view of a 14-year-old Jewish boy. For mature children ages 14 and up. (Unabridged audiocassette ISBN: 1-883332-40-0 and CD ISBN: 1-883332-50-8 available from Audio Bookshelf.)

## AFRICAN AMERICAN HISTORY

*Only Passing Through: The Story of Sojourner Truth.* This is a remarkable account of the life of Sojourner Truth. Once a slave, she earned her freedom and became an advocate for the abolishment of slavery. Ages 10 and up. (Unabridged audiocassette ISBN: 188333280X and CD ISBN: 1883332842 available from Audio Bookshelf.)

*Roll of Thunder, Hear My Cry,* by Mildred Taylor. This is the story of a 9-year-old African American girl and her family who live in the Deep South in the 1930s. They survive racism, poverty, sickness, and betrayal as the young girl learns firsthand about social injustice. Ages 9 and up. (Unabridged audiocassette available from Bantam Books; ISBN: 0807206210.)

*The Watsons Go to Birmingham,* by Christopher Paul Curtis. A funny, tragic, and heartwarming story about an African American family's visit to Alabama in the summer of 1963 and the events that forge the Civil Rights movement. Ages 10 and up. Levar Burton does a terrific job of narrating this story. (Unabridged audiocassette available from Bantam Books; ISBN: 0553477862.)

## NATIVE AMERICAN HISTORY

*Island of the Blue Dolphin,* by Scott O'Dell. This is the award-winning, real-life story of a 12-year-old Native American girl who was abandoned with her younger brother on an island off the coast of California. Her brother died and she survived alone for 18 years. (Unabridged audiocassette available from Bantam Books; ISBN: 0553474057.)

*Julie of the Wolves,* by George Jean Craighead. This is the compelling story of a 13-year-old Inuit (Eskimo) girl who runs away from an unhappy arranged marriage and becomes lost on the Alaskan tundra. She must call upon her recollection of the "old ways" to survive, and she gets some help from a pack of wolves. (Unabridged audiocassette ISBN: 1559940476 available from Harper Audio.)

# Making Historical Fiction

These books, while not available on audiocassette or CD, are well worth reading in the car. Read them out loud on long car trips for the whole family to enjoy, or make your own recordings of these books and listen to them while on the road. All are available at your local bookstore or public library.

## Ready Resources

*Ben and Me: An Astonishing Life of Benjamin Franklin as Written by His Good Mouse Amos,* by Robert Lawson. Benjamin Franklin's mouse gives his side of the story on what life is like with Benjamin Franklin. Ages 8 and up.

*Mr. Revere and I: Being an Account of Certain Episodes in the Career of Paul Revere, Esq. as Revealed by His Horse,* by Robert Lawson. The title says it all. Ages 9 and up.

*Patty Reed's Doll: The Story of the Donner Party,* by Rachel K. Laurgaard. Recounts the journey of the Donner Party and the hardships they endured. In this story the more horrific details of the tragic journey are not revealed. Ages 8 and up.

*By the Great Horn Spoon,* by Sid Fleishman. Follow the adventures of Jack and his butler as they travel by ship from the

## From the Information Highway

The United States Pledge of Allegiance was originally written by Frances Bellamy in 1892. Bellamy's original pledge read: "I pledge allegiance to my Flag and the Republic for which it stands, one nation indivisible, with liberty and justice for all." Congress officially established the pledge in 1954 as: "I pledge allegiance to the flag of the United States of America and to the Republic for which it stands, one nation under God, indivisible, with liberty and justice for all."

East Coast, around the horn of South America, to California
to stake their claim in the 1850s Gold Rush. Ages 9 and up.

*Can't You Make Them Behave, King George?; And Then What Hap-
pened, Paul Revere?; What's the Big Idea, Ben Franklin?; Where
Was Patrick Henry on the 29th of May?; Why Don't You Get a
Horse, Sam Adams?; Will You Sign Here, John Hancock?;* and
*Shh! We're Writing the Constitution!* by Jean Fritz. Jean Fritz is
a master at writing historical fiction that can be enjoyed by a
wide age range; the titles mentioned here are for ages 7 and
up. She introduces readers to historical figures through clever
stories laced with humor and keen insight into the politics,
culture, and principles of the times. Her tales include lots of
interesting trivia facts—details that will make you and your
kids feel as if you really know the characters who lived so
long ago.

IN THIS chapter we'll explore how maps and highlighter pens provide hours of fun on the road for student navigators. Learn how out-of-state license plates make convenient tools that you can use to jump-start a lesson in geography. Carschoolers share innumerable resources and activities for learning geography from singing the names of states and capitals to using flags, coins, and inflatable globes! Carschooling just naturally lends itself to the study of geography, so keep your eye out for learning opportunities you'll find along the road.

## GEOGRAPHY TOOLS

Here is a list of the items that are needed to do most of the activities in this chapter:

| | |
|---|---|
| Balloons | Foreign coins |
| Camera (Polaroid preferred) | Highlighter pens/markers |
| Compass | Crayons and colored pencils |

| Maps | Postcards |
|------|-----------|
| Atlas | Quarters |
| Globe | Rubber stamp rings |

# GLOVE COMPARTMENT GEOGRAPHY

Not surprisingly, maps (tucked neatly in the glove compartment when not in use) are the number one tool carschooling families use to learn geography. Here are some activities that will help your carschoolers acquire an understanding of where places exist in relation to one another as they learn to chart their location and destination.

## Road Navigators

Let your carschoolers take turns being the family navigator or map reader. As one carschooling mom said, "Even our 7-year-old has learned to keep track of where we are by reading the exit numbers on the freeways and finding how far across the state we traveled. All of my kids are excellent map readers, not a small thing since I know many adults who still can't tell the difference between a black line (highway) and a blue line (river)."

Maps usually have a key that shows what different symbols on the map represent. For example, a square with a flag on top is symbolic of a school, and a square with a cross on top is a church. Lines of different widths represent certain types of roads and highways. Color has meaning on topographic or road maps, too:

**Blue** indicates water (rivers, lakes, oceans, and so forth)
**Brown** indicates elevation above sea level
**Green** indicates vegetation (trees, forests, and so forth)

**Black** indicates human-made structures (roads, boundaries, buildings, railroads, and so forth)

**Red** indicates major roads and survey lines

These symbols are standard on United States maps, but they
can differ in other countries. While your road navigators are keeping you on track, see if they can tell you what other features shown
on the map are near your present position.

*Ready Resources*

You can print out U.S. topographical map
symbols and their meanings at the USGS
Web site at http://mac.usgs.gov/mac/isb/pubs
/booklets/symbols/roads.html.

> **From the
> Information Highway**
>
> *Vexillology* is a word
> used to describe the
> flags.

# Where in the World?

Provide each player with a copy of the same
map. The first player chooses a location on
the map (a city, river, mountain range, park, and so forth) and tells
everyone the name of the location. Then all of the other players
have 10 minutes or 10 miles to find the location on their maps. The
first person to find it wins 10 points. Play then passes to the second
player who chooses a location, and so on, until there have been as
many searches (or rounds) as there are players in the car. The person with the most points wins.

*Ready Resources*

At this Web site (www.maps.com) you can print out free maps
of states and countries. You can even customize the maps to suit
your needs.

# Charting a Course

Encourage your road scholars to learn to read maps by letting them plot your route to wherever you are going. Tell them that you need to get from one city (or state) to another. Then ask them to look on a map, find the departure and destination points, and pick a course of roads and highways to follow. You can provide younger

children with extra help by telling them the names of cities and landmarks you will pass along the way, so they can easily locate the roads to follow on the map. If you have several children, simply divide the trip into segments and follow a route chosen by each child for a portion of your trip.

Carschool mom Sher taught her kids to be navigators and said, "This method helped our children develop skill and speed at reading maps. They used their map to guide the driver and explain what road or exit to look for next. This process helped them to really understand distance as portrayed on a map and how that relates to real time traveling in the car. We tried to allow time to take back roads when they were chosen and discovered some off-the-beaten-path surprises and real educational opportunities as a result."

This activity can be used for short in-town trips as well. Charting routes using local maps will help your children learn where they live in relation to the store, bank, post office, church, library, a park, or a friend's house.

## Ready Resources

Ride With Me Audiocassettes produces audiotapes that tell the entertaining history, trivia, folklore, and geography of the region you are passing through on your car travels. It's like having a tour guide in the car with you. The audio programs are synchronized to milepost markers, so as you come upon a marker, you listen to a story about the locality you are driving through. The narrator (often a celebrity) instructs the listener to turn off the tape and return when you reach a particular milepost, exit, or landmark. The tapes alert listeners to interesting side trips along the route as well. You can select the tapes by the highway route you will be traveling through, or by state, historic place, or national park; there are a few countries to choose from, too. Listen to samples of the tapes, view a catalog, or place an order at their Web site at www.rwmaudio.com.

*Educational Travel on a Shoestring: Frugal Family Fun and Learning Away from Home,* by Judith Waite Allee and Melissa Morgan, is a value-packed, practical information guide for parents who want to learn through vacations and field trips without spending a fortune. This book should be in every carschooler's library. It contains ideas for learning about geography and many other subjects while traveling and includes an extensive resource guide for inexpensive destinations and activities that both instruct and entertain (ISBN: 0877882045). Available through bookstores and online at http://eaglesnesthome.com.

## Alphabet States and Capitals

Here's an activity suggested by a carschooling mom that uses the alphabet to help name all of the states. Say each letter of the alphabet and see if your carschoolers can name a state that begins with that letter. (There are four states beginning with A, three that begin with C, and so forth.) Give clues when needed, based on information you already know, or based on geographical facts that you can find from looking at a map of the United States. For example, here are some clues for states that begin with the letter A:

> President Clinton came from this state and it's in the South.
>     (Arkansas)
> It's the largest state. (Alaska)
> It borders California on the southeastern side. (Arizona)

While you are playing this game, carschoolers learn many interesting facts about different states as they are mentioned and discussed as clues.

### Ready Resources
Here is a terrific Web site (www.50states.com) that has free information about every state, including size, state flower, nickname, motto, history, and more.

Everyone remembers things better when they are set to music. The Audio Memory Publishing *States and Capitals Songs Kit* teaches U.S. states and capitals. It includes eight practice songs and four test songs and a large 25 × 36 inch map of the United States with 172 items to label. Students can color the map while they listen to the songs. The lyrics of the songs are on the map. One side of the tape teaches the states and the other side teaches the capitals. (All ages.) Visit their Web site at www.audiomemory.com to hear song samples and to order the tapes.

## Stamp Out States

Here is a really clever idea submitted by carschooling mom Leita S. of Arkansas. Before going on a car trip, she copies or prints a map of the United States for each carschooler. Next, she purchases an inexpensive package of stamp rings. (Each stamp ring has a different symbol or picture on it, so the kids can tell them apart.) The kids pick the ring they want and put it on their finger. As they ride, carschoolers watch for license plates from other states. If they see one, they locate that state on their map and stamp it with their ring.

## Mapping the Highlights

Carschooling mom Dawn B. explained that her family travels frequently because her husband's job requires it. Her children (ages 9 and 5) enjoy following the family's route on a map. She gives each carschooler a regional map and folds it so that it is easy for them to see the roads they will be traveling that day. She has the kids mark their starting point and their destination with a star. Then, using a highlight pen, they mark their route as they travel.

Carschooling mom Emily G. of Canada marks their family's travel route on a map with a highlighter pen. Then she glues the map to a piece of cardboard and laminates it with clear contact paper so it will last for the entire trip. Her kids use the map to track their progress on road trips.

If you are not going on a long trip, try this out with your carschoolers. Give your road scholars a city map and let them track your way as you do errands all around town.

## Searching for the Weird and Wacky

When carschoolers get antsy on long trips, pull out your car atlas or map and challenge them to search for cities with weird and wacky names—the United States is full of them! You could also challenge them to find (in the atlas) the following cities and towns and ponder the meaning of the names:

| | |
|---|---|
| Unalaska, Alaska | Bald Head, Maine |
| Why, Arizona | Boring, Maryland |
| Greasy Corner, Arkansas | Hell, Michigan |
| Bummerville, California | Hot Coffee, Mississippi |
| Last Chance, Colorado | Tightwad, Missouri |
| Two Egg, Florida | Square Butt, Montana |
| Hopeulikit, Georgia | Worms, Nebraska |
| Normal, Illinois | Truth or Consequences, |
| Gnaw Bone, Indiana | New Mexico |
| Monkey's Eyebrow, Kentucky | Tick Bite, North Carolina |
| Belcher, Louisiana | Hicksville, Ohio |

Idiotville, Oregon

Defeated, Tennessee

Hoop and Holler, Texas

Satans Kingdom, Vermont

George, Washington

Big Ugly, West Virginia

Imalone, Wisconsin

## Color the States

Photocopy a map of the United States for each carschooler. Whenever someone spots a license plate from one of the states, have them use crayons to color in that state on their map. Even very young children can scribble-color on the map. Sue R. of New Mexico says her kids enjoy this activity and adds, "We seem to have better luck finding out-of-state plates in our hometown during summer vacation time—Memorial Day to Labor Day—there are just more people on the road then."

**From the
Information Highway**

A star on a map usually symbolizes the location of a capital city.

## Mapping Roadside Attractions

Stop at the visitor's bureau to procure maps of the area you are driving through. Then, whenever you stop at tourist spots, historical attractions, or points of interest along the way, ask carschoolers to find that spot on the map and mark it with a highlighter pen. Carschooling mom Annette of North Dakota says, "It's a neat record of where we've been and improves the kids' map reading skills."

# LICENSE PLATE GEOGRAPHY

Next to maps, carschoolers named out-of-state license plates as their favorite resource for introducing the subject of geography.

Here are a few ways license plates can become catalysts for a geographical exploration.

## License Plate Junkyard

Danni, a carschooling mom from Texas, suggested this game that her family enjoys. The object is to spot the most out-of-state license plates that are the farthest away from your own home state. Each player calls out the name of the state when they see an out-of-state license plate. Then they write down that state on a piece of paper and refer to a map to figure out the distance from their own home state. The person with the most license plates from the farthest distance away at the end of the hour, day, or trip, wins. The only other rule is that if you see a junkyard you can say, "Junk your cars (<u>fill in name of another player</u>)," and that person loses all the license plates he or she had collected.

## Stranger Plates

Keep a spiral notebook in the car that has a picture of the United States on the front. Whenever you spot an out-of-state license plate, write it down in the notebook. Then locate that particular state on the map and talk about that region of the country and whatever you may know about the state. Carschool mom Peggy explained that this activity encouraged her children to look up state information on their own so they could wow everyone in the car with their knowledge. She acknowledged that finding all 50 state license plates can be difficult but discovered that airport parking lots produce good results. Peggy reports that "out of 50 states our list is almost two-thirds complete. We have been working on this project for a year and it has been lots of fun."

## State Mottos

Every state has an official motto or saying. For example, Alaska's motto is "North To The Future," California's is "Eureka," and New Hampshire's is "Live Free or Die." Many mottos are included on state license plates. Every time you are carschooling, have carschoolers look for state mottos on license plates. Whenever they see a state motto on a license plate, they must say the name of the state and read the motto out loud for everyone to hear. Then write it down in a state motto journal or notebook. Some state mottos are in Latin. For example, Virginia's motto is "Sic semper tyrannis," and it means "Thus always to tyrants." Hawaii's motto is in the Hawaiian language, and Washington's is a Native American word. See how many your carschoolers can find as you travel.

### Ready Resources

You can print out a list of all 50 state mottos to keep in the car by visiting this Web site: www.factmonster.com/ipka/A0801718.html.

## What's in a Name?

Did you know that states have nicknames? Here are the nicknames for every state. Ask your carschoolers to try to figure out why each state has that nickname.

| | |
|---|---|
| Alabama = Heart of Dixie | Delaware = First State |
| Alaska = The Last Frontier | Florida = Sunshine State |
| Arizona = Grand Canyon State | Georgia = Peach State |
| Arkansas = The Natural State | Hawaii = Aloha State |
| California = Golden State | Idaho = Gem State |
| Colorado = Centennial State | Illinois = Prairie State |
| Connecticut = Constitution State | Indiana = Hoosier State |
| | Iowa = Hawkeye State |

Kansas = Sunflower State

Kentucky = Bluegrass State

Louisiana = Pelican State

Maine = Pine Tree State

Maryland = Free State

Massachusetts = Bay State

Michigan = Wolverine State

Minnesota = North Star State

Mississippi = Magnolia State

Missouri = Show Me State

Montana = Treasure State

Nebraska = Cornhusker State

Nevada = Silver State

New Hampshire = Granite State

New Jersey = Garden State

New Mexico = Land of
   Enchantment

New York = Empire State

Rhode Island = Ocean State

South Carolina = Palmetto
   State

South Dakota = Coyote State

Tennessee = Volunteer State

Texas = Lone Star State

Utah = Beehive State

Vermont = Green Mountain
   State

Virginia = The Old Dominion
   State

Washington = Evergreen State

West Virginia = Mountain
   State

Wisconsin = Badger State

Wyoming = Equality State

# License Plate Photo Safari

Collect photographs of license plates from every state in the United States. Grab a camera, hop in the car, and go on a License Plate Safari. Barbara Phillips, a carschool mom and homeschool activist suggests, "Every time your carschoolers see a parked vehicle with an out-of-state plate, pull over (if it's safe to do so) and have them take a close-up picture of it. Keep a list of all of the states, and as you collect pictures of the license plates, check off the states on the list. Good places to find license plates from out of state are on college campuses and at tourist attractions."

### Variation
Collect pictures of license plates from other countries.

# JUST FOR FUN GEOGRAPHY

Here are some really innovative ways to learn geography by using the things that you find in the world around you.

## Ashtray Numismatists

A carschooling mom explained that her husband travels all over the world on business and always brings back a coin from each of the countries he visits to show to the kids. On the drive home from the airport, he talks about the country he was in, what language the people spoke, and he shows the kids a coin from that country. Since no one in the family smokes, the ashtray in the car became a collection box for the foreign coins. They developed a game in which one player randomly selects a coin from the ashtray and holds it up for the others to see. The first person to name it, identify the country it is from, and tell something about the country gets to pick the next

| Country | Currency | Language |
| --- | --- | --- |
| China | Yuan | Chinese |
| Costa Rica | Colon | Spanish |
| France | Franc | French |
| Germany | Mark | German |
| India | Rupee | Hindi |
| Israel | Shekel | Hebrew |
| Italy | Lira | Italian |
| Japan | Yen | Japanese |
| Mexico | Peso | Spanish |
| Thailand | Baht | Thai |
| United Kingdom | Pound | English |
| United States | Dollar | English |

coin to hold up. They play this game until they go through all of the coins or they arrive at their destination—whichever comes first. If you don't have a traveling family member, you can purchase coins from other countries at coin shops or make play coins from cardboard cut outs. Use this list of countries and coins to create your own coins so you can play the game, too.

## Ready Resources

Here are two more ways to provide international geography learning for carschoolers without ever leaving your home town.

**GeoSafari Talking Globe Traveler:** This is the handheld version of the GeoSafari Talking Globe and is ideal for car travel. It contains more than 5,000 geography questions for ages 8 and up. It also provides timed geography games and multiple-choice quizzes with arcade-like lights and sound. Available at most toy stores.

**Leap Frog World Globe:** This globe comes with a computerized pen that initiates a response when you touch it to the globe. Touch it to any country or area on the globe and you will learn encyclopedic information about that location. There is a quiz setting, too, so carschoolers can test their knowledge. Although not designed specifically for travel, it is compact enough to take along in the car. Available at most toy stores or order at 1-800-701-LEAP (5327).

# Two Bit Geography

One carschooling family uses out-of-state license plates and the U.S. Mint's introduction of individual state quarters to help them with an informal study of United States geography. While riding in the car, they enjoy searching through pocket change for the new state quarters. If they find one, they use the Official United States

Mint 50 State Quarters Collector's Map to learn interesting facts about that state. Additionally, as the carschoolers spot license plates from various states, they look up that state on their Collector's Map to find out more about it. As they collect the quarters to fill in the map, they fill their heads with knowledge about each state. Here is a description (taken from the U.S. Mint Web site at www.usmint.gov) of what The Collector's Map includes:

★    A topographical state map of the United States with push-fit holders in which to collect all 50 state quarters from circulation.

★    Each of the 50 states listed by date of entry into the union with the upcoming year it will be featured on a U.S. quarter.

★    Information on each state of our union including state flag, state capital, date of statehood, state bird, state flower, state tree, and state nickname.

★    Photography and history of U.S. quarters from colonial times to today. Find out the origins of the term "two bits"!

★    A history of the U.S. Mint with many little known facts, photos, and anecdotes from the Mint's historical files. Find out how a dead rat helped improve the Mint's security system!

★    Option to customize maps for collection of either Denver or Philadelphia mintmarks. In reality, there will be 100 quarters, not just 50!

## Ready Resources

To order the map, visit the U.S. Mint Web site at www.usmint.gov /catalog/ and click on 50 State Quarters on the menu on the left side of the screen, and then click on the icon for The Official United States Mint 50 State Quarters Collector's Map. The map costs about $25 and unfolds to three feet in length.

The mint sends free information, lesson plans, and quarter collector sheets to educators. You can order this material at www.usmint.gov (click on Mint Programs and then click on Educational Initiative).

## Keep Moving

Geography is a classic car game that is great to play on extended road trips. Helene of California explained the rules of the game: "The first player picks the starting geographical site, usually where the trip commences, for example, Los Angeles. Los Angeles ends with the letter S, so the next player has to think of a geographical item that begins with S. Perhaps they would say, San Francisco. That ends in an O, so the third geographical item must begin with O. The next player might say, Oregon Trail. That ends with an L, so the next person says something beginning with an L, perhaps Lima. The game ends when you arrive at your destination. This game can go on for hours. Anything geographical is fair game. You just can't repeat items. Use mountain ranges, cities, landmarks, continents, and so forth."

## Stateline Geography

Carschooler Kris Y. of Pennsylvania says her road scholars appear in pictures: "My kids love visiting new states on car trips. Every time we enter a new state we stop at the visitor and information kiosks along the way and find out about interesting things to do and see in that state. We also take the kids' pictures next to the road sign that says 'Welcome to Maryland' or whatever state we're visiting. They have an album of these pictures that include California, Nevada, Arizona, Pennsylvania, Maryland, Florida, Oregon, Washington, and even though it's not a state, Washington D.C., the nation's capital." Get your carschoolers started on collecting all 50 states as you photo-shoot the stateline on your next trip.

# Flag Photography

Take pictures of any and all flags you see as you travel. Some places to look for them are at gas stations, industrial parks, stadiums, post offices and other government buildings, car dealerships, tourist attractions, theme parks, and airports. If you use a Polaroid camera you can make a scrapbook as you go of the flag pictures you collect. Try to identify the flags and label them in your scrapbook.

> **From the Information Highway**
>
> The three countries with the largest land area are Russia, Canada, and the United States.

*Ready Resources*

If you can't identify a flag, visit the Flag Detective Web site at www.flags.av.org/flags/. There you can search for different flags based on the colors, symbols, and shapes that are on the flag to discover its origin and what it represents.

At the *Maps of the World* Web site (http://fotw.vexillum.com/flags/) you can view more than 23,500 flags. If you look up the flag of a particular state or country, you can also find information about its history and the meaning behind the symbols on the flags.

Audio Memory Publishing *World Geography Songs Kit* sets geography to music and makes memorization much easier. This cassette includes 27 songs; a workbook with maps, lyrics, illustrations and tests; and a world map. Songs teach the names and locations of the continents, oceans, planets, and 225 countries. The kit includes famous landmarks and 23 maps to label and color. You can visit the Web site at www.audiomemory.com to hear song samples and to order the tapes.

# Around the World with Street Signs

Tell your carschoolers to look for street names that are the names of foreign countries and their capital cities and to write them down.

The person to find the most in 30 minutes or 30 miles of travel time wins. Once the game is over, have players take turns finding their list of names on a globe or map.

---

### Just for Road Scholars

Ask your road scholars to tell you if the country or capital city named on a street sign is located east or west of your home. Is it located in the northern or southern hemisphere? If you have a globe in the car, ask them to find the longitude/latitude location.

---

# Compass Capers

Carschooling provides many opportunities for teaching kids how to read a compass because you travel in so many different directions as you go from the post office to the bank to the grocery store, and so forth. Each time you stop the car, have the kids take a compass reading. (To get an accurate reading, the compass must be level, so take the reading when the car is not moving.) To ease frustration and arguments over who gets to use it, you might want to buy a compass for each carschooler. Explain that the needle on the compass moves so that one end of it (usually with a red arrow on it) is always pointing toward the magnetic North Pole. North, South, East, and West are the four major points on the compass and are called cardinal points.

Have your carschoolers compare their compass to a clock: North is located at the 12 position and South is at the 6; West is at 9 and East at 3. As you look at the face of the compass, North is at the top, South is at the bottom, West is on the left, and East is on the right. Points that are marked halfway between the cardinal points are called intercardinal points but are referred to as Northeast, Southeast, Southwest, and Northwest. Finally, there are eight more points on the compass that are located between the cardinal and intercardinal points and are referred to as secondary intercardinal points. They are North-northeast, East-northeast, East-southeast, South-southeast, South-southwest, West-southwest, West-northwest, and North-northwest. With this information, have the kids look at their compass, determine where North is located, and tell you what direction they think you will have to travel to get to the next destination.

## Just for Road Scholars

The compass, like all circles, is divided into 360 degrees. North is at 0 degrees, and the degrees increase in a clockwise direction. The cardinal points are 90 degrees apart from each other on the compass. If North is 0 degrees, then East is 90 degrees, South is 180 degrees, and West is 270 degrees. In the beginning of the twentieth century it became more customary to state compass direction or bearing in "degrees" from North. In other words, instead of saying you are heading East, you would say your heading is 90 degrees.

1.  Challenge your road scholars to figure out what degree each of the intercardinal points represents. (Answer: NE = 45, SE = 135, SW = 225, NW = 315)
2.  What is the degree of each of the secondary intercardinal points? (Hint: NNE = 22.5 degrees) (Answer: NNE = 22.5, ENE = 67.5, ESE = 112.5, SSE = 157.5, SSW = 202.5, WSW = 247.5, WNW = 292.5, NNW = 337.5)

Did your road scholars discover that each compass point is separated by 22.5 degrees?

# Inflate the Globe

Keep an inflatable world globe in the car. You can blow it up when you need it, and it is lightweight and easy to pass around. As you listen to audiobooks, encourage carschoolers to find the different states, countries, and locations mentioned. For example, Harry Potter's home is in England; Laura Ingalls Wilder lived on the prairie in Wisconsin, Missouri, Kansas, Minnesota, and Iowa in the United States; Ernest Shackleton's ship, *The Endurance*, was shipwrecked in Antarctica; Julie of the Wolves lived on the Alaskan tundra. Try to find mountain ranges, rivers, and oceans that are mentioned in books as well. Young children may just bat the globe around—but they will hear the family discussion and begin to become familiar with geography vocabulary.

> **From the Information Highway**
>
> Continents are the large masses of land on Earth. There are seven continents: Africa, Antarctica, Asia, Australia, Europe, North America, and South America.

*Ready Resources*

You can purchase inflatable world globes from Einstein's Emporium 1-800-522-8281 or www.einsteins-emporium.com.

## Just for Road Scholars

Explain time zones and how time changes depending on where one is located on the globe. Point out the International Date Line. Name a location mentioned in a story and have your road scholars determine what the current time is there.

*Ready Resources*

Print out the U.S. Naval Observatory World Time Zone Map at http://aa.usno.navy.mil/faq/docs/world_tzones.html and keep it handy in case they get stuck. If you have Internet access in the car, you can find the time anywhere in the world at www.worldtime server.com/.

## Make Balloon Globes

Blow up a white or pale blue balloon for each carschooler. Give each person a fine, black, felt-tipped marking pen. Ask them to try to draw the seven continents on their balloon globe from memory, and have them draw any other global features they would like to include. In addition to the continents, they may want to use colorful markers to indicate oceans, seas, rivers, fjords, mountain ranges, volcanoes, deserts, countries, islands, the equator, longitude lines, latitude lines, and more.

**From the Information Highway**

*Cartography* is the art and science of making maps.

## Postcard Travel Journal

Nothing is more effective in teaching geography than traveling to different places. Have your carschoolers keep a simple record of the places they've been. Each time you visit a new city, state, or country, let the kids buy a picture postcard that depicts their favorite aspect of the place you visited. Have them write a note on the postcard about what they enjoyed most about that particular place, and then tell them to address the postcard to themselves. Take the postcard to the post office in that town and ask the postal employee to "round date" the postcard. That way you will have a collection of postmarks from each of the places you visited when you get home.

# Carschooling VISUAL AND PERFORMING ARTS

# CHAPTER 8

CARSCHOOLERS TAKE art projects on the road, and in this chapter you will find out which ones have proved most effective and fun. Let your voices be your instruments and use some of the ideas here to start a family carschool choir. Engage in art and music appreciation by listening to educational CDs and audiocassettes. Make your own instruments to tap out rhythmic beats while heading down the highway. Discover how to expose your kids to art, music, and drama in ways that make them beg for more!

## VISUAL AND PERFORMING ARTS TOOLS

Here is a list of supplies that will allow you to engage in most of the suggested activities in this chapter:

| | |
|---|---|
| Aluminum foil | Camera and film |
| Audiocassettes and CDs | Chalk |
| Black construction paper | Crayons |

| | |
|---|---|
| Dry-erase markers | Musical instruments |
| Children's songbook | Paper |
| Coloring books | Paper bag |
| Drama scripts | Paper plates |
| Modeling beeswax | Rope |
| Music flash cards | Wikki Stix |

# ART PROJECTS AND ART APPRECIATION

Art is a favorite subject in carschools. Don't let the lack of easel space in the backseat deter you from trying some of these terrific ideas for artistic expression on the road.

## Silver Sculptures

Carschooling mom Ellen S. of Utah always keeps a roll of aluminum foil in the car. When the kids start to wiggle and squirm, she passes a roll of foil around the car and tells the kids to make silver sculptures. Ellen said, "Sometimes they just wad up a bunch of foil and then start to shape it into something recognizable. Other times they carefully fashion dogs, snakes, people, cars, hearts, stars, action figures, and whatever else their imaginations dictate. They have also made crowns, hats, masks, chains, rings, bracelets, and other accessories. My son occasionally wads up a ball of aluminum foil and the kids have fun batting it around in the backseat of the car."

## Black and White Masterpieces

Chalk is not only good for sidewalks and blackboards—it's a great medium for carschoolers. Give each carschooler a piece of black construction paper and a piece of white chalk, and tell them to draw whatever they like. It's sort of like drawing on a blackboard—

and the white doodles and scribbles look interesting on the black background. Chalk also has the added advantage of easy cleanup—no melted crayons or marker stains in the car.

## Make a Flat Family!

Carschooler Hallie of California makes a Flat Family on long car trips. She uses varying sizes of paper plates and draws faces and other features on them, and then attaches paper straws (folded back and forth so they are accordioned) for arms and legs. She plays with them constantly and presses them against the car window to say hello to people passing by in their cars. Her mom, Katy, says, "Whenever we stopped along the way, people who saw her flat dolls were completely amused, and would often donate stuff to make hair and accessories for the Flat Family. She spent many hours on the road happily engaged making members of the Flat Family and playing with them. Another great feature was that they didn't take up much room in the car and could be stored easily in a box or bag."

## Picture This!

Most children really enjoy using a camera and taking pictures. Have them keep their very own photographic journal of your carschooling adventures. Polaroid cameras and digital cameras are great fun because you can see how the picture looks instantly. Let carschoolers take turns photographing interesting things along the way. They will learn quickly how to adjust the way they hold the camera and where to position themselves for the best light and distance to get a really good picture.

Purchase inexpensive photo albums, or just have carschoolers tape or glue their pictures into a notebook as soon as the pictures are developed. Keep some blank address labels handy so that they can write a note about the picture, where it was taken, and the date it was taken on the labels and then stick them next to the photo in the album. They will have fun reminiscing about their journey whenever they flip through the album.

### Ready Resources

For some great tips on how to take good pictures, pick up a copy of *How to Take Good Pictures: A Photo Guide by Kodak,* published by Ballantine Books (ISBN: 034539710X). It may be available at your local library, or you can purchase it online at www.amazon.com.

## Pass It Along Art

This is a fun drawing activity to do in the car. Give every carschooler a piece of paper and a pencil. Have everyone draw a head and neck on their paper—it can be the head and neck of a person, animal, insect, monster, or whatever. Have them fold the paper in half so that no one can see the drawing—and pass it to the person next to them. That person unfolds the paper and draws a body attached to the head and neck that was already drawn on the paper. It can be any kind or shape of a body they would like to draw. When they are finished drawing, tell them to fold the paper so no one can see the drawing and pass it to the person next to them. That person draws legs, arms, hands, and feet on the body. When everyone is finished drawing, hold up the papers and show off the results of your progressive artwork!

## Box Full of Fun

Christy in Canada keeps art boxes in the car for each child with things they usually don't play with at home—rubber stamps, paper, stickers, chalk, pipe cleaners, and so forth. She says, "When we are driving from place to place, they enjoy opening their art boxes and creating whatever their imaginations inspire."

# Colorful Knowledge

If you haven't explored the incredible variety of educational coloring books available for every age and grade range, you are missing out on a terrific opportunity to teach your kids about a variety of subjects through the simple art of coloring. There are coloring books that teach the alphabet, African American history, anatomy, art, biology, literature, foreign languages, social studies, world history, U.S. history, Native American history, science, and more. Surprise your carschoolers with a topical coloring book to reinforce their learning.

## Ready Resources

Here are a few carschool coloring book favorites available at your local bookstore or online at amazon.com:

> **From the Information Highway**
>
> The three primary colors are red, yellow, and blue. The three secondary colors are green, orange, and purple.

- ★ *Color Your Own Modern Art Masterpieces,* by Muncie Hendler, Dover Publications (ISBN: 0486293289). Black outline pictures of famous modern art masterpieces that kids can color, with information about the artwork and artist.
- ★ *Gray's Anatomy,* by Fred Stark, Running Press (ISBN: 0762409444). The text describes each organ of the body and its function.
- ★ *Great Inventors and Inventions* (Dover Coloring Book), by Bruce Lafontaine, Dover Publishing (ISBN: 0486297845).

Learn the story of a great inventor while coloring his or her invention.

★ *Let's Learn French Coloring Book*, by Anne-Francoise Hazzan, S. William Pattis, and Minerva Figueroa, National Textbook Company (ISBN: 0844213896). Learn a French word a day while coloring a picture that illustrates the word.

★ *The Marine Biology Coloring Book*, by Thomas M. Niesen, HarperCollins Publishers (ISBN: 0-06-273718-X). This coloring book looks more like a field journal with black and white illustrations that carschoolers can color. The drawings are exquisitely detailed and accompanied by text filled with scientific information about habitat, behavior, and symbiotic relationships among marine organisms.

For a terrific selection of educational coloring books visit this Web site: www.schoolcatalogs.net (click on "coloring books" in the alphabetical index).

START EXPLORING by Running Press is an entire series of educational coloring books that provide detailed illustrations to color as well as interesting text explaining concepts on diverse subjects. Here is a list of some of the titles currently available:

*Ancient Egypt,* by Peter Der Manuelian
*Architecture,* by Peter Dobrin
*Forests,* by Elizabeth Corning Dudley, Ph.D.
*Masterpieces: 60 Famous Paintings and Their Stories,* by Mary
    Martin and Steven Zorn
*Oceans,* by Diane M. Tyler and James C. Tyler, Ph.D.
*The Age of Dinosaurs,* by Donald F. Glut
*The Civil War,* by Blake A. Magner

All can be ordered at any bookstore or online at www.running press.com.

# The Mobile Art Gallery

Dry-erase markers, those handy pens used for business and school presentations on special wipe-off boards, have been commandeered by carschooling parents to provide hours of car window art activities. The markers come in a variety of colors for drawing and doodling. Let the kids decorate the windows and transform your car into a mobile art gallery. Cleanup is easy, too—just wipe clean with a dry or damp tissue or paper towel. You can even use the pens to keep travel game scores right on the window or to play Hangman or Tic-Tac-Toe without having to hassle with a paper and pencil.

For those who are hesitant to use markers on the windows, carschooling mom Dorinda suggests purchasing clear, plastic Avery Cling Sheets. They are the size of drawing paper and cling to the car windows. Kids can use dry-erase markers to draw on them. They wipe clean when you are through and, in the event your child has created a work of art you want to save, you can peel it from the window without destroying the drawing.

## Ready Resources
Here are two resources for nontoxic markers to use on windows:

★ Dry-Erase Markers can be purchased at business and school supply stores or online at www.dryerase.com.
★ Crayola Window FX Washable Markers, made with a special marker formula designed to work on windows, mirrors, and more, are available in eight colors in a reusable package at toy stores and online at www.crayola.com/store/.

★ Avery Cling Sheets can be purchased at office supply stores or online at www.avery.com.

## Shape Up Wikki Stix

Wikki Stix are a combination of nontoxic yarn and wax formed into pliable sticks that can be bent into an endless variety of shapes. They stick to each other and to almost any surface when you apply slight pressure. They are also reusable. Jennifer's 2- and 4-year-old children love to play with Wikki Stix in the car. Jennifer reports, "Not only are they great for free-form twisting and shaping, but my set came with a white board (the kind you use with dry-erase markers). Wikki Stix cling to the surface if you press them onto the board, so the kids can make 'flat' designs, too. We draw letters, shapes, and numbers and the kids press the Wikki Stix onto the board to match the design."

*Ready Resources*
The Wikki Stix Travel Fun Pack contains 48 Wikki Stix with an eight-page booklet of activities, designs, and games for up to four players, lightweight playboard, and a sturdy carrying case. Other kits are also available at www.wikki stix.com.

## Mind Your Own Beeswax!

Modeling beeswax is pliable and smooth when warmed in your hand, and it has the light fragrance of pure beeswax. It can be molded into all kinds of shapes—like people, gnomes, and animals. It's much neater than other modeling

### From the Information Highway

The world's largest art gallery is the Winter Palace and Hermitage in St. Petersburg, Russia, where 322 galleries contain 3 million works of art. To see the entire collection, you have to walk 15 miles!

clays, as little bits don't fleck off quite so much. The only precaution is not to leave it unattended in a hot car as it will melt and make a mess. One carschooling mom said, "The kids find the feel of working with the warm wax relaxing when they are bored of singing and other car activities."

## Ready Resources
Modeling beeswax comes in thin sheets that can be warmed easily to a pliable texture in the hand. It is available from some art supply and specialty toy stores, and it is also available online at www.naturalplay.com.

# All Tied Up

Knot tying is a practical art form that many carschoolers learn and practice in the car. *The Klutz Book of Knots: How to Tie the World's 25 Most Useful Hitches, Ties, Wraps, and Knots,* by John Cassidy (ISBN: 0932592104), not only provides complete instructions for tying a variety of knots but includes some rope to get you started. You can also find free knot-tying instructions at this Web site: www.realknots.com/knots/.

## Ready Resources
*Lives of the Artists*: *Materpieces, Messes (And What the Neighbors Thought)*, by Kathleen Krull, is an audiobook in which 20 artists are respectfully exposed for their idiosyncracies as well as their contributions to the history of art. Some of the artists lives featured include Da Vinci, Michelangelo, Bruegel, Rembrandt, Van Gogh, Matisse, Picasso, Chagall, O'Keeffe, Dali, Noguchi, Kahlo, and Warhol. This series is geared for ages 10 and up (ISBN: 1-883332-25-7 for audiocassette; ISBN: 1-883332-63-X for CD). Available at bookstores and online at www.audiobookshelf.com.

# SINGING AND MUSIC APPRECIATION

Singing is one of the simplest ways to foster music appreciation in the car. Remind shy vocalists that—just like singing in the shower—the car provides privacy so they can sing their hearts out and not worry about critics' complaints to stay on key. True nonsingers can accompany the carschool divas with instruments or just enjoy the many resources suggested to enhance musical awareness.

**From the Information Highway**

Leonardo da Vinci, who painted the "Mona Lisa," could write with one hand while drawing with the other simultaneously.

## Learning the Lyrics

Carschoolers love to sing out loud in the car. However, "One Hundred Bottles of Rootbeer on the Wall" doesn't last as long as you might think, and the "Song That Never Ends" can get on one's nerves after the fifth or sixth round. If you simply rely on the passengers to suggest songs to sing, you may discover that everyone knows the first line or two of a song but not all of the lyrics to the entire song. This can be very frustrating for backseat divas and tenors. To solve that problem, keep a good book of children's songs or popular tunes in the car. Let carschoolers take turns calling out a number, then turn to that page number in the songbook and start crooning. Kids will memorize the lyrics quickly after just a few repetitions, and all of you will increase your repertoire for future performances.

### Ready Resources

There are lots of resources for song lyrics. Here are a few ideas to get you started:

★ *The Reader's Digest Children's Songbook* contains the sheet music and lyrics for lots of classic children's songs, along-with Disney tunes and a few light rock songs, too. Available at bookstores and at www.amazon.com (ISBN: 0895772140).

★ Free Lyrics to Songs. The National Institute of Environmental Health Sciences offers a nifty Web site where you can print out (for free) the lyrics to hundreds of songs kids love to sing. It includes patriotic music, Broadway musicals, old favorites, holiday music, and more. You can even listen to the tunes while you print out the lyrics and assemble them into a binder for use in your carschooling. Visit their Web site at www.niehs.nih.gov/kids /music.htm.

★ The MacScouter. The Scouting Resources Web site has lots of songs sung at camp-outs that can easily be used in carschooling. Visit their Web site at www.macscouter.com.

## Name That Tune!

Carschooling mom Kellie and her 6-year-old daughter drive 40 miles three to four times a week for various classes, dance lessons, gymnastics, and so forth. On the way they like to play "Name That Tune." They take turns humming a song, and the other person tries to guess the song's title. Kellie says her daughter loves this game and asks to play it every time they are in the car.

One fun variation on this game is to pick a song category—for example, the opera, Broadway musicals, country/western songs, rock 'n' roll, campfire tunes, or religious hymns—and only hum tunes from that category.

Another variation on this game that is fun for a group of carschoolers is to limit songs to a particular theme, such as love, friendship, a broken heart, patriotism, sunshine, dogs, surfing, rain, money, or the environment. Challenge each player to sing a line from any song with that theme. If a player can't think of a tune for that theme, the player sits out the next round of theme songs.

## Car-Tuning

Carrie, a carschooling mom in Nebraska, said that on a field trip with another family they were introduced to a game called "Name That Car Tune." Each player had to sing a line from a song that had words pertaining to cars in them. Some examples are *car, ride, road, highway, street,* and *Mustang.* If it is about a car or traveling in a car, it is fair game. Carrie explained, "The first player sang a verse from 'Baby, You Can Drive My Car' by The Beatles. The next player sang 'Route 66.' The next one sang, 'On The Road Again,' and a young player sang a camp song called 'There Was a Little Ford.' Play continued with each player singing a verse from a car or road song. When a player couldn't come up with a song, he or she was out. Play continued until there was only one player left—the winner! By the way, when a player began to sing a car song, everyone else joined in. It was a great way to pass the time while sharing songs. Because everyone sang along, even those players who were officially out of the game still participated and had fun, too."

*Ready Resources*

For inspiration, try "Car Tunes" by Sugar Beats. This album for kids is designed specifically to be played in the car. In fact, all of the tunes are associated with cars. The Sugar Beats take familiar popular tunes and rework them slightly for some knee-slapping, toe-tapping fun. Some of the songs include "Car Wash," "She Drives Me Crazy," "King of the Road," "Hitch Hike," "Mustang Sally," and "Fun, Fun, Fun." This album is available at children's book and music stores and online at www.amazon.com.

## Singing in the Rain—or Sunshine!

Christy in Canada said that her family divides into two teams when they sing in the car. One team sings songs about rainy or cloudy days, and the other team sings songs about sunny days. The team that comes up with the most songs in their category wins.

## Whistle a Happy Tune

Whistling is a fun activity to do in the car. Challenge everyone to whistle an entire song from beginning to end. Or have one player whistle a tune, and let everyone guess the name of the song. Whistling is a musical art form that takes skill and practice. You can whistle with just your mouth or put your fingers in your mouth to create certain sound techniques. Give young whistlers a few tips, and you will be able to get your carschoolers whistling in no time.

### From the Information Highway

Eamonn McGirr, an Irish songwriter and performer, holds the world record for nonstop singing. In January 1996 he sang nonstop for 11 days and 20 minutes.

### Ready Resources

Here are some great resources that are sure to turn your carschool whistlers into pros:

★ *How to Whistle Like a Pro (Without Driving Anyone Else Crazy),* by David Harp, Jason Serinus, and Don Mayne, Musical Idiot Press (ISBN: 0918321603).

★ *How to Whistle With Your Fingers,* by Candy Hendrix, Hendrix Publishing (ISBN: 0966758706).

★ Free Whistling Lessons (that you can print out and bring along in the car) from legendary professional whistler, Robert Stemmons, are available at his Web site: www.the whistler.com.

## Speak the Language of Music

Musical flash cards are a great tool to bring along in the car to help carschoolers learn music theory. You can purchase laminated (very practical for carschooling) music flash cards from Notes and Strings (1-800-587-3056) or at most music stores. Many carschoolers create their own flash cards on index cards. Here's a game to play using the flash cards.

Have one person be the "Keeper." The Keeper will need a notepad and pencil to keep track of the players' scores. The Keeper puts the cards in the bag and shakes them up. Then the Keeper reaches into the bag and pulls out a card and asks the first player to name that note, rest, or whatever other musical symbol is on the card. If the first player names it, the player scores a point, and the card is put in a discard pile. A new card is drawn for the next player to identify. Play continues until all of the cards have been drawn from the bag. The player with the most points wins!

## Got Rhythm?

This extremely simple, cooperative activity will develop rhythm awareness. Ask each carschooler to take a turn clapping a rhythm. Then each person in the car tries to clap that exact rhythm, too. Play continues as long as everyone is having fun.

## Songs in a Bag

Pass a paper bag around the car and ask everyone to put one small object into the bag—for example, a penny, chewing gum, candy, a peanut, a tiny doll. To start the game, pull an object out of the bag and challenge everyone to sing a line from a song with the object in it. The game continues until there are no more objects in the bag. (In this example, some songs the players might sing are "Pennies from Heaven," "Does Your Chewing Gum Lose Its Flavor on the Bedpost Overnight," "The Candy Man," "Found a Peanut," and "Playmate.")

## Ready Resources

There are lots of wonderful collections of children's songs. The more songs your children know, the more fun they will have choosing songs for these games. Here are some suggestions to add to your carschoolers' repertoire:

- ★ *Raffi* is the quintessential children's musician. His wonderful collection of children's songs encourage a love of nature and the environment with catchy tunes and singable lyrics. For more information or to order tapes and CDs, visit www.raffinews.com.

- ★ *Brianboy!* offers two musical albums for very young children ages 1–7. Electric Kids' Tunes includes lively, upbeat versions of "Twinkle, Twinkle," "The ABC Song," and more. How High the Sink is an eclectic mix of tunes from traditional children's songs like "She'll Be Coming 'Round the Mountain" to more sophisticated fare such as Pachelbel's "Canon." Both cassettes come with illustrated booklets that contain the song lyrics. For more information, e-mail brianboy @Houston.rr.com or call 1-281-955-7402.

- ★ *Linda Arnold* is an award-winning, popular musical artist whose songs explore themes that range from world friendship to the joy of reading. She is a regular on the Disney Channel and hosts the nationally syndicated radio show *Pickleberry Pie.* To view her library of album titles, order a catalog from AmeriCam (1-800-451-3827) or go online at www.americam.com.

> **From the Information Highway**
>
> Ludwig van Beethoven lost his hearing at the age of 26, and when his *Ninth Symphony* premiered in Vienna, he was completely deaf.

★ *Tom Chapin* has achieved critical acclaim for his recordings aimed at 4- to 11-year-olds and their families. His many album titles include songs about peace, the environment, and the treasures of childhood. To view and order his album titles, visit his Web site at http://members.aol.com/chapinfo/tc/.

★ *Charlotte Diamond* is another award-winning children's music performer. Charlotte has many albums with fun and singable themes about nature, diversity, creating a better world, and silly kid stuff, too. See a list of titles to order at her Web site: www.charlottediamond.com.

★ *Mary Miche* specializes in songs that teach science, ecology, and cooperative peacemaking. For a list of album titles and to order, visit her Web site at www.marymiche.com.

## Musical Hot Potato

Pam in Alabama reports that her family plays a fun musical game in the car on long trips. It takes a little bit of preparation before you leave, but she claims it's worth it! Buy small gifts for each passenger (for example, one pack of chewing gum, a candy bar, fruit leather, or peanuts) and buy one "special gift" (for example, a toy, a crossword puzzle, or a comic book). Gift wrap these presents and put them in a bag, setting aside the special gift. When the time is right, announce that it's time to play Musical Hot Potato. Remove one small present from the bag. Tell the carschoolers to pass the present around the car while the music plays. When the music stops, the carschooler who is holding the present gets to keep it and is out of the game. Keep playing until only one carschooler is left. Give that person the last small present in the bag as well as the special present you set aside. Pam says,

"I use a CD player and bring classical music. I tell the kids the name of the song, and who the composer is before each round. Because they are motivated to cooperate to get the prize, they are willing to listen to the music. It's a great way to introduce classical music appreciation as we carschool."

# Sing and Spell

Terri C. of Tennessee says her son loves singing in the car. When he was 2 years old, she began making up lyrics to familiar songs to teach him things she felt he needed to learn. The first song included his name, age, address, and telephone number to the tune of "Farmer in the Dell." Using this method, Terri said that he also learned the days of the week, spelling, colors, science and nature facts, and even foreign language vocabulary. Terri reports, "My son is 4 now and has surprised me many times with things he remembers that were learned when we set them to music while riding in the car. Here is a sample of a song I adapted to teach him about colors and spelling." (Sing this to the tune of "Are You Sleeping?")

R - E - D
R - E - D
I spell red, I spell red.
Stop signs are red,
Fire trucks are red,
R - E - D
R - E - D

"I used the same tune for Blue (the sky is blue, *repeated twice*), and by stretching the tune a little, I used it for Green (leaves and grass) and other colors, too."

## Musical Math Facts

Math tutor Marnie Ridgeway of California discovered that her kids learned anything that she sang, so she set a lot of math facts to music. Marnie said, "There are math fact tapes of all kinds on the market (Math-U-See [www.mathusee.com] has a skip counting tape and School House Rock [www.amazon.com] has some as well). We made up our own—or as my daughter, Hannah, would put it, I ruined most of her favorite songs by setting the multiplication tables to them."

Marnie suggests setting to music any kind of facts kids should have on instant recall: math facts, spelling words, word definitions, states and capitals, parts of speech, verb conjugations, foreign phrases, countries and their capitals, the Periodic Table of Elements, dates in history, lines in a play, quotations from famous speeches, poetry or scriptural passages, and the laws of math and physics like the Pythagorean Theorem, Newton's Laws, the Laws of Thermodynamics, or the four-coupled second order differential equations that govern electricity and magnetism (although Marnie admits that by the time you get to this subject your carschoolers have usually developed their own paradigms for remembering what they need to know). Marnie believes you can set anything you want kids to memorize to music and, if they like the music, they will learn the material.

## Musical Sing-Alongs

Chris B. of California said that singing is one of her family's favorite things to do in the car. They like to listen to musicals, talk about the storyline, and then sing along with the cast. Chris says, "The kids particularly enjoyed doing this with *Man of La Mancha*. After listening just a few times, they were singing the story as gustily as the performers. We have no television, so many of these classic musicals are fresh to my children. We try to supplement our musical studies by attending a live theater presentation of the musical, too."

# Teaming Up for Sound Effects

You will need a minimum of four people for this activity. Each person repeats one line of the following verse over and over in rhythm with the other players. The result that your synchronized voices produce is a sound effect. One person begins, setting the rhythm or beat (not too fast); then the next person joins in at the same tempo, but says a different phrase; then the third and fourth players join in too, each with his or her own phrase, one after the other. Let's try one and see what it sounds like!

> *Person 1:* Cold liver, cold liver, cold liver (keep repeating)
>
> *Person 2:* Bean soup, bean soup, bean soup (keep repeating to same rhythm)
>
> *Person 3:* Wish-wash, wish-wash, wish-wash (keep repeating to same rhythm)
>
> *Person 4:* Washing machine, washing machine, washing machine (you have to say this fast to keep up with the preset beat)

Everyone keeps repeating, never stopping, until they can all hear the effect. What sound did your special effects carschoolers get? You guessed it—a washing machine!

Here's another one to try. What do your carschoolers sound like this time?

> *Person 1:* Bananas, bananas, bananas (say this in a low voice, and don't say the word too fast)
>
> *Person 2:* Knee deep, knee deep, knee deep (in a medium or normal tone of voice)
>
> *Person 3:* Tea and coffee, tea and coffee, tea and coffee (in a high-pitched voice)
>
> *Person 4:* "Hear the lively song of the frogs in yonder pond." (keep the same beat, and use a normal voice)

Everyone keeps repeating, never stopping, until they can all hear the sound effect of frogs croaking.

## Ring Around Rhymes

Repeating songs and rhymes are great fun in the car. One player says a line of a song or rhyme, and everyone else repeats it. Here's a simple one to get you started:

> Boom chick-a-boom (everyone repeats it)
> I said a boom chick-a-boom (everyone repeats it)
> I said a boom chick-a-boom (everyone repeats it)
> I said a boom chick-a-ricka chick-a-ricka chick-a-boom (everyone repeats it)

Then the player that started the song asks everyone to say it louder. So the next round is done in loud voices. The following round may be done in higher voices, or lower voices, or softer voices, or faster, or slower, or with a British accent. You just keep playing and inventing ways to say the song until everyone agrees to stop.

## Make a Joyful Noise

Keep a supply of musical instruments in the car. You can purchase inexpensive plastic harmonicas, kazoos, castanets, triangles, bells, tambourines, drums, maracas, recorders, flutes, and other nifty handheld music makers at toy stores and at school supply stores. Distribute the instruments, and let everyone make their own joyful noise. Or invite the kids to play along with a favorite song on the radio or cassette or CD.

## Ready Resources

Here is a Web site with instructions for making simple musical instruments, most of which you can take along in the car: www .preschooleducation.com/art31.shtml.

Classroom musical instruments can be purchased online at www.music123.com (click on "Classroom Music" on the menu).

# Radio Classics

Jeni S. of Guam reports that public radio is a wonderful resource for music education in the car. She says, "My children study classical music and right after school there is a classical music program on our public radio station. My children regularly contact the host and request particular pieces that they have not heard but are studying. It is exciting for them to hear the host announce their names as regular listeners and supporters of classical music."

## Ready Resources

For information on National Public Radio programming and stations in your area, visit www.npr.org.

Here are some other great classical music resources:

★ *Lives of the Musicians—Good Times, Bad Times (And What the Neighbors Thought)*, by Kathleen Krull, provides biographical information about composers along with bits of trivia and gossip. It is punctuated with music by the featured composers. Some of the composers highlighted are Mozart, Beethoven, Chopin, Verdi, Foster, Tchaikovsky, Gilbert and Sullivan, Joplin, Prokofiev, Gershwin, and Guthrie. Geared for ages 10 and up (ISBN: 1-883332-23-0 cassette; ISBN:

1-883332-60-5 CD). Available at bookstores and online at www.audiobookshelf.com.

★ *The Classical Kids Series* is a great way to introduce all ages to classical music. Each title is a fictional story that includes real historical information about the composers, little anecdotes about their lives, and samples of their work. Some of the titles are *Beethoven Lives Upstairs*, *Mr. Bach Comes to Call*, *Mozart's Magic Fantasy*, and *Vivaldi's Ring of My*stery. All are available on audiocassette and video from online bookstores such as amazon.com.

★ *The Music Masters Series*, by Vox, is an audiotaped music appreciation course. The tapes or CDs contain a narration of each composer's life as well as sample selections of their music. Composers featured include Bach, Mozart, Chopin, Mendelssohn, Schubert, Schumann, Grieg, Handel, Beethoven, Haydn, Wagner, Vivaldi, Corelli, Dvorak, Tchaikovsky, Brahms, Johann Strauss, Foster, Sousa, Berlioz, and Verdi. The six-cassette or CD sets are reasonably priced and available from Builder Books (1-800-260-5461) or online at www.bbhomeschoolcatalog.com.

Carschooling families recommend these audio productions for learning about the different instruments of the symphony orchestra:

★ *Elmo and the Orchestra,* a CD by Sesame Street. It introduces instruments and the musical sections of the orchestra peppered with silly puns and humor. Available from bookstores and online at www.barnesandnoble.com.

★ *Peter and the Wolf and Young Person's Guide to the Orchestra* is a re-release of a popular classic. It helps children become acquainted with the names and sounds of the various instruments. Available on audiocassette or CD from bookstores and online at www.bbhomeschoolcatalog.com.

★ *Peter Ustinov Reads the Orchestra,* produced by Mark Rubin Productions, introduces the different instruments in the orchestra. Released in 1987, this title is available at many public libraries.

# DRAMA

Take advantage of having a captive audience in the car and stage some backseat performances. Ask your carschoolers to read or recite poetry or scenes from books or fairy tales with dramatic flair. Visit your local library to find one-act plays that the kids can act out in the car. Don't forget to check the audiovisual department for recorded plays that you can listen to in the car as well. Here are a couple of ideas that might inspire your carschooled thespians.

## Shakespeare on Wheels

Maureen of New Hampshire shared that her 15-year-old son is in a homeschool theater group that specializes in performing Shakespearean plays. They have discovered that learning lines from the different scenes is a perfect activity to conduct in the car. Her 10-year-old daughter "prompts" her son by following along in the script and reading the other lines for him. Maureen declares, "He learns his lines, she gets to read Shakespeare, and there is momentary calm in the backseat."

## Drama to Go

When her children became interested in performing, one carschooling mom reported that she ordered scripts for one-act plays with just a few characters in them so the kids would each have just one or two parts to perform. She said it was great fun to put on a play in the backseat on long car trips. They kept a bag of simple costume props (scarves, hats, sunglasses, eye patch, beard, wig, and so forth) handy so they could really get into their parts. By the time they arrived at their destination, the children knew their parts so well they would perform a skit for their grandparents or whomever they were visiting.

### Ready Resources

Pioneer Drama Service offers a selection of scripts for musicals, full-length plays, children's plays and musicals, melodramas, one-act plays, and plays for Christmas and other special occasions. From Shakespeare, to heroines tied to railroad tracks, to silly soda fountain scenarios, you'll find a suitable vehicle for your backseat actors. For a selection of available scripts, call for a catalog (1-800-333-7262) or view it online at www.pioneerdrama.com.

★   ★   ★

BE SURE TO look in Chapter 6, "Language Arts," for more dramatic performing ideas, including storytelling, recitation, and puppetry.

A CAR IS the perfect environment for learning a new language. Listening to foreign language programs suits a captive audience, and the passing scenery provides endless opportunities for practicing vocabulary. In this chapter, carschoolers reveal their favorite foreign language programs and explain how they reinforce foreign language skills through interactive games and activities in the car. From listening to audiotapes and CDs or music in another language, to calling out colors seen in the landscape, to translating mileage and road signs to the foreign language they are studying, carschoolers have plenty of ideas for practicing foreign language skills without boring drills. There are some ingenious methods for practicing finger-spelling while on the road, and carschoolers share these sign language learning techniques with you.

## FOREIGN LANGUAGE TOOLS

You don't need a lot of tools to study a foreign language in the car, but here are a couple of absolute essentials:

Foreign language dictionary in the language of your choice.
Foreign language program and/or supplemental curriculum on audiocassette or CD.

# LANGUAGE FUN

Carschoolers love to make learning fun, and they readily turn drill and practice work into entertaining games. Here are a few of their ideas for using roadside scenery to improve foreign language proficiency.

## Translation Game

Carolyn M. carschools in California where many towns, cities, and streets have Spanish names because much of the state was settled by Spanish explorers, ranchers, and missionaries. She said that her kids, who were studying Spanish in school, began to notice this phenomenon and created the Translation Game. Players take turns calling out a town or street with a Spanish name, or a Spanish word on a billboard, and the other player has to translate it into English within 60 seconds to earn a point. The person with the most points at the end of the game wins. Of course, it helps to keep a Spanish/English dictionary handy to keep everyone honest. Carolyn provided this list of common Spanish words (along with their English translations) that seem to be repeated on street signs and billboards regardless of what town her family travels through:

| | |
|---|---|
| Arboles = Trees | Fortuna = Fortune |
| Bonita = Pretty | Gordo = Fat |
| Colores = Colors | Hacienda = Estate |
| Diablo = Devil | Joyeria = Jewelry |
| Estrella = Star | Luna = Moon |

Mercado = Market
Nopales = Cactus
Osos = Bears
Perros = Dogs
Rio = River

Sol = Sun
Tierra = Earth
Uvas = Grapes
Verde = Green

# Map Interpreters

Many cities and towns in the United States have Spanish names, and Erin W. of New Mexico and her family call out Spanish names they find on road maps and then translate them into English. She says, "It gives my daughters practice in Spanish pronunciation and translation."

# Global Language

Karen S. of Virginia keeps an inflatable globe in the car, and her children use it to point to a country and challenge each other to say "hello" in the language of that country. She said, "Initially, they didn't know many languages. We found a site on the Internet called 'Say Hello To The World' at www.ipl.org/youth/hello/. You just click on a country name and the word for 'hello' in that country's main language appears and you can hear a native speaker say the word so you can learn the correct pronunciation. They used a notebook to create a list of countries, the predominant language spoken there, and the word for 'hello' (including the phonetic spelling so they would remember how to pronounce it). They take the notebook along in the car and use it in their global game. One player points to a country, and the other looks it up and says 'hello' in that language. Once they mastered 'hello' in a particular language, they began to search for how to say 'good-bye' and other words or phrases as well. Not only have they learned a lot about the many languages of the world, but they also learned a lot about geography and where different countries are located on the globe."

## Drive-By Foreign Languages

Practice foreign languages by translating the names of common things you see through the car window into the language you want to practice. To practice nouns, one player calls out whatever he or she sees in English—car, boy, cow, and so forth—and the other players try to say the word in Spanish, French, or any other language. You can also translate street signs for danger, police, fire, stop, hospital, and so forth. To practice numbers, have a player call out in English the numbers of passing car license plates and mileage signs—and have the other players say them in a foreign language. Eventually, as you gain proficiency in a language, try to translate complete phrases and sentences on billboards. It helps to keep a foreign language dictionary handy in the car for words that you don't know.

### Variation

Katie M.'s family has refined this game slightly. They pick a category (animals, numbers, colors, and so forth) and call out what they see in Spanish. For example, let's say the category is "numbers." Her carschoolers take turns spotting road signs with numbers on them (mileage or speed limit signs) and saying the number in Spanish instead of English. Or if the category is "animals" and someone sees a cow, they all say *vaca* instead of *cow*. She says it has really helped everyone to improve.

## Signing Signs

Shannon H. of California has a degree in American Sign Language/ Interpreting for the Deaf. When she was a student, her instructor, who was deaf, suggested practicing signing signs as a way to practice finger-spelling. First, get a chart of finger-spelling sign symbols for the letters of the alphabet. To play, try to finger spell any word that you see on road signs. Shannon says, "You'll be surprised at how fast you will learn to finger spell 'Stop.' Try to read what other passengers in the car are signing. Have a race to see who can sign 'Exit' the fastest!"

> **From the Information Highway**
>
> The Japanese word "karate" means "empty hand."

*Ready Resources*
ASL finger-spelling dictionaries with charts are available at the library and at bookstores. You can also find an interactive finger-spelling dictionary, along with a downloadable finger-spelling chart for free online at http://where.com/scott.net/asl/abc.html.

## Foreign Tongue Twisters

Tongue twisters are fun in any language! At the International Collection of Tongue Twisters Web site (www.uebersetzung.at/twister/index.htm), you can print out a tongue twister in every foreign language to practice in the car. This index file contains one tongue twister for each language. More tongue twisters can be accessed through links under each language category, where you can also find some "rough" translations.

## Sing Along with Me!

Set anything to music and it is easier to remember. Look for songs in other languages and start your carschoolers singing. Your local library may carry children's song books and songs on audiotape or

CD in foreign languages. Check with your librarian (and don't forget to ask about interlibrary loans).

*Ready Resources*

Here are some Web sites that have lyrics to familiar children's songs in many languages that you can print out and take along in the car:

> **Mama Lisa's World: Children's Songs and Rhymes.** This fantastic Web site (www.mamalisa.com/world/europe.html) offers printable lyrics of children's songs and rhymes that are popular in other countries. Not only can you print out the song lyrics and rhymes in the language of the country chosen but the English translations appear right next to them. Most of the songs are sung to very familiar tunes, so if you print out the lyrics you can easily figure out how to sing them to the tune you already know. In no time at all your carschoolers will be conducting a multicultural songfest as you travel down the road! You will find songs from countries in North America, Europe, Asia, Africa, and South America.
>
> **Foreign Languages for Children.** This Web site (www.geocities.com /Athens/Delphi/1794/) offers printable lyrics to songs in German, Latin, and Spanish, sung to familiar tunes. A neat feature is that they also have ideas for finger spelling American Sign Language to familiar tunes.

# Fairy Tale Foreign Languages

Michelle carschools her kids in Maine, and she came up with a clever way to practice learning French in the car. She said, "Our library has many children's fairy tale books in foreign languages. We have been learning French, so I borrow the books in French. Then I tape-record the members of my family as we take turns reading the story out loud and use the tape in the car to reinforce our French lessons. The kids like to follow along in the book as the tape plays."

## Multilingual Gaming

Play traditional car games such as I Spy, 20 Questions, Scavenger Hunt, alphabetical games, and number games using a foreign language. Carschoolers will learn vocabulary and how to construct simple sentences in a really fun and painless way.

Instructions in English on how to play some traditional car games are provided in Chapter 12, "Carschooling Recess." Use a foreign language dictionary to translate to the language of your choice.

### From the Information Highway

The Lone Ranger's sidekick, Tonto, had a nickname for his friend. It was "Kemo sabe." In the Navajo language that translates roughly to "soggy shrub."

## Guess the Word

Carschooling mom Pam V. figured out a relatively painless way to help her kids learn Spanish. She explained, "I sometimes introduce a new word from our textbook while we are on the road. I will say a sentence in English and insert just a word or two in Spanish. For example, recently I introduced the word *buzon*. My kids know the name of most colors in Spanish already, so I said, 'The first *buzon* is *blanco*. The next *buzon* is *verde*. The next *buzon* is *negro*.' They had to guess what a *buzon* was (it is a mailbox). (By the way, for those who don't speak Spanish, *blanco* is white, *verde* is green, and *negro* is black.) The kids have to figure out the new Spanish word based on the clues I give. I usually introduce only words that name things that we can see along the way: *cielo* for sky, *camion* for truck, *arbol* for tree, and so forth."

## Yummy Foreign Languages

Ellen Z. of Ohio and her carschoolers have learned a lot of foreign language words through food. They look for billboards and signs that have pictures of different kinds of foods and then say the name of the fruit, vegetable, or dairy product in the foreign language they are studying. Whenever they get stuck on a particular word, they refer to the foreign language dictionary that they keep tucked in the glove compartment.

# FOREIGN LANGUAGE PROGRAMS

Carschoolers rely on an array of audiotapes and CDs to learn a new language. From simple audio lessons designed for young children that set vocabulary words to music to comprehensive lesson plans narrated by native speakers to assure correct pronunciation and fluency, the choices can seem limitless and overwhelming. To help you sort through the products that are available, I asked carschooling  families to recommend their favorite foreign language programs. I have included the manufacturer's recommended age range at the end of each description. Age range can be a useful guide, but remember that older students studying a brand new language may benefit from products designed for younger children as the simplicity may make initial comprehension much easier. Likewise, if you have a very young carschooler who learns quickly (and young children generally do assimilate foreign languages much more readily than adults), by all means offer your road scholar more sophisticated material. Let your carschoolers' interests, abilities, and desire to learn guide you toward the best programs for them.

I have one more piece of advice. If you have more than one carschooler, and you order a foreign language program that comes with an activity book, consider ordering as many books as you have carschoolers. (Companies that manufacture kits may offer additional books that can be purchased separately—just call the company and ask.) Kids love to use the books to follow along while the tape plays. They also enjoy doing the activities in the books (crossword puzzles, word searches, and so forth). Ordering books for each carschooler will keep everyone satisfied, and the additional cost is a small price to pay to maintain the driver's sanity.

# I Can Speak French

**Driving French for Kids.** This kit (specifically designed for use in the car) includes a book and audiotape with songs in French that teach different words and phrases. The narrator suggests a game to play in the car that reinforces what is learned in each song. Call 1-800-298-4883 or find it at www.homeworks-online.com. (Ages 3 to 8)

**Hear/Say: Kids Guide to Learning French.** This kit includes a 60-minute audiocassette with more than 200 sound effects that kids will enjoy learning and repeating, and a 32-page colorful activity book with activities to reinforce the information learned on the audiotape. Comes in other languages, too. Available from Home Works, Inc. Call 1-800-298-4883 or order online at www.homeworks-online.com. (Ages 5+)

# I Can Speak Greek

**Greek 'N' Stuff.** This company has materials for parents and children who want to learn Greek. The materials are biblically based. The workbook series, "Hey, Andrew! Teach Me Some

Greek!" uses activities to teach Greek to preschoolers. "Alone With God" gives mid-elementary students a verse-by-verse study of scripture. Their Web site has a special free feature where you can learn a Greek letter or a Greek word each month. Visit www.greeknstuff.com or call 1-309-796-2707. (Preschool–high school)

## I Can Speak Latin

**Artes Latinae.** This a favorite Latin course among carschoolers, and it is available in book with audiocassette form or on CD-ROM. Comprehensive and self-teaching, the course covers two years of high school Latin and meets the foreign language requirements for university entrance. All items in the program are available individually or in complete packages. This company also carries a bibliography of books in Latin. They even have Latin versions of some Dr. Seuss books! See their Web site for catalog and prices at www.bolchazy.com /alindex.html or call 1-800-392-6453. (Ages 10+)

**Greek 'N' Stuff.** This company has materials for parents and children who want to learn Latin. The materials are biblically based. "Latin's Not So Tough!" introduces students to classical Latin. Their Web site has a special free feature where you can learn a Latin word each month. Visit www.greeknstuff .com or call 1-309-796-2707. (Preschool–high school)

## I Can Speak Spanish

**Driving Spanish for Kids.** Specifically designed for use in the car, this kit includes a book and audiotape with songs in Spanish that teach different words and phrases. The narrator suggests a game to play in the car that reinforces what is learned in each song. Call 1-800-298-4883 or find it at www.homeworks-online.com. (Ages 3 to 8)

**Learning Wrap-Ups Spanish Intro Kit.** Learning Wrap-Ups is famous for it's math wrap-up manipulatives, but this kit helps students learn 480 key Spanish words and phrases. It includes four sets of Wrap-Ups, two audiocassettes to teach proper pronunciation, and a 16-page teacher's guide. ISBN 0-943343-76-3, Spanish only. Available from bookstores and online at www.learning-wrapups.com. (Ages 8+)

> **From the Information Highway**
>
> The Cambodian language has the largest alphabet of any language with 74 letters.

Carschoolers are innovative when it comes to teaching foreign languages. Pam V. reported that her kids liked Learning Wrap-Ups for math and Spanish, but the company didn't make a foreign language version in French. Pam decided to make her own and managed to put together a "wrap-up" out of poster board in about 15 minutes. She put the French interrogative words down one side and the translations down the other side. She plans on making a few more and keeping them in the van.

**Road Scholar, Learning Spanish Is Fun.** This unique board game lets the players go on a road adventure in search of treasure. Along the way, players learn words or phrases in Spanish (or whatever foreign language you select). The audiocassette can be used in the car and features the game board story along with correct pronunciation of words and phrases. The Game includes 300 bilingual language cards along with assorted game pieces. Available from Home Works, Inc. Call 1-800-298-4883 or order online at www.homeworks-online.com. (Ages 8+)

**VocabuLearn Beginners Spanish Series, Learn Language with a Beat.** Listeners review vocabulary and useful phrases to rock 'n' roll music. Listeners learn nouns, verbs, phrases, and conversation and use an accompanying text as a word and grammar guide. Available from Home Works, Inc. Call 1-800-298-4883 or order online at www.homeworks-online.com. (Ages 13 to 22)

## I Can Speak . . .

**Audio-Forum.** With the world's largest selection of self-instructional language courses—285 courses in 103 languages, from Afrikaans to Zulu, including a large selection of Native American languages—pick a language from Audio-Forum and select from an assortment of audio products (in that language) that include complete courses for children and adults as well as games, songs, vocabulary builders, poetry, literature, dictionaries, and drama, all on audiocassette and/or CD. In addition, Audio-Forum offers language courses on CD-ROM, and flash cards, electronic translators, and foreign language films on video. Call 1-800-243-1234 or visit their Web site at www.audioforum.com. (Products for all ages)

**LinguaFun! Travel Series.** This kit contains an audiocassette and 54 game cards, which lets your carschoolers learn languages while playing Gin Rummy, Solitaire, Concentration, and Go Fish. By combining colorful game cards, carschoolers can construct more than 5,000 sentences about everyday family activities, along with days of the week and numbers. Use the audiocassette to learn correct pronunciation and sentence combinations along with interactive language building games. The card games reinforce the lessons learned. Comes in several languages including Spanish and French. Available from Home Works, Inc. Call 1-800-298-4883 or order online at www.homeworks-online.com. (Ages 7 to adult)

**Learn in Your Car for Kids.** This kit was created especially for parents and kids to enjoy learning a foreign language during commute time. Listen to the interactive audio program and learn basic vocabulary, phrases, colors, numbers, and sentences. Games and exercises to reinforce concepts introduced on the audiocassette are included in the laminated, wipe-clean pages of the activity book. It comes in French, German, Italian, Spanish, and Japanese. Available from Home Works, Inc. Call 1-800-298-4883 or order online at www.homeworks-online.com. (Ages 7 to 12)

**Lyric Language Audios.** Lyric Language Audio introduces a foreign language by setting the basics to music on audiocassette and CD. Available from Home Works, Inc. at www.homeworks-online.com or call 1-800-298-4883. (Ages 4 to 8)

> **From the Information Highway**
>
> The world's most widely spoken language is the Mandarin dialect of Chinese. It is estimated that 500 million people speak Mandarin Chinese.

Elise E. is an elementary bilingual teacher. In her family's car travels, she has been using the Lyric Language Audio Spanish CD recommended for ages 4 to 8, and her older son loves it! Elise said, "My 16-year-old has struggled with learning Spanish, but he likes the catchy songs and can't help but sing along (although he pretends he is doing it for his 6-year-old brother). He says he is actually learning some of the vocabulary he didn't understand in class at our public high school. The songs repeat the phrases in both Spanish and English and teach lots of vocabulary. The music is really good, too. You can get it on CD, cassette, and there are videos as well."

**Power-Glide Foreign Language.** Courses include six, 90-minute cassettes and a workbook to reinforce learning. Power-Glide offers fun, easy-to-use, effective methods of natural language learning through storytelling. Additional products include tests, an interactive CD-ROM, teacher's guides, and more. Available in German, Spanish, Japanese, Russian, French, and Latin. Call 1-800-596-0910 or go online at www.power-glide.com. (Programs for all ages)

Susan C. of California uses Power-Glide Junior in the car. She said, "I like the way my children (ages 3 and 6) hear Spanish through a kind of ongoing storyline that introduces new words into the tale and then reviews the words during breaks in the story. If you used Power-Glide consistently and moved into the older program for grades 6 and up, you'd probably have a pretty good understanding of the basics of conversational language, although you might have to find supplemental programs to learn grammar."

**Sybervision.** This program (known as the Pimsleur Language Learning System) comes with a guarantee to work for you on a conversational level in 30 days or your money back! They have language programs available in Spanish, French, German, Italian, Russian, Japanese, Arabic, Chinese, Greek, Hebrew, Portuguese, Armenian, Croatian, Dutch, Hindi, Lithuanian, Korean, Norwegian, Polish, Swahili, Swedish, Vietnamese, and more. No rote memorization, complex grammar, or conjugation drills. The Pimsleur System uses a spoken, not written, question and answer method. All you have to do is listen to native speakers say words, phrases, and sentences and repeat. A tutor provides the clues needed to understand the meanings, and then you are asked to respond to a similar question directed to you. Available on CD or audiocassette. Call 1-800-275-6940 or visit the Web site at www.sybervision.com. (All ages)

Marge, a carschooling mom, says, "Our family has really enjoyed using the Sybervision foreign language course in the car."

**Teach Me Tapes.** A series of individual kits designed to introduce basic Japanese, Spanish, French, Italian, Chinese, Russian, Hebrew, and other languages to children, these audiotapes come with an activity book so that kids can follow along and reinforce what they learn. Teach Me Tapes is a Parents' Choice award-winner. Call them at 1-800-456-4656 or check out their Web site at www.teachmetapes.com. (Ages 2 to 12)

Kristine Yoder of Pennsylvania recommends Teach Me Tapes and said, "My kids really like Teach Me Tapes. We bought the entire series. It was a great way to introduce them to a variety of foreign languages so that they could decide which one they wanted to study in more depth."

**The Learnables Foreign Language Course.** This program was mentioned repeatedly by carschoolers as one they rely on for foreign language studies. Courses are available in Spanish, French, German, Russian, Hebrew, Chinese, and Japanese. Parents do not need to know the language to help with the lessons. Call 1-800-237-1830 or visit their Web site at www.learnables .com. (Ages 7+)

Kelly K. uses The Learnables language program with all four of her children, ages 4 to 11. She said, "The Learnables uses a book and tape method that is ideal for the car. We've been using it on and off over the last few years. One suggestion I have is to spring for a second book so that the carschoolers in the middle seat and backseat can each have a book to follow."

Christine is another carschooling mom who thinks The Learnables is a great program because of the logical progression. She said, "It starts out teaching you to count and then it gives vocabulary words on tape and directs your attention to the correct picture in the book. Then it moves to the next level that is reading. All students do on the first level is listen. They do not have to respond in Spanish, but by the time they begin to read they will recognize and pronounce many words. I am currently using it with my 7- and 10-year-old boys. I had one year of college Spanish and rarely have opportunities to use it, so prior knowledge isn't required. If you choose to learn another language, the vocabulary book (that is all pictures, no words) will work with other languages in the program, so you only need to purchase the tapes."

**Usborne Language Packs.** Learn German or French or Spanish with this kit, which includes a full-color book and an audiocassette. The book includes a story about three cartoon characters who go on an adventure. As they travel along, words, phrases, and more complex grammar are introduced in a step-by-step manner. There are quizzes and puzzles, too. You can listen to the tape and follow along in the book. Native speakers teach correct pronunciation. Available at bookstores. ISBN 0-7460-1440-6. (Ages 11+)

# OTHER LANGUAGE DELIVERY SYSTEMS

## Foreign Language CD-ROM Program

**Rosetta Stone Language Library.** This product is only available on CD-ROM, but it has been recommended by many carschooling families. If you have a laptop computer, this program is a great one to bring along in the car. The Rosetta Stone's award-winning method uses thousands of real-life images, written text, and voices of native speakers to teach you to speak, read, and write the new language quickly, naturally, and easily. No translation. No memorization. No drills. Acquire everyday proficiency in all key language skills: listening comprehension, reading comprehension, speaking, and writing. Available languages include Spanish, French, German, Dutch, Danish, Portuguese, Italian, Latin, Russian, Polish, Welsh, Hindi, Arabic, Hebrew, Turkish, Chinese, Thai, Japanese, Vietnamese, Korean, Indonesian, and Swahili. Selected by the Peace Corps, the U.S. State Department, and NASA! Call 1-800-788-0822 or check out their Web site at www.rosettastone.com. (All ages)

Miki, a carschooling mom says, "My family uses the Rosetta Stone CD-ROM on our laptop that we take along in the car. One of the great features is that you can purchase the entire language program, or rent it monthly on the Internet. Free demonstrations are available at the Web site, so you can try it before purchasing or signing up for the rental program."

# Foreign Language Videos

**Llama Lips Spanish Videos for Kids.** International Language School offers videos that emphasize hearing the word, saying the word, and doing the word. It includes an activity book to use along with the video. Call 1-859-331-6002 for a free catalog. (Ages 1 to 10)

**Muzzy, The BBC Language Course for Children.** From Early Advantage, this video course for teaching Spanish, French, German, and Italian to young children comes with two audiotapes to use in the car as well. Muzzy is a bear-like character (from outer space). He has adventures with myriad characters in the language you choose. By watching the stories and listening to songs, kids begin to learn the language. Activity books accompany the videos. Five videos, two audiotapes, script book, guides, and CD-ROM are included. You can try it risk-free for 30 days. Order online at www.early-advantage.com or call customer service at 1-888-999-4670. (Ages 5 to 10)

Carol F. of Oregon was able to get Muzzy at her local library. She had this advice for parents: "My kids enjoyed the Spanish version of Muzzy, but the minute they found out there was an English version (every course comes with both versions) it was difficult to get them to listen to the Spanish version. My advice is to avoid showing your kids the English version."

**Video Learning Library.** More than 15,000 how-to and special interest videos in 40 or more subject categories from academics to home improvement are available. View the extensive catalog of foreign language video titles online at www.videolearning .com/S2702.HTM or call for a catalog at 1-800-383-8811. (All ages)

## Foreign Language Books

Elise E., an elementary bilingual teacher, recommends two books that are useful in the car: *Spanish in 10 Minutes a Day* and *Learn Spanish the Fast and Fun Way*. She said that both books are easy to understand, progress at an even pace, have easy-to-read text, and contain interesting pictures. The books begin by substituting Spanish vocabulary words in place of English words in sentences as the student works through the text. This gives practice in recognizing the word in context, which helps with understanding the meaning. These books are available at www.amazon.com. (Ages 12+)

Check with your local library as well as local and online book-stores. Many carry books that teach foreign languages. They also carry children's books written in foreign languages that provide practice in reading foreign languages while in the car.

## Electronic Translators

Lingo 10 Talk (10 Language Talking Translator) is a top-of-the-line multilanguage translator that translates characters (alphabets), words, and phrases into foreign languages and shows you how to pronounce them phonetically through sound and an easy-to-read LCD display. You can draw on more than 60,000 words and 1,200 useful phrases and learn how to pronounce foreign words properly. Equipped with a powerful data bank, it also has a currency conversion feature and world times in more than 200 cities. The Lingo 10 Talk translates in all directions for these languages: English, German, French, Spanish, Italian, Portuguese, Russian, Chinese, Japanese, and Korean. Visit the Web site at www.lingodirect.com or call toll free at 1-877-546-4677.

Beth C. of Texas said that her husband travels for business and has learned to depend on an electronic translator when traveling in foreign countries. Her children were so fascinated with it that she bought one to use in the car to practice foreign languages. She said, "With a push of a button we can translate words and phrases into about 10 different languages!"

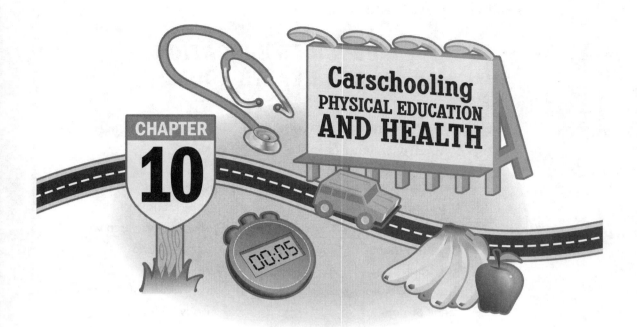

# CHAPTER 10

## Carschooling PHYSICAL EDUCATION AND HEALTH

CARSCHOOLERS FREQUENT highway rest areas and public parks to shake their sillies out and get some exercise. Most suggest carrying sports equipment in the car that kids can use at rest stops such as balls, hackeysacks, chalk for hopscotch, jump ropes, and frisbees. In addition to more traditional methods of getting exercise, this chapter contains some unique ideas for satisfying that PE requirement while on the road. For example, Car Seat Calisthenics is one way to get fit, and Car Dancing provides a great cardiovascular workout. Physical education goes hand-in-hand with health—a subject that carschoolers have developed very creative ways to learn. One example is Climb the Pyramid, which uses advertisements for food products on billboards to test road scholars' knowledge of the nutritional value of various foods. Songs about body parts and Road Sign Harvest Time teach about anatomy and nutrition. Try these carschooling family favorites with your road scholars.

# PHYSICAL EDUCATION AND HEALTH TOOLS

Here are a few items that will enable you to enjoy the activities in this chapter with your carschoolers:

Audiocassette or CD player and dance music on CDs and cassettes

Measuring tape

Notebook

Package of balloons

Pencil or pen

Sports equipment (balls, jump ropes, and so forth)

Stopwatch or watch with second hand

Towel

Water (plenty of it to keep the body hydrated)

# ROAD WORK

For those of you who thought PE could only take place in a gym, here's proof that you can get a good workout in the car or on the road.

## Rest Stop Olympics

Rest stops along highways are great places to pull over and stretch your legs. Why not make the stop memorable and get some real physical exercise, too, by conducting a Rest Stop Olympics? Your kids will think of lots of ways to test everyone's mettle. Although not absolutely necessary, it might be helpful to have a stopwatch or watch with a second hand, and a tape measure. Here are a few ideas to help get you started. Gather the family together in an area with plenty of room to move and then it's off to the races. Award points or prizes in each of these categories (or in others your carschoolers create):

Who can run from one landmark to another in the least amount
of time?

Who can skip from one location to the next in the shortest
amount of time?

Who can hop on one foot for the longest time?

Who can stand in one spot and jump the farthest distance forward (without a running head start)?

Who can do the most jumping jacks in 30 seconds?

Who can do the most consecutive cartwheels in one minute?

Who can jump the highest?

Record the winners of your Rest Stop Olympics and each
carschooler's personal best time or distance in a notebook. Each
time you stop for a Rest Stop Olympics, the athletes can try to beat
their previous best scores.

## Car Seat Calisthenics

Carschool mom Carole M. of Florida was a personal trainer before
she had children, and exercise is very important to her. She advises
that just because the kids are safety-belted into a car seat doesn't
mean they can't exercise. Here are a few fun and easy exercises to
do in the car:

**Shrug and Slump:** Sit up straight, and let your hands rest on your
lap. Shrug your shoulders up toward your ears. Hold that position for five seconds (count one-one thousand, two-one
thousand, and so forth). When you finish counting five seconds, let your shoulders drop and slump forward, relaxing
completely for five seconds. Repeat the shrug-and-slump at
least three times.

**Stretch to the Ceiling:** Sit up straight. Clasp your hands together in
your lap and then stretch your arms over your head, reaching

for the car ceiling. (Adults may have to bend their elbows slightly or stretch their arms straight out in front of their bodies to accommodate low car ceilings.) Hold that position for five seconds. Then lower your arms until your hands are resting in your lap. Relax for five seconds and repeat.

**Cross-Overs:** Sit up straight. Put your right hand across your body to touch your left knee as you raise it. Then put your left hand across your body to touch your right knee. Keep repeating this movement, back and forth, for about one minute.

**Knee Grip:** Place a towel, book, or some other object between your knees. Push your knees together as tight as possible and hold it for five seconds. Then relax, letting your knees come apart for five seconds (hold onto the towel or book so it doesn't fall). Repeat the exercise several times.

**Shake It Up:** Keeping your hands loose and relaxed, shake them as fast as possible for 10 seconds. Lift your feet up off the floor, and do the same thing to them. Repeat several times.

Here are some general safety guidelines you should consider whenever you exercise: Stop exercising if you experience pain, discomfort, nausea, dizziness, lightheadedness, chest pain, irregular heartbeat, shortness of breath, or sweaty hands! Keep water available and drink plenty of fluids. Don't forget to have fun!

## Car Dancing!

Just because you are sitting down doesn't mean you can't dance. You can get the exercise you need to help tone the body, strengthen muscles, and improve cardiovascular health by "car dancing." Simply turn on your favorite music and start by tapping your toes and/or fingers to the beat of the music. Use the room you have in the car to bend your toes and fingers, rotate your ankles and wrists, bend your knees and elbows, raise your legs and arms up and down, bend down at the waist while reaching for the car floor with your hands, or stretch and reach for the ceiling all to the beat of your favorite tunes! Try to car dance without stopping for 20 minutes to get the most benefit from the activity.

## Just for Road Scholars

Your pulse rate goes up when you exercise because your heart beats faster as you increase your movement. Your heart has to pump so much blood through your body that you can feel the blood pulse each time your heart beats! To demonstrate this, have your road scholars check their heart rate before they start car dancing. To do this, tell them to hold out their left hand, palm turned up. Then grasp their left wrist between the thumb and index finger of their right hand. Place the index finger on the upturned wrist near the base of the thumb and feel the pulse. Count the number of pulses or heartbeats that they feel in 15 seconds. Multiply the number by four, and this is the number of times their heart beats (in a relaxed state) per minute. Next, turn on the music and start car dancing. After 20 minutes of continuous car dancing, stop the music and have the road scholars check their heart rate again. The rate should be higher.

# Thumb Wrestling

This is a great game to help expend a little energy in the car. Two players clasp hands in a handshake, keeping their thumbs straight up. Then the players move their thumbs in a criss-cross motion while saying, "One, two, three, four, we declare a thumb war. Five, six, seven, eight, try to keep your thumb up straight." Each thumb wrestler tries to pin down the other's thumb with his or her own, keeping their hands clasped the entire time. If more than two people want to play, the winner can take on other challengers in the car.

## Musical Rest Stops

On long car trips, tell the kids you will stop at every rest area along the way. When you pull into the rest stop, park the car safely out of the way of other cars and traffic. Turn some music on (or sing), and tell everyone to get out and skip around the car. When the music stops, everyone gets back in the car. This is a great way to get everyone to stretch their legs, and it breaks the monotony of long car rides.

## Hand Jive

Clapping hands is a great way to get some physical activity in the car. Performing specific hand motions while reciting rhymes helps kids develop coordination and rhythm. Set your road scholars to work creating hand-clapping routines for their favorite songs.

### Ready Resources
*Hand Clap! 'Miss Mary Mack' and 42 Other Hand Clapping Games for Kids*, by Sara Bernstein, has lots of great hand-clapping activities with easy instructions (published by Adams Media Corporation; ISBN: 1558504265).

## Batty Balloons

Keep a few small, deflated balloons in the car. When the kids get antsy on car trips and need to release some energy, just blow up a balloon and let them bat it around the backseat, from one player to the other.

# HEALTHY HABITS

School curricula cover a wide range of health topics, from fire and bicycle safety to sex and drug education. The car provides a private and distraction-free place to discuss many issues of importance with your children. Numerous publications, audiotapes, and videos are available for parents and educators to use with children, many of which can be used in the car. Your local library is the first place to check for suitable materials. The U.S. government and many nonprofit organizations also have developed materials to help families find information about everything from nutrition to poison prevention.

Learning about the human body and how to keep it healthy are key components of a health class. Carschoolers have devised some ingenious ways to tackle this subject on the road.

## Ready Resources
Free or low-cost public health and safety materials can also be found at these Web sites:

U.S. Department of Health and Human Services at www.dhhs.gov/
Center for Disease Control at www.cdc.gov/
Parent's Patch at www.parentpatch.com/pe_and_health.htm

## Skeleton Hokey Pokey

To teach children the bones of the body, substitute the words in the "Hokey Pokey" song for actual names of bones. First sing a verse the traditional way, and then sing it with the correct bone name. To accommodate the fact that you are seated in the car and can't turn around, change the words "and you turn yourself around" to "and give high-fives all around." Here's how it goes:

> You put your right foot in,
> You put your right foot out,
> You put your right foot in
> And you shake it all about.
> You do the Hokey Pokey
> And give high-fives all around,
> That's what it's all about.

Next, repeat that verse but substitute the word "tarsals" for "foot" as follows:

> You put your right tarsals in,
> You put your right tarsals out,
> You put your right tarsals in
> And you shake it all about.
> You do the Hokey Pokey
> And give high-fives all around,
> That's what it's all about.

Repeat the verses, using the traditional words first and then substituting the correct bone names as follows:

> Left foot: left tarsals
> Right hand: right carpals
> Left hand: left carpals
> Right arm: right humerus, radius, or ulnar
> Left arm: left humerus, radius, or ulnar
> Right shoulder: right scapular

Left shoulder: left scapular

Right hip: right upper ilium or right lower ischium

Left hip: left upper ilium or left lower ischium

Right knee: right patella

Left knee: left patella

Right leg: right femur, tibia, or fibula

Left leg: left femur, tibia, or fibula

Right ankle: right talus

Left ankle: left talus

Head: Cranium

Point out to your carschoolers that the arm has three major bones. The large bone between the shoulder and elbow is called the *humerus*. The two smaller bones between the elbow and the wrist are the *ulnar* and *radius*. Likewise, the leg has three major bones. The large bone between the hip and the knee is the *femur*. The two smaller bones between the knee and ankle are the *tibia* and *fibula*. When you sing the song, substitute whatever arm or leg bone name you want to use.

## Just for Road Scholars

Not all of the bones of the body were included in the "Hokey Pokey" song activity. See if your road scholars can figure out a way to include these other bones in the song so they can learn the names of all of the bones of the body:

Jaw bone: mandible

Neck bone: cervical spine

Collar bone: the clavical

*(continues)*

Chest bone: the sternum

Tip of the chest bone: the zyphoid process

Ribs: costals

Mid-upper spine: thoracic spine

Lower spine: lumbar spine

Finger bones: metacarpals

End of the spine: sacral spine

Tail bone: coccyx

Heel bone: calcaneus

Toe bones: metatarsals

# MOBILE ANATOMY LAB

Turn your car into a mobile anatomy laboratory by investigating the human body and its functions with these activities that you can do as you hit the highway.

## Explore the Largest Organ

Skin is an organ. In fact, it is the largest organ of the human body. Skin forms a protective layer over the body to help prevent injury and disease, keeps moisture in the body, regulates the body temperature, produces vitamin D, and excretes waste.

Looking at skin through a magnifying glass or jeweler's loop is a terrific way to see the many features of it. Have the kids scan the skin on their hands and arms to view hair, wrinkles on their knuckles, freckles, scabs, scars, warts, moles, pimples, pores, bruises, calluses, and whatever else they can find that demonstrates the complexity of this marvelous organ.

# A Circulating Highway

The heart and blood vessels (veins and arteries) make up the circulatory system. The heart pumps blood that carries oxygen and nutrients to all parts of the body including the eyes, skin, bones, and teeth. The heart is the size of a fist and acts like a pump to circulate blood. Tell your carschoolers to put their hands over the center of their chest to feel their heart pumping (beating).

Veins and arteries are tubes of varying sizes that act like a highway system in the body, transporting blood to all of the body parts. The heart pumps blood through the lungs where it collects oxygen and then heads out through the arteries to deliver the oxygen-rich blood to the body. When the blood has delivered the oxygen, it is pumped back to the heart and lungs through the veins to get more. When blood is rich in oxygen, it is red. When it has little oxygen, it is blue. That's why veins are blue in color; they are returning oxygen-depleted blood to the heart and lungs.

Have your carschoolers look at the inside of their wrists to find their own circulating highways. They should be able to see some blue blood vessels near the surface of their skin. These are veins returning oxygen-poor blood to the heart and lungs.

> ### From the Information Highway
>
> *Melanin* is a natural pigment that gives skin its special color. The darker someone's skin color is, the more melanin that person has. The lighter someone's skin color is, the less melanin the person has.

# Mighty Muscles

The muscular system includes all of the body's muscles that contract to move bones and body parts. Muscles are either voluntary or involuntary. You control voluntary muscles, and they move whenever you want them to. Involuntary muscles work automatically inside your body.

Muscles need the oxygen that blood supplies to work efficiently. To demonstrate this, have carschoolers hold their arms straight out in front of them, or up over their heads for one minute. When the arm muscles are in this position, they are using up more oxygen than they are receiving. They get weak and tired and may start to ache.

## Who's a Bonehead?

Bones make up the skeletal system. They are living, and they protect the body's internal organs, support the body, make blood cells, store minerals, and provide a place for muscles to attach. Inside bones is a substance called marrow. It's a thick fluid that makes blood cells that help the body fight off infection, and it delivers oxygen to the body as well. Bones are hard, unlike another substance in the body called cartilage. Cartilage is a rubber-like substance such as that found in the nose and ears.

To demonstrate the difference in flexibility between bone and cartilage, have your carschoolers feel the bones in their wrist. Then have them feel their noses and ears, pull on them gently, and squish them with their fingertips. The difference should be quite apparent.

## Traveling Treats

The digestive system helps us digest our food. Digestion starts in the mouth where the teeth, tongue, and saliva break down food into smaller pieces. When you swallow, the *esophagus* is the tube that takes the food from your mouth to your stomach. In the stomach, gastric acid and enzymes break down the food some more. The food then leaves the stomach and goes to the small intestine where the nutrients from broken down food are absorbed into the blood. The large intestine absorbs water and minerals and eliminates the solid waste.

The adult intestine is a long tube that is about 20 feet in length. To demonstrate this fact, have your carschoolers find an 18-wheeler truck on the road. Now, tell them to imagine a piece of tubing the length of the truck, all curled up inside their body. They will marvel at how such a huge organ can fit in such a small space.

## Airborne

The respiratory system enables your body to breathe. When you breathe in, your lungs expand to take in air that is made up of oxygen, nitrogen, and other gases that are essential to the body's health.

> **From the Information Highway**
>
> There are more than 600 muscles in the human body.

To demonstrate how the lungs expand, ask your carschoolers to put their hands on their chests and take a deep breath. They can feel their chest expand or get larger as air fills the lungs. Then, as they exhale, they can feel their chest shrink or get smaller as air containing carbon dioxide leaves the lungs.

## Did You Get the Message?

The nervous system includes the brain and the nerves that connect to it. The nerves are like a highway system running throughout the body. The brain controls this nerve network and sends and receives messages rapidly along it to control all of the systems in the body. It's what allows the body to move, think, and feel. From kicking a ball, to laughing so hard that you cry, to feeling cold snowflakes as they fall on your tongue, your brain and nerves are what enable you to experience these things.

Would your carschoolers like to feel a nerve? Tell them to bend their arm slightly and use their other hand to feel the back of their elbow. The elbow is a joint that connects the bones of the arm. Have them look for an indentation between two bones in the back of the elbow. If they run their finger up and down that groove, they can sort of feel the nerve that runs along it. Tell them to press on it and they are sure to feel a "funny" sensation or perhaps even a little minor discomfort. That's a nerve with a familiar nickname. It's called the "funny bone."

# A YUMMIE FOR YOUR TUMMY

## Climb the Pyramid

Carschool mom Carla K. of Ohio developed a game that teaches how choosing the proper foods helps to keep bodies healthy. She introduced her carschoolers to the five major food groups using the Food Guide Pyramid published by the U.S. government:

### THE FIVE MAJOR FOOD GROUPS
### (AND THE RECOMMENDED DAILY PORTIONS)

1. **Fats, Oils, and Sweets:** Eat sparingly.
2. **Milk, Yogurt, and Cheese:** Eat two to three servings per day, with one serving being equivalent to one cup of milk or yogurt; or one to two ounces of cheese.

3. **Meat, Poultry, Fish, Dry Beans, Eggs, and Nuts:** Eat two to three servings per day, with one serving being equivalent to two to three ounces of cooked lean meat, fish, or poultry; or one egg; or two tablespoonfuls of peanut butter or nuts; or one-half cup of cooked dried beans.

4. **Fruits and Vegetables:** Eat three to five servings of vegetables, with one serving being equivalent to one cup of raw leafy vegetables; one-half cup of cooked or other raw vegetables; or three-quarters of a cup of vegetable juice. Eat two to four servings of fruit, with one serving being equivalent to one medium-sized apple, orange or banana; one-half chopped, cooked, canned fruit; or three-quarters of a cup of fruit juice.

5. **Bread, Cereal, Rice, and Pasta:** Eat six to eleven servings, with one serving being equivalent to one slice of bread; one-half cup of cooked rice, pasta, or cereal; or one ounce of raw cereal.

The pyramid calls for eating a variety of foods in recommended portions to get the nutrients a human body needs to be healthy. Once carschoolers are familiar with the different food groups, have them practice classifying food advertised on

> **From the Information Highway**
>
> Why do cut apples turn brown? Oxygen in the air reacts with a substance in apples called *phenolase* and turns the cut surface brown. Tossing the apple slices in a mild acid, such as lemon juice, will keep the apples from turning brown and help them look more appetizing.

billboards and street signs according to their food group. Some, like milk, are simple. Others, like a cheeseburger, require a little more thought and effort. Cheeseburgers include several groups: Fats (mayonnaise), Cheese, Meat, Vegetables (lettuce, pickle, tomato, and onion), and Bread (bun).

To make the activity more challenging for her older carschoolers, Carla asked them to try to determine how many servings of each food group a particular food supplies. In the case of a quarter-pound cheeseburger, her teens estimated that it provided one serving of Cheese, one to two servings of Meat, less than one serving of Vegetables, two servings of Bread, and probably too much Fat as the mayonnaise is rarely "used sparingly" at fast food restaurants. The kids subtracted those servings from the recommended daily allowance to determine how many more servings in each food group they would be able to eat after munching down a cheeseburger. Carla says, "It was an eye-opening exercise for my whole family."

### Ready Resources
You can print a free copy of the U.S.D.A. Food Guide Pyramid to use in the car by visiting their Web site at www.usda.gov/cnpp/Kids Pyra/.

## Road Sign Harvest Time

This is a cooperative learning game and everyone is on the same team. Designate one person to be the Scorekeeper. Pretend that you own a family farm and as you begin your car trip it is harvest time. The fruits and vegetables on your farm must be harvested before the first frost of fall arrives (the end of your car trip). Challenge your carschoolers to harvest or collect as many fruits and vegetables as possible from passing signs and billboards (your farm). Score 1 point for every fruit or vegetable they call out. Score 5 points if a player knows the name of a vitamin or mineral that the fruit or vegetable provides. Score 10 points if a player knows what benefits that vitamin or mineral provides for the body. Score 20 points if the player knows what symptoms a person might have if they were deficient in that vitamin or mineral. When in doubt, have the players use this Fruit and Veggie Vitamin and Mineral Chart to discover some answers.

# Fruit and Veggie Vitamin and Mineral Chart

### VITAMIN: A

Fruit sources: Cantaloupe, apricots, papayas, mangoes, watermelon.

Vegetable sources: Carrots, sweet potatoes, pumpkin, mustard greens, hot chili peppers.

Benefits: Keeps eyes, skin, hair, bones, and teeth healthy. Helps body resist infection.

Deficiency symptoms: Night blindness, dry eyes, dry and itchy skin, reduced hair growth in children, improper tooth or bone formation, lowered resistance to infection.

### VITAMIN: B$_2$ RIBOFLAVIN

Vegetable sources: Leafy green vegetables such as spinach; mushrooms.

Benefits: Healthy skin, tissue repair, antibody and red blood cell formation.

Deficiency symptoms: Cracks and sores around mouth, dry skin, vision problems, and light sensitivity to eyes.

### VITAMIN: B$_6$ PYRIDOXINE

Fruit sources: Bananas.

Vegetable sources: Broccoli, spinach.

**From the Information Highway**

Do you know the difference between sweet potatoes and yams? Sweet potatoes are roots of a vine in the morning glory family and are rich in vitamin A. Two varieties are sold in U.S. stores, one with light skin and one with dark skin. Dark-skinned sweet

*(continues opposite)*

Benefits: Healthy red blood cells, gums, teeth, blood vessels; absorption and metabolism of proteins and carbohydrates; promotes healthy nerve and brain function.

Deficiency symptoms: Anemia, irritability, fatigue, insomnia, nerve dysfunction.

## VITAMIN: C

Fruit sources: Kiwi, cantaloupe, grapefruit, orange, papaya, strawberries, tangerine, blackberries, raspberries.

Vegetable sources: Bell pepper, broccoli, brussels sprouts, cabbage, hot chili peppers, mustard greens, rutabagas, potatoes, tomatoes.

Benefits: Antioxidant; heals wounds; maintains healthy gums, skin, and blood.

Deficiency symptoms: Bruise easily, bleeding gums, slow wound healing, and in extreme cases, scurvy.

## VITAMIN: E

Vegetable sources: Spinach, collard greens, mustard greens, Swiss chard, corn oil.

Benefits: Antioxidant; helps protect red blood cells, cell membranes, muscles, tissues, and preserves fatty acids.

Deficiency symptoms: Poor muscular, circulatory, and nerve performance.

## VITAMIN: K

Vegetable sources: Green leafy vegetables such as spinach, collard greens, mustard greens, Swiss chard, and alfalfa.

Benefits: Needed for normal blood-clotting.

Deficiency symptoms: Excessive bleeding, poor coagulation of blood.

## MINERAL: CALCIUM

Vegetable sources: Broccoli, turnip greens.

Benefits: Healthy bones and teeth, nerves, and muscles.

Deficiency symptoms: Soft bones, osteoporosis.

## MINERAL: IRON

Fruit sources: Raisins (dried grapes).

Benefits: Helps make hemoglobin to transport oxygen to body, prevents anemia.

Deficiency symptoms: Weakness, fatigue, headaches, shortness of breath.

## MINERAL: MAGNESIUM

Vegetable sources: Leafy greens, broccoli, spinach.

Benefits: Activates enzymes to release energy in body; promotes healthy bone growth and proper heartbeat.

Deficiency symptoms: Nausea, muscle weakness, cardiac arrhythmias.

## MINERAL: POTASSIUM

Fruit sources: Bananas, oranges.

Vegetable sources: Green beans, mushrooms, broccoli.

Benefits: Maintains fluid balance for proper nerve, muscle, and heartbeat function.

> potatoes are usually mislabeled as "yams." Real yams are tubers of a tropical vine that grow up to seven feet in length and weigh up to 150 pounds! Yams have a bark-like dark brown skin, and the flesh can be off-white, purple, or red. Real yams contain no vitamin A and you rarely see them in U.S. supermarkets.

Deficiency symptoms: Nausea, anorexia, muscle weakness, irritability.

Designate a target score that you think is reasonable for the duration of your trip. When you reach your goal, give everyone a yummy fruit or vegetable snack.

## Salad Toss!

Look for vegetables on roadside signs. When players see a picture or the printed name of a vegetable, they call it out, write it down, and award themselves a point. Two players cannot use the same sign. The idea is to collect as many as possible during your car ride, and the person with the most wins. However, each time a player accumulates a list of five new vegetables the player can shout "Salad toss!" and everyone else has to start over.

### Variation

Search only for vegetables that are good sources of vitamin C or vitamin A. When in doubt, check the Fruit and Veggie Vitamin and Mineral Chart.

# Carschooling ELECTIVES

## CHAPTER 11

CARSCHOOLERS HAVE ideas for learning everything from vocational training and home economics to developing interpersonal and critical thinking skills while cruising down the highway. A few subjects fall outside the realm of traditional studies, and carschoolers have tackled them all. In this chapter carschoolers share their methods for exposing their kids to career possibilities by using billboards and watching for company logos on passing trucks and cars. News flashes on the radio provide a basis for a study of current events, politics, and economics. Talk radio shows and public broadcasting programs offer an opportunity to develop critical thinking skills as carschoolers examine the pros and cons of issues raised. Also, discover the techniques carschooling parents use to encourage open discussions and share family values in the cozy confines of the family car.

## ELECTIVES TOOLS

The essential tools for elective studies that encourage critical thinking skills are a working car radio and/or the daily newspaper.

# RESOURCES FOR ACADEMIC ELECTIVES

Certain academic electives (philosophy, psychology, business, religions of the world, and so forth) are generally reserved for high school and college. Check with your local library for a selection of lectures on audio- and videotape that you can use in the car.

One source for quality lectures that are not only educational but entertaining as well is the Teaching Company, which offers a catalog of full-length audio and video courses for high school and college level taught by "the finest teachers in the country." They have a money-back guarantee: Call them at 1-800-832-2412 or shop online at www.teach12.com.

# VOCATIONAL TRAINING

Schools spend a good deal of time preparing students to join the workforce, with "Career Day" or "Take Your Child to Work Day" being the annual crowning achievement in vocational training. Carschoolers learn about career opportunities every day by noticing the occupations of other people on the road and by using corporate billboards to role-play possible career choices. Here are some activities carschoolers enjoy that help road scholars discover a range of career opportunities for the future.

## When I Grow Up

When I Grow Up is a game one carschooling family plays that introduces the many different jobs and careers people have. One player looks out the window and spots an occupation portrayed on a billboard or a sign or on a passing truck, van, or car. The player writes down the occupation on a slip of paper and tucks it into the glove compartment or a pocket for safekeeping. Then the player says, "When I grow up I want to be a _____." That is the cue for the other players in the car to begin asking a series of 10 questions that have yes or no answers in an effort to figure out what that person wants to be. The player who guesses correctly based on the answers to the questions gets to choose an occupation for the other players to guess. If no one guesses, the slip of paper with the occupation written on it is shown to all of the players. Then the player that stumped everyone gets to choose another occupation for everyone to guess. Some of the jobs carschoolers may discover from this game are real estate agent, police officer, truck driver, florist, school bus driver, emergency medical technician, tow truck driver, fast food clerk, and road worker.

## Guess Your Job Title

In this game, one player is designated as the "Job Applicant." Another player writes down a job title (for example, firefighter) on a piece of paper and passes it around to all of the players except the Job Applicant. Each player then tells the Job Applicant one thing he or she will need in order to do this job (for example, a uniform, CPR training, a hose, courage). After hearing each clue, the Job Applicant must try to guess what the job title is. If the Job Applicant does not guess the correct job title by the time everyone has given a hint, the Job Applicant does not get the job and must apply again for another job. If the Job Applicant guesses correctly, then another player is chosen and play continues until everyone has had a turn to be the Job Applicant.

> **From the Information Highway**
>
> According to Citizens for a Scenic Spokane, four states do not allow billboards: Maine, Vermont, Alaska, and Hawaii.

# Mechanically Inclined

Deanna, a carschooling mom from Maryland, reported that sitting in the car doesn't stop her kids from exploring how things work. Her wanna-be mechanics like to take things apart and put them back together again. So she keeps a bag of easy-to-pull-apart and reassemble items and toys in the car. Here are some of her children's favorite things to take apart and put together again in the car:

Flashlights
Pens
Keys (take them off and put them on the key ring)
Nesting boxes or dolls
Parlor Puzzles

## From the Information Highway

According to the World Development Report 2000, almost half of the world's population, 2.8 billion people, live on less than $2 a day. Of these people, 1.2 billion live on less than $1 a day.

*Ready Resources*

Parlor Puzzles are a boxed set of five interesting, portable, handcrafted metal puzzles similar to brain teasers. The idea is to take them apart, but it requires analysis and dexterity to accomplish the task. Available from the Museum Company at 1-877-213-9778 or online at www.museumcompany.com.

# High Finance

Ed is a carschooling dad who lives in Washington. He and his teenage sons listened to *Rich Dad, Poor Dad* by Robert Kiyosaki on audiocassette in the car (it is available at most bookstores). They have had many discussions about assets and liabilities, money management, and investing and sheltering income. Ed and his sons highly recommend this book to other carschoolers who want an engaging introduction to business and finance. There is also a version for younger children called *Rich Kid, Poor Kid*.

## Pre-Driver's Ed Course

Bonnie of Fayetteville uses car travel time to give a "Pre–Drivers Ed Course" to her kids. She says, "We discuss slower speed limits in residential areas, near schools, and downtown, and then faster speed limits for highway driving. We also talk about safe following distances and how so many accidents could be avoided by not tailgating. I have demonstrated making a complete stop at stoplights and stop signs, and explained what the dotted yellow lines mean in comparison to the solid yellow line. We've deciphered the meaning of various traffic signs, too. Sometimes we even see someone driving erratically and I take the time to mention the dangers of drinking and driving, or driving under the influence of drugs (including prescription drugs), driving when overtired, and driving while talking on a cell phone. I have filled my kids in on what to do in case of an accident and have emphasized the importance of courtesy toward other drivers as a method for avoiding road rage. Who says a child has to wait until driving age to begin learning the rules of the road and how to be a safe driver?"

## Home E-*Car*-Nomics

Just because you're riding in the car doesn't mean you can't teach your kids how to cook. Have a Car-B-Cue right on the car engine!

There are three major benefits to cooking on the car engine: You stretch your gas dollar and conserve energy by not using the stove at home; you save time when you cook as you drive; and you can teach your kids about food preparation—an important life skill!

Cooking on the engine of the car is like steaming food; it doesn't brown food, and the results will not be anything like baking, broiling, frying, or barbecuing. You simply place the food and seasonings in heavy-duty aluminum foil and seal it tightly like a package. The food is wrapped so it (and the car engine) will stay clean. Secure the food in the aluminum foil package onto the hottest part of the engine. The easiest way to find the hottest part is to drive the car around town for 30 minutes or so, and then stop the car and let it cool down for 15 minutes. After this cool-down period, lightly touch the various metal parts under the hood—the hottest parts will still be warm to the touch. You can tuck the food package snugly between metal parts so that it won't fall out or use wire to secure the food against the manifold. Be sure not to block airways.

Once your food is securely on the engine, just drive until it's cooked. If you're cooking a boneless chicken breast, you will probably drive 45 to 60 miles at 60 mph. Fish will take less time—maybe 35 to 45 miles at 60 mph. You may have to pull over and test it to see if it's done. Also, if you get stuck in a traffic jam, remember that the food can burn, so shorten your cooking mileage to adjust for traffic snarls. You will need tongs, an oven mitt, and a plate to handle the hot aluminum pouches safely. Be careful removing the food from the engine as the pouches can tear on sharp edges, spilling the contents and making a mess. Here's a recipe your carschoolers might like to try:

### INGREDIENTS

1 small chicken breast cut in strips (smaller pieces cook faster)
1 teaspoon olive oil

season with salt, pepper, and garlic powder
    to taste
$^1/_2$ teaspoon fresh rosemary

**Directions:** Combine ingredients in aluminum foil packet, place next to manifold, drive 55 mph for 40 miles.

Cooking is not an exact science in the car. Older model cars may cook things faster than newer energy-efficient cars. You just have to try it. Stop the car and check the food every so often to determine how much longer you will need to drive for the meal to be cooked. Once you experiment a few times you will get the hang of it.

Heating up hot dogs or tofu dogs is a good way to try cooking on the car engine without investing a lot of time and effort. Just wrap them in aluminum foil, secure them next to the manifold, and have the car-chef with a driver's license start your engine!

> **From the Information Highway**
>
> Do you know what it costs to raise a child? According to the Department of Agriculture, a middle-income ($38,000–$64,000) couple will spend $165,630 for food, shelter, and other basic necessities to raise a child to age 17.

## Ready Resources

Here are two books on car cuisine to hone your road scholar's cooking skills:

*Manifold Destiny: The One! The Only! Guide to Cooking on Your Car Engine,* by Chris Maynard and Bill Scheller (Random House; ISBN: 0-375-75140-8), is entirely devoted to the subject of cooking on the car engine and includes recipes.

*Off the Eaten Path,* by Bob Blumer (Ballantine Books; ISBN: 0345421507), contains just a few tips and recipes for preparing meals on the car engine.

# CAR TALKS

~~~~~~~~~~~~~~~~~~~~~~~~~~~~~~~~~~~~~~~~~~~~~~~~~~~~~~~~~~~~~~~~~~~~~~~~~~~~

Lots of parents have commented that their children are more comfortable in the intimate setting of a car discussing topics that might otherwise make them uncomfortable. It seems to have something to do with the fact that when the driver and passenger talk there is no direct eye contact. Carschoolers will often engage their parents in conversations about important issues, things that are embarrassing or frightening, or things they are confused by or trying to make sense of, such as sex, politics, religion, or relationships. One carschooling parent shared this experience:

> My husband and I had an argument and it frightened my eight-year-old daughter. She was unable to say, "You and Daddy had an argument and I was scared." Instead, in the safety and close quarters of the car, my daughter said, "When people shout at each other they're mad." It didn't occur to me at that moment that she was referring to the argument between her dad and I. So I said, "Did somebody shout at you?" She said, "No, I hear other people shouting at each other sometimes." I asked, "Where did you hear people shouting?" My daughter replied, "Oh, just places." Well, I knew she hadn't been anyplace without me, and suddenly it dawned on me what she was referring to and I said, "Oh, Daddy and I were shouting at each other yesterday, weren't we? And that was scary, wasn't it?" She said yes and we had a long conversation about arguments, shouting, relationships and how even though people raise their voices or get angry, it doesn't mean they will stay angry with each other or stop loving each other. I reassured her that her dad and I can disagree and have words with each other and continue to love each other very much. I gave her similar examples of how she can get angry with a friend because they won't

share a toy, but that she still likes her friend and still wants to remain friends.

Parents tackle many difficult topics in the car. Often they are introduced unexpectedly. For example, you may turn on the news to get a traffic report and a controversial or sensational news headline is broadcast on war, terrorism, rape, murder, or anthrax. You might be quick to turn the radio off, but if the broadcast was heard by everyone, you may need to talk about it as this carschooling parent discovered:

I was stuck in traffic and didn't have a watch or a working clock in the car. I turned on the radio to get the time. We heard that a father had left his baby in the car and that the baby died. My kids were horrified. I had to explain how such a thing could happen.

We talked about how important it is for babies to get their sleep. We talked about how we don't like to disturb people or babies when they are sleeping soundly, so it can be a big temptation to leave them in the car to allow them to sleep undisturbed. I explained that it is something no one should ever do because it is so dangerous. The temperature inside the locked and closed car can rise higher than the human body can tolerate, which can result in death. We also talked about the fact that someone could see the baby and kidnap it. We talked about how sometimes parents run errands and that it can be tempting to leave a child in the car while they run into the store to make a quick purchase. We talked about how a quick errand can turn into a 20-minute stop.

We talked about how quickly a life-threatening situation can occur. We talked about how a child could inadvertently take the brake off and that the car could roll causing an accident. We talked about how horrible it would make a parent feel to have caused the death of his or her own child through carelessness or an error in judgment. Helping my children to see that ignorance of these possibilities or thoughtlessness can lead to disastrous and tragic results really impressed upon them the consequences of our actions in any given situation.

Other complex subjects may be opened innocently enough by listening to audiobooks. What we may consider to be a relatively benign children's story or fairy tale can raise issues (like wicked step-mothers) that may cause confusion. Stories by popular children's author Roald Dahl are filled with archetypes that beg for discussion, as do the Harry Potter series of stories in which we meet the hero, a young boy, who is forced to live under the stairs and is abused physically and verbally by his relatives. Many children's books deal with themes of death, catastrophes, natural disasters, environmental woes, and more. Even though the stories may have "happy endings," kids often want to talk about the circumstances, conditions, and solutions presented in the story. These are wonderful opportunities to provide additional information that will help your kids understand the story scenarios, to listen to what your children have to say, and to offer your opinion and imbue your values as they relate to these matters.

Talking about contemporary social issues is especially interesting to teen carschoolers. You don't have to manufacture a big idea; they are all around us in the news, in movies, in books, in music, and in advertisements on billboards. The car is a great place to continue conversations started at home, too, or to reintroduce subjects that you have thought about and have more information to share or another perspective to offer.

## The Key to Car-Versations

The key with car conversations is to be well prepared. As an adult, you have to educate yourself about these topics. You have to do more than just read the local newspaper because the conversation can go in so many different directions. You may want to present a topic from several perspectives so that you're not preaching to your children but providing them with many points of view. You don't want to make things up or bluff your way through a discussion; you want to give your children the facts.

Let's suppose you are discussing a law that requires motorcyclists to wear helmets. Perhaps a study was released that showed a significant decline in fatal accidents since the law went into effect. Give your kids additional information to consider as they form their own opinion about the merit of such a law. What if the speed limit had been lowered at the same time the helmets were required? It would beg the question, "Was the drop in fatal accidents a result of wearing helmets or a reduction in speed or both?" Provide your kids with as much information as you can to understand a subject. You may not want to draw any final conclusions because many of these discussions will be open to interpretation.

Just allowing your children to take part in all kinds of conversations opens the door for developing critical thinking and good communication skills. Encourage your kids to participate as good listeners in the beginning and then to express their thoughts on the matter. Don't forget to use the strategy of sometimes couching your own opinion by simply telling your children what you know and your current thoughts on the matter. Let them know that you understand that they may discover other information that will cause them to develop a different opinion from yours. You might encourage them to talk to their grandparents or other respected relatives and friends who may have different opinions as well. Never forget to advise them to conduct their own research that will help them to support whatever conclusions they draw. Carschooling families encourage conversation in the car in a variety of ways.

## Headline Heart-to-Hearts

A Texas carschooling mom reported that she always brings the daily newspaper along in the car. She has her children read headlines about world politics, local issues (concerning everything from redevelopment to leash laws), cloning, sports contract negotiations, art acquisitions at the local museum, and whatever else is in the news. They discuss the topics at length, and each family member is encouraged to ask questions and offer an opinion. "As a result," said the mom, "our family has become more tolerant of each other's point of view, and *that* has brought us all closer together."

## Psy-*car*-logy: The Doctor Is In

Carschooling mom Carol B. of California said her family uses the car as an analyst's couch! Her children often wait to get in the car to talk to her about important stuff. Likewise, if she suspects there is something bothering one of her children, she just asks that child to accompany her on an errand and inevitably the conversation begins before they've backed out of the driveway. Carol said the discussions continue even though there are interruptions as they stop to do the errands. They get back in the car and the train of thought isn't lost. She noted:

> Sometimes my kids will take several weeks to process everything related to a particular subject or concern or problem. We may start a conversation on a Tuesday and not finish until three weeks later. This is particularly true if a situation requiring some serious thought has occurred. The kids may give me portions of the story, wait for my response, take some time to mull it over, and then approach the topic with a little more information factored in a few days later. When I see these kinds of conversations coming, I

usually hold back all judgment calls until I get the full story. I have discovered that what my kids really want is just someone to listen. Sometimes just talking about it out loud is enough for them to figure out what to do on their own, without my input. I love it when that happens! By listening to their point of view, I get a real feel for who they are becoming and it helps keep the communication channels open, especially as the kids are getting older.

## From Nag to Confidant

Mary O. of Illinois says that time spent in the car with her teenage son improved their rocky relationship. Mary said, "When we're in the car alone, without other family members around, it can be a very positive experience. At home, if I bring up a topic like getting a job, my son thinks of me as a nag. In the car, I'm transformed into someone who is just interested in him and his life. I think I'm inclined to listen more in the car—instead of talking all the time—because I do have to concentrate on driving. He really seems to like it when I listen, and he is more forthcoming about the people and things that are influential in his life."

## The Facts of Life

Melinda carschools in Florida and reiterates what other parents have discovered. "Our van trips are my family's grab-mom-for-the-difficult-questions time. I think it really does have a lot to do with the fact that they can be rather 'anonymous' by not having to look you in the eye. I know a few of our discussions have given me some white-knuckle, pray-on-the-fly moments. I have a 10-year-old daughter and a 6-year-old son. We have discussed teenage pregnancy, drugs, and sex. I never pushed it, I just answered questions as they came up while we traveled in the car."

## A Safe Place to Vent and an Effective Parenting Tool

Louanne R. shared that her family experienced a series of losses, a new crisis every two to three months (a family pet died, her grandmother died, she had a miscarriage). She could see that these events were really bothering her 9-year-old son, but he wouldn't discuss them at all. She got grunts and single-syllable replies to any attempt to open a discussion at home. She tells how things changed when they got in the car:

> My son seemed willing to listen and even discuss what was going on in our family as we were driving. Now that he has found a comfortable place to express his emotions, he has moved our car discussions on to other topics that kids his age often don't discuss with their parents. Instead of filtering everything through his peer group, he'll ask his dad or me for guidance. When we're in the car I mostly just let him talk and sometimes try to guide his decision by asking questions like, "What do you think you should do," or "How would you feel if the situation were reversed?" By asking questions, I can lead him to think through the consequences of any given action. For me, car conversations are an effective parenting tool.

## Father–Son Bonding Time

Stephen L. is another parent who has discovered the value of talking to his children in the car. He said, "Sometimes I just drive in silence, without any distractions, knowing that within a few minutes my son will start talking about something important to him or asking questions about something he is curious or worried about. As a result, some of our best and deepest conversations have taken place in the car."

# Family Debate Team

Mary and Michael Leppert, the authors of *Homeschooling Almanac* and publishers of *The Link* homeschool newspaper, use car talks to learn debate techniques. "Besides being a great conversation place, the car provides all three of us (our 14-year-old son, included) an excellent environment to follow some sort of Parliamentary procedure. We don't break out *Robert's Rules of Order*, but we do use the Toastmasters' technique of not interrupting each other, and conversely, keeping each statement short enough to be to the point. In other words: if we listeners can't interrupt, the speaker can't ramble. For us, the car becomes like a mobile living room, where we can all sit and talk in intimate proximity. It provides a time for all of us to be together without any distractions, as we can turn off the cell phones and really stretch out to discuss important topics for an hour or more, without interruption. We invariably get into at least one long and deep discussion per trip that at times becomes heated, because at least one of us feels passionately about it. Usually these topics are about social issues such as illegal immigration, the treatment of Taliban POWs, capital punishment, welfare, corporate crime, religion, etc. Sometimes one of these conversations will be sparked by a news story on the radio. Getting into a powerful discussion is also a great way to fight road fatigue! The time just flies by!"

# One Thing I Like About You

Jen from Texas says that her family plays a game in the car that is fun, easy, and relationship building. She invented it in an effort to improve her relationship with her daughter. In the afternoon when Jen picked her daughter up at school, it seemed like they spent most of the ride home griping at each other and being together was generally unpleasant. In a desperate attempt to rebuild their relationship (and make going places in the car more enjoyable), Jen made up a game called One Thing I Like About You. Here's how you play it.

Each time you are in the car you must play the game at least once at a stoplight. At the red light, the driver (or other adult) starts the game by saying, "One thing I like about (<u>name</u>) is (<u>fill in the blank with something positive</u>)." You must say one thing nice about each person in the car. Then the next person continues the game, saying something nice about the first person and each other person in the car. The game continues even if the light turns green!

Jen said, "My daughter is 11 years old, and she still likes to play this game. I've even done it with other kids (besides my own) in the car. I provided childcare for a friend of mine for about six months and played the game with her son a few times. Then, for some reason, we forgot about the game and didn't play for a few weeks. Finally, he cried out at a red light, 'Please! I want to play One Thing I Like About You!' It was so sweet! One Thing has made being in the car a lot more fun for our family."

## The Question Book

Katy Hunt of California said that her kids often took advantage of having her undivided attention on car trips to ask questions. When she didn't have a satisfactory answer, they wrote the unanswered questions in a notebook in the car that they dubbed the "Question Book." She occasionally used a tape recorder for this purpose, especially when she was driving and couldn't write down the children's questions. They simply pressed the record button and asked their question. When they got home they looked for answers in their reference books and on the Internet. Katy said that occasionally the children wouldn't be interested in looking up the answers, and she would simply go ahead and research the question. Then she would jot down a note or two in the Question Book or record a comment that provided more information about whatever question they had asked. When they got back in the car, she'd bring along the Question Book and the tape recorder. As they drove along, eventually the kids would look in the Question Book and read the answer, or turn on the tape recorder and listen to the answer that had been recorded. Katy said, "That always resulted in more conversations, and inevitably, more questions."

## Lie Detector

In this game, players learn interesting things about one another by trying to guess which of three statements another player makes is the lie. The first player makes three short statements about him- or herself. For example, a player might say, "I sang a solo in my choir. My rabbit won first prize at the country fair. I broke my toe while Irish step-dancing." All of the other players hold up one, two, or three fingers to indicate which statement they think is a lie. The player who made the statements tells the others which statement was a lie. Those who guessed correctly get a treat like a peanut, raisin, or M&M. Then another player takes a turn by making two truthful statements and one lie.

## Bad, Glad, Mad, Sad

This is a great game to play on the ride home from school or work because it helps everyone in the car to know what kind of day each person had. It can stimulate conversation and help you to learn more about each member of your family. Each player takes turns telling the others about something bad that happened, or something that made them feel glad, mad, or sad.

## To TV or Not to TV? That Is the Question

The latest trend in family car design is the "entertainment system," complete with television screens and VCRs. Car manufacturers site the benefits of these systems especially on long trips. In addition to entertainment, they provide a distraction that can restore order in the backseat when the behavior of cooped-up kids gets out of hand. It's also nice to have a diversion for the children when you're trying to negotiate four lanes of 65-mph bumper-to-bumper traffic. The advantages seem notable, but many carschooling parents have expressed concern about overuse of VCRs in the car and what that will do to family car conversations. One parent had this to say:

> Car conversation ranks right up there with dinner table conversation in our family. The car has provided a safe and secure place for us to have uninterrupted time alone together. My concern is that families raised on VCR cars will miss out on the best part of carschooling—and that is the intimacy and bonding that occurs during conversations, and the little things that happen that help us to appreciate each other in the quiet moments in the car. Our car talks have added a thread of commonality that makes us treasure these little moments that we share in the car. I know that when my children grow up they will look back and remember these conversations just as most of us remember the special moments we had with our families in the car.

This parent's comment reminded me of a car trip my family took when I was a child. On a winter's day in the mid-1960s my parents loaded my brother, sister, and me into an overpacked station wagon and headed toward Lake Tahoe to enjoy some snow skiing. In those days we didn't have CD players or even Walkmans, so we listened to the radio until we lost the signal about an hour into our trip. From that point on we knew the drill: songs, games, storytelling, and conversation. As we drove, it began to snow. Within a short distance the mounting snow made the two-lane highway treacherous. We stopped to put chains on the car and continued to our destination, although traffic was moving at a snail's pace. Visibility worsened as we approached the mountain summit. My dad could only use the taillights of the car in front of him to guide our car along the road. Suddenly the freezing cold wind snapped the windshield wiper off the driver's side of the windshield. There was no place to pull over on the narrow mountain road, which was bounded by the craggy mountain face on one side and a steep cliff on the other. Our car, which had been filled with laughter and conversation, became very quiet. It was understood that my dad needed to concentrate as he rolled down the window and tried to use his gloved hand to wipe away the blinding snow as he maneuvered the car over the summit and down the other side of the mountain. My sister asked my mom what we should do. "Pray," she whispered. As frightened as we all were, we drew strength from being together, silently supporting each other with our thoughts and prayers.

> **From the Information Highway**
>
> Nearly half of U.S. children between the ages of 8 and 16 watch more than two hours of television a day.

While winding our way down the mountain, my father spotted a turnout. He stopped to jerry-rig a tree branch to use as a windshield wiper so that he could see the road. In spite of the driving snow, we all got out of the car to stretch. My brother noticed something near a small, ice-covered pond by the side of the road. It was a duck, and it looked half frozen. Feeling sorry for the creature, he picked it up and asked my folks if he could care for it until we could get it to an animal shelter. My mother welcomed the diversion, and the duck was soon tucked beneath a blanket on my brother's lap as we continued on our perilous journey. Near the bottom of the mountain my brother broke the prayer-filled silence and whined, "Ooooh, the duck pooped on me." My mom shined a flashlight beam on his lap. The duck stood up, quacked, hopped to the front seat and flew out of my father's snow-encrusted open window. We were all stunned—and even more surprised when my brother said, "Hey, the duck laid an egg," and held it up for all of us to see. In a moment of fear-filled anxiety, when we all thought we would surely die before reaching our destination, that duck laid a message of hope right in my brother's lap. We all burst out laughing, and within minutes my father turned down the road that led to our rented cabin. We got out of the car and hugged one another in relief—happy to be together and alive. None of us has ever forgotten that car trip, but I'm certain the distraction of a video would have produced a very different, and far less of a bonding or memorable experience.

Other families offered these comments on the subject of using videotapes in the car:

> When my children were younger, we watched a lot of videotapes in the car. We have found, though, that as the boys got older we've enjoyed conversations more and have used the tapes less. It seems as if the boys are more comfortable opening up about certain topics when they are in the van, when we're not face-to-face. I think a video player would eliminate some of those opportunities for questions and conversations that only take place in the van. (L. R.)

★   ★   ★

> We have recently discovered the idea of not using the radio, cassette player, and videos in the car! We have been singing songs and playing more games together. I read out loud to the kids while my husband drives. It gives the kids a chance to have my

undivided attention, and they do not seem to fight at all when I am reading or talking to them. (Dorinda O.)

The ultimate test of your parenting is your relationship with your children. Carschooling and car discussions improve your relationship, keep you connected, and provide occasions to interact in profound and meaningful ways. The key to using any resource, including VCRs in the car, is to use it intelligently and in moderation. That way, you can take full advantage of every opportunity that presents itself, not only to learn about every subject but to develop close bonds and goodwill in your family.

# Carschooling RECESS

**CHAPTER 12**

CARSCHOOLERS TAKE breaks from academic subjects to relax and just have fun. Recess in the car includes many traditional and familiar car games, but ingenious carschoolers have also created their own games that provide hours of fun in the car. Travel games, such as checkers, chess, battleship, and handheld electronic toys have been road tested by carschoolers, and their recommendations for the best of these products are included here as well. Even food provides some fun for carschoolers—try playing Bubble Gum Blowout or go on an Animal Cookie Car Safari!

## RECESS TOOLS

Some recommendations for products and toys in this chapter are *not* included in this tool list. Scan the pages of this chapter prior to starting your car engine to be sure you have the items that will bring the most enjoyment to your family when on the road. Here is a list of many of the tools that will help you get the most out of carschool recess:

Crayons or markers

Graph paper

Gum (chewing gum in many flavors; many varieties of bubble gum)

Index cards

Junk mail

Latex balloons

Paper

Paper lunch bags

Pencil

Roll of pennies

Roll of quarters

Tape

Stapler and staples

String

# YIPEE! IT'S RECESS!

All work and no play makes for grouchy road scholars and frustrated carschooling parents. Be sure to schedule recess times for your road scholars. Here are some activities seasoned carschoolers recommend for recess at your carschool.

## Off-Ramp Romps

When taking long car trips with young children, plan for frequent road breaks. Call ahead to the chamber of commerce of various cities along your route, and ask where the closest public park is located to the freeway off-ramp in that town. Tell them you prefer a park with a swing, slide, and a restroom. (The staff may also be able to suggest other kid-friendly places to visit in their city.) Instead of having to stop for a snack at a restaurant and let the kids play in the parking lot, you can take a nice break at a park, use the picnic table, playground, and the park restrooms, and get back in the car refreshed and ready to go. Your children will think it's neat to

**From the Information Highway**

The first state to have roadside picnic tables was Michigan.

see so many parks and try out all the new playground equipment. They might even meet a few new playmates along the way!

## My Father Owns a Grocery Store

Carschool parent J. A. Rock says that her favorite family car game when she was a child was My Father Owns a Grocery Store. The person who is "it" thinks of an item sold in a grocery store and says, for example, "My father owns a grocery store and in it he sells something that starts with the letter B." Everyone guesses B items (bread, bananas, boysenberries, broccoli, and so forth), and the person that guesses correctly gets to go next. She passed the tradition of playing this game along to her children, who enjoy it as much as she did. She said, "When my daughter was too young to understand the alphabet and think of words that began with B, we would play this game by color instead. For example, we would say the grocery store sold something yellow and then she could easily guess items like lemons or bananas. You can modify the game with each round. Whoever is 'it' picks the *type* of store and *who* owns it. For example, 'My *sister* owns a *pet* store and sells something that meows.' Even the youngest toddler can guess a 'cat' from this clue."

When played traditionally, the game helps with learning the alphabet and what letters different words begin with. In other forms, it helps children learn colors or animal sounds. You can also play "music store" with instruments, "realtor" for architecture, "restaurant" to learn about different foods, and "travel agent" to learn about different countries and cultures.

## U Is for Ugly

Leslie M.'s son came up with a fun, cooperative game to play on long road trips that involves searching for car names in alphabetical order, for example, names that start with A (Aerostar), B (Buick),

C (Chevrolet), and so forth. She said the only letter they couldn't find a car name for was U and they finally accepted "ugly" car! The game works for lots of different things (animals, states, countries, rivers, and so forth). Everyone plays and works together to find an object for every letter of the alphabet—so everyone wins!

## Travel Scavengers

Alicia E. of South Carolina said that her oldest son likes to think of a word for the rest of the carschoolers to find on road signs and billboards. The first person to find it gets to choose the next word to find. They have varied the game by searching for numbers, too. Their favorite version is searching for a list of specific things. It's similar to a scavenger hunt. For example, they may have to find one of each of the following items:

Airport control tower

Ambulance siren

Baseball cap

Bicyclist

Billboard advertising a fast
    food restaurant

Bus stop

Car with skis on top

Car with something dangling
    from the rearview mirror

Cellular phone

Church steeple with a bell

Convertible

Detour

Dog in a car

Drawbridge

Flag

Graveyard

Hitchhiker

Kids waving in a car

Mattress dumped along the
    roadside

Mobile/motor home

Out-of-state license plate

Police car

Purple semi truck

Somebody's head moving to
    the beat of music

Stadium

Truck driver who will honk
    his horn

Two horses

Yellow caution tape

The first person to find everything on the list wins. This can also be a cooperative game where everyone works together to find all of the items on the list. Alicia warns, "Some items are hard to find. We once drove three-and-a-half hours before finding that purple semi truck!"

### Variations

Make theme lists, for example, a list of street signs: Wrong Way, Dead End, Speed Limit 25, Road Work Ahead, and so forth. Look for different makes of cars or for drivers wearing shirts of different colors (red shirt, orange shirt, yellow shirt, green shirt, blue shirt). Look for different kinds of animals (horses, cows, birds, dogs, cats, deer, and so forth).

Carschooling mom Donna T. keeps a bag of pennies in the car and a list of things to find on car trips. If any of the kids find something on the list, everyone receives a penny. However, if anyone asks, "Are we there yet," everyone has to give up a penny!

## Fifty in Fifty

This cooperative game is lots of fun on long car trips. You will need 50 index cards, pencils for every player, a bag or box to collect discards, and 50 cents for every player. Distribute the cards among the players. Tell them to write (or draw a picture of) something they might see on the trip on each card (for example, a truck, a billboard, a stop sign, a cow). Collect the cards, shuffle them, and deal them out among the passengers. The object of the game is to find all 50 items in 50 minutes or 50 miles—whichever comes first. Players find the items on their own cards first. As each player finds an item, the matching index card is discarded. (Use one bag or box for all of the discards.) Players who have found all of their items can help the others. If the group finds all 50 items in 50 miles or 50 minutes, each player wins 50 cents to spend at the next stop.

## Sounds Like Fun

One player imitates a sound. The rest of the players try to guess what makes this sound. For example, you could make the sound of a door creaking, or try to imitate the sound of a saw, or horse, or a crowd going wild at a sporting event. Young children will have fun with animal sounds. Older kids and adults can try more complicated sounds.

## Looney Ballooney

You will need latex balloons, paper, and a pencil. Write several notes with silly instructions, such as "cluck like a chicken," "sing the National Anthem," "howl like a wolf," or "cross your eyes." Insert each note in a deflated latex balloon. Then blow up the balloon (with the note inside) and tie the end closed. Pass balloons to all the players in the car and tell them to squeeze the balloon between their knees for five seconds. Players who break their balloons must do whatever the message inside says. If the balloon doesn't break, it is passed to the next player. Play continues as long as everyone is having fun.

## Sound Off

This is a fun and very noisy game. Each player picks one thing that happens when driving on the road and creates a sound to represent that thing. For example, whenever the driver stops the car, the player could make the sound of screeching brakes. Or, if another car passes you, a player could make the sound "Whoosh!" Each player thinks of an event (for example, crossing a bridge) and makes up a sound to represent it (clicking his tongue). Whenever that event occurs, the player who chose it must make the appropriate sound. This gets to be really fun when several events occur at the same time—for example, while crossing over a bridge the driver hits the brakes and you see a car pass you, all at the same time. You would hear the sound of a clicking tongue, screeching brakes, and someone saying "whoosh" all at once. It's fun!

## What's Missing?

Try this fun observation and memory game to play in the car. Have players each remove one object from their pocket and put it into a bag. Pass the bag to each player to look at what's in it. Then the first player removes one object from the bag—without letting the others see what it is—and passes the bag to each player to look into again. Players write down their name and the object they think is missing on a piece of paper. The guesses are turned into the player who removed the object, and that player identifies the winner. If there is a tie, players with correct answers play another round to break the tie. The missing object is returned to the bag, and the winner gets to remove an object for the others to guess. To keep the game interesting, replace all of the objects with new items from time to time.

## I Want to Go for a Limousine Ride

All of the car passengers can play this game, which requires players to listen attentively to figure out the "secret." Designate one player as the "Chauffeur." The Chauffeur will determine who gets to go on the limousine ride by thinking of a method each player must use in order to go on the limousine ride—but don't reveal it to the other players! The Chauffeur begins the game by saying, "I want to go on a limousine ride, and I am taking an ape." The next player thinks about what the Chauffeur said, tries to figure out the "secret," and then says the same thing as the Chauffeur but changes the item to bring on the limousine ride. For example, the player may say, "I want to go on a limousine ride, and I am taking a (<u>baseball</u>)." In this example, the player is guessing that the secret is to select something in alphabetical order because the Chauffeur started the game with an item beginning with the letter A, so the player thinks of a word beginning with the letter B. Depending on whether or not the player has figured out the secret, the Chauffeur tells the player whether he or she gets to go on the limousine ride. If the player is correct, the other players will soon catch on to the secret and everyone will name items in alphabetical order. If, however, the player has not guessed the secret, then the next player tries. Let's say that the secret was not listing items in alphabetical order. The next player might guess that the secret is that the items must be animals—because an ape is an animal. So the player might say, "I want to go on a limousine ride, and I am taking a giraffe." If that is the secret, the Chauffeur tells the player to come along on the ride. Players take turns until everyone has guessed the secret, named an appropriate item, and been admitted into the limousine for the ride.

What is the secret? In this example "the secret" is that the item players are going to bring has to begin with the same letter as their name, otherwise they cannot take the limo ride. The Chauffeur's name in this example was Alex, and he selected an "ape" because it begins with the same letter as his name. The player who selected "giraffe" would not have been correct unless his name happened to begin with G. Play would have continued until the secret was guessed by all. You can see that this game requires attentive listening and reasoning and may be frustrating for very young players, which is why it is generally recommended for ages 10 and up. However, this is a fun game for older players, and it can be quite complex and challenging to play.

# Rainy Day Raindrop Race

Patricia of Oregon suggested this simple game to play on rainy days. On the count of three, have carschoolers select a raindrop at the top of one of the car windows closest to where they are sitting. Tell them to put their finger on the window over the raindrop they have chosen and trace its path as it runs down the window. The raindrop that gets to the bottom of the window first wins!

# Car Make Tally

Give each player a pencil and paper and ask them to choose a particular make of car: Chrysler, Honda, Toyota, Ford, BMW, Volkswagen, Lexus, Volvo, and so forth. Have them write down the make on a piece of paper. Now each player tries to spot as many cars of the make they chose in 10 minutes or 10 miles, whichever comes first. Each time they spot one, they write a tally mark on their paper. When the time or mileage is up, the player who spotted the most cars and has the most tally marks is the winner.

# Your Smelly Socks

Joan from California explained that her carschoolers like to play a game they call Your Smelly Socks. They draw straws to determine who will be *it*. The other players think of a silly saying or phrase such as "Your smelly socks." Each time the player who is *it* is asked a question, the player must answer "Your smelly socks." Players take turns asking questions. For example, a player might ask, "What would you like for dessert tonight?" *It* must reply, "Your smelly socks." Another player may ask, "What did you wear to the prom?" Again, *it* must reply, "Your smelly socks." Pretty funny, right? The catch is that *it* cannot laugh. If you are *it* and you laugh, you lose.

The other players work really hard to think of questions that will be really funny when answered by the saying or phrase that *it* must say. If *it* survives a full round of questions without a giggle fit, then *it* wins. If *it* succumbs to a laughing attack, then *it* loses and has to sit out one round. Play continues until everyone has had a chance to be *it*.

## These Are a Few of My Favorite Things

You'd be surprised what you can learn about your carschoolers by playing this game. Ask each person in the car to name his or her "favorite" things in each of several categories. Start the game by saying, "What's your favorite (fill in the blank with a category)?" Here are some categories suggested by carschoolers: color, music, song, instrument, fruit, vegetable, ice cream, cookie, candy, book, magazine, TV show, movie, pet, wild animal, board game, computer game, toy, sport, vacation spot, restaurant, season, or time of day. You will be surprised at the conversations that erupt due to these revelations!

## Name That TV Tune!

Each person takes a turn humming the tune to a favorite TV show, and everyone else tries to be the first to guess the name of the TV show correctly.

If this seems too easy for your carschoolers, challenge them to start the game by humming only the first three notes of the song. If someone guesses the name of the TV show correctly, that player gets to hum a new tune for players to guess. If no one guesses correctly, then the person who hummed the first three notes, hums four notes, then five notes, and so on until someone guesses correctly. If the players give up, the hummer gets to start a new game by humming a new TV tune.

## Tiny Bubbles

Julia of Phoenix, Arizona, and her family attended a wedding where the hosts did not dispense the traditional rice or birdseed to throw at the happy couple after the ceremony. Instead, wedding guests were given tiny vials filled with bubble liquid and miniature bubble wands so that they could blow itty bitty bubbles to celebrate the marriage of the bride and groom. She said that seeing all of those shimmering bubbles floating around the happy couple was a sight to behold. On the way home from the wedding, Julia's 9-month-old baby was fussy. Her 4-year-old remembered his bubble vial and began to blow bubbles in the car. The baby calmed right down upon seeing the wondrous sight. Her 6-year-old joined in the bubble blowing and everyone delighted in the marvel of bubbles drifting throughout the car. The bubbles were so tiny that they popped fairly quickly and didn't obstruct the driver's view at all. Julia said, "It was a lovely way to enjoy the ride home. I have found these bubble vials in many toy stores. They are really inexpensive but have provided lots of happy, quiet moments in our car travels."

## 20 Questions

This is a classic game, with lots of variations. In the traditional game, one player thinks of something that is either an animal, vegetable, or mineral and announces the category to the other players. Players try to guess what that player is thinking of by asking questions in turn. The questions must be phrased so that they can be answered with "yes" or "no." If the answer to a question is "yes," the player who asked the question gets to guess the answer. If the player guesses correctly, that player gets to try to stump the group. If the player guesses incorrectly, play continues until 20 questions have been asked. At the end of the 20 questions, everyone has one last

**From the Information Highway**

The *Guinness Book of Records* reports that the longest bubble was 50 feet long by 2 feet in diameter and was made by David Stein using his own invention called "The Bubble Thing."

opportunity to guess the answer. Whoever guesses correctly gets to stump the group next. If no one guesses the answer, the player that stumped everyone gets to try to stump the group again.

## Car Fishing

Carolyn of California claims that her children like to go fishing in the car! She gives them a short dowel with a long string that has a magnet attached to it. She places magnetized letters, numbers, and toys in a shoebox under their feet. Then they go fishing for whatever will stick to the magnet on their dowel.

## Alphabetical Animals

Have your carschoolers take turns naming various kinds of animals in alphabetical order. For example, select the category of "birds." Each player would then name a particular kind of bird in alphabetical order. The first player might say "Albatross," the next "Bluebird," the next "Canary," and so on. The letters Q, X, and Z can be tricky in all animal categories, so keep field guides handy in case you get stuck. Don't play for points; just have fun seeing if you can get through the entire alphabet.

## Wacky Tourist Attractions

Take a carschool recess break at a really wacky location and give those belly laugh muscles a workout! There are a lot of goofy and bizarre tourist attractions in America, and (wouldn't you know it) there's a book to guide you to them all. It's called *New Roadside America: The Modern Traveler's Guide to the Wild and Wonderful World of America's Tourist Attractions,* by Doug Kirby, Ken Smith, and Mike Wilkins (Fireside; ISBN: 0671769316).

## Car Comedy Competition

Nothing relieves the tedium of a long car ride like a little humor. Plan ahead and tell everyone to bring two good jokes to tell in the car. When things get a little dull, have a Car Comedy Competition. Everyone tells one joke—the person who tells the funniest joke wins. What do they win? They get to tell their second joke!

To facilitate the Car Comedy Competition, keep a good joke book in the car or print out a few jokes gleaned from the Internet and tuck it in the glove compartment. When you need a little humor, pass the book or printout around and let everyone pick one joke to tell.

*Ready Resources*
Here are two resources for kids' jokes that you can consult to add to your repertoire:

> *Goofy Good Clean Jokes for Kids,* by Bob Phillips (Harvest House Publishers; ISBN: 1565074912), has lots of jokes your kids will enjoy telling.
>
> This Web site (www.azkidsnet.com/JSknockjoke.htm) has jokes for kids, including knock-knock jokes, elephant jokes, riddles, silly rhymes, and more.

## What Kind of Car Will I Drive on My 16th Birthday?

Debbie S. of Illinois plays this game with her children. "I tell them to add up all of the numbers in their birthday. For example, a child whose birthday is 10/18/95 would add all of the individual numbers together as follows: 1 + 0 + 1 + 8 + 9 + 5 = 24. The sum of their birthday digits is their special number. Then I tell the kids that when I say 'go' they should start counting the cars that go by. When they reach their special number, they shout out what kind of a car it is. I tell them that will be the kind of car they will drive on their 16th birthday."

## What If?

C. Boynton of Washington described an activity she enjoys with her carschoolers: "When we're driving down the road, my kids (ages 8 and 10) frequently ask me questions that begin 'What if _____?' The questions often are speculations about how they would react in any given (usually dire) situation. For example, we might be driving alongside the ocean and they would ask, 'What if a tidal wave struck right now?' Or we might be driving through a forest and they would ask, 'What if someone cut down all of these trees or a forest fire burned them all up?' Or they might ask, 'What if a swarm of bees flew in the car window right now?' I have learned to simply ask them what they would do. Sometimes their imaginations come to the rescue, and sometimes they have very practical suggestions for how to handle such situations. I listen to their thoughts, and if needed, offer an idea or two for them to consider about how to handle the emergency in question. I often remind them of the emergency supplies in our car and a procedure for getting help. This 'game' has been a favorite of ours. We laugh at some of the silly solutions we have entertained,

> **From the Information Highway**
>
> The name Jeep came from the initials "G.P.," which were used in the army as a nickname for the "General Purpose" vehicle.

and I know the kids have more confidence about what to do in any emergency."

## Scribble Chains

You will need some plain white paper, crayons or markers, and tape or staples. Have the kids scribble on both sides of several pieces of paper, but tell them they will be cutting or tearing the paper into pieces when they are through to make Scribble Chains (that way, no one will be upset if their artwork gets destroyed). When they are through scribbling, cut or tear the paper into strips about 1 inch wide and 8 inches long. (The size doesn't have to be exact and can be any measurement you think will work best.) Take a strip of scribbled-on-paper, form it into a loop, and tape or staple the ends together to form a circle. Take a second scribble-strip of paper and pass it through the first loop. Tape or staple this into a circle as well. Keep on going until you form a nifty Scribble Chain! Challenge the kids to make the longest chain they can. They can pass the chain back and forth to add links.

To help carschoolers learn how far they have traveled, try having them add a loop in the chain each time the odometer logs five miles. The chain will help the kids keep track of the number of miles they have traveled—just count by fives!

## Comical Car Rules

Lots of families have funny "rules" when riding in the car that are fun to do on long or short car trips. Here are some silly rules of the road carschoolers may follow:

★ Lift your feet up as the car goes over a railroad track.
★ Hold your breath as the car goes through a tunnel.

★   Say "beep-beep" when you go through a toll booth.

★   Sing as the car travels over a bridge.

★   Clap when you see a fire truck.

★   Snap your fingers when you see a bumper sticker with radio station call letters.

★   Touch your nose when you see a yellow car.

★   Say "Moo" when you see a cow.

★   Stomp your feet when you see a convertible VW Bug.

Add your own road rules to this list and have fun!

## The Name Game

D. Thompson's family plays this game, and it is perfect for kids of all ages. Think of a name. Then tell the group whether it is a boy's or girl's name, and tell them the first letter of the name. Players try to guess the name by taking turns calling out names they can think of that start with the appropriate letter. That's it. Simple, but fun!

## Crazy Names

One carschool mom said that her family invented a game that was inspired by the funny names of towns, rivers, and roads they passed by. She said, "It all started in Montana where a sign announced Wild Horse Creek. A few miles later a sign said Dead Horse Creek. Our family, having a bizarre sense of humor, thought this was amusing and came up with all sorts of stories about what happened to the horse. We passed so many strange and funny names for creeks, roads, and towns that we started guessing the names of the next creek, road, or town. For instance, we passed Fox Road. The object of the game was to guess a humorous name for the next road. Someone thought the next road might be Chicken Road. Then someone else said, 'Then the one after that should be Why-

Did-the-Chicken-Cross-the-Road?' We crossed Leggins Creek and someone shouted, 'The next one will be Arms Creek!' The best was when we crossed Crazy Woman River; my kids pleaded with me to stop so they could take a picture of me in front of the sign! We did, and that started a photographic collection of funny and unusual names for towns, creeks, rivers, and roads that we enjoy looking at to this day!"

## Hug-a-Bug

Peggy is not a fan of the Slug Bug game, which has simple, if not moronic, rules—when you see a VW Bug, you slug or punch the person sitting next to you. She developed a much more peaceful version of this game called Hug-a-Bug. When her family sees a VW Bug, they hug each other in the car or extend their hands to touch each other in a symbolic hug. Her kids really enjoy playing this peaceful version of the game.

## Paper Bag Puppet Show

Dana O. of Nevada exclaims, "My kids adore puppets! They think it's so funny when I put a puppet on my hand and have it tell them what to do—like make funny faces or sing a silly song. They like to talk to the puppet, too. We even have a game called Tell Me All Your Troubles. The puppet asks each child to tell it about anything that is bothering him or her; sometimes they mention serious things ("My brother punched me."), and other times they come up with funny problems for the puppet to listen to ("I can't decide if I want to eat the blue or the red jelly bean."). Of course the puppet always responds appropriately. They will actually talk to the puppet as if it is real, and they seem very satisfied to have the puppet's undivided attention and complete sympathy and support. My kids like to interact with any kind of puppet, so I keep a stack of brown lunch bags in the car along with a marker pen. When we need a change of pace while riding in the car, I can pull out a bag, slip it over my hand, draw a mouth and some eyes on it, and provide an instant puppet show. The kids like to get in on the act, too. I pass out bags all around, they draw a face on them, and then we play with the puppets. It's great fun!"

## Mail Call

This is a great activity for young children to do in the car. Save all of your junk mail and bring it along in a bag. When the kids get a little antsy, just say, "Mail call!" and divide up all of the mail evenly and let them open it. Have them tell you, as best as they can, what it is about based on the pictures in the brochures, and so forth. If they can read, have them read the mail to you.

## Rest Stop Leaf Search

Diana K. of Arizona reports that whenever her family arrives at a rest stop she and her husband wander around the area and pick a few leaves from different trees, plants, and bushes while the kids use the restrooms. When the kids come back to the car, they give a few leaves to each boy and challenge them to find an identical leaf. When they get back on the road, they use field guides to identify what kind of leaf they have. She said, "We press the leaves in a travel journal as little mementos of our trip."

## Odds and Evens

This game requires two players. One of the players will be "odds" and the other "evens." Each player makes a fist, and then they count to three simultaneously. On "three" they each stick out one, two, three, four, or five fingers (the whole hand). Then they count the total number of fingers showing on the hands. If the total is an odd number, the player called "odds" wins. If the total is an even number, the player called "evens" wins.

## Rock, Scissors, Paper

This games requires two players. Players put one hand behind their back. While their hand is out of view, they make one of three hand gestures:

* ★ Make a closed fist (rock)
* ★ Use the index and middle fingers to form a V-shape (scissors)
* ★ Make the hand and fingers flat with an open palm (paper)

Both players count to three and reveal their hand positions at the same time. The rock wins over scissors because it can break them, the scissors beat paper because it cuts paper, and the paper beats rock because it can cover the rock. Some kids declare a winner after the best two out of three tries. Others like to play the game indefinitely.

## I Spy

This is another classic car game. One player, the "Spy," looks at something that can be seen either in the car or on the road and announces, "I spy, with my little eye, (<u>fill in the blank with something the Spy can see</u>)." For example, the Spy might say, "I spy, with my little eye, something round and black." Players call out what they think it might be (for example, "a steering wheel"). If that is the correct answer, the person who guessed correctly gets to be the Spy. If no one guesses the object on the first clue, the Spy continues to give more clues until someone guesses the right answer.

## Car Colors

Erin D. of Missouri described this simple game that her kids enjoy playing: "The children take one minute to watch cars go by as we're driving down the street. Then they each pick a color of a car they have seen go by and try to find 25 things that we pass on the road that are the same color. (They keep a tally with a pencil and paper, but they have to call the item out before making a tally mark so that everyone else can verify the find.) The first person to spot 25 items in that color wins. Of course, picking common colors makes this game much easier to play."

## Silly Alphabetizing

This is an old favorite—but with a funny twist. The first person starts with the letter A and says "A is for (<u>funny word or phrase beginning with the letter A</u>)." For example, a player might say, "A is for *ants* in your pants." The next player must repeat what the first player said and add a word or phrase for the next letter of the alphabet, for example, "B is for *birdbrain*." Each player repeats everything that has been said previously and adds another word or phrase for the next letter of the alphabet. Play continues through "S is for *smelly* toes," and the remainder of the alphabet. Of course, by the time you get to Z, the players have to recite each item from A to Z—so it really challenges their memory and takes some time to play.

# TOYS AND GAMES

~~~~~~~~~~~~~~~~~~~~~~~~~~~~~~~~~~~~~~~~~~~~~~~~~~~~~~

Homemade or store-bought toys find their way into most family cars. They really help to pass the time on long car journeys. Before you stock your carschool with toys, consider these tips to ease frustration and keep the game pieces tidy and intact.

### TIDYNESS TIPS

★ Using toys and games with a lot of pieces in the car frustrates some children. The pieces fall on the car floor and the kids can't get to them while the car is moving (they have to stay buckled in their car seats and seat belts). To solve the problem, carschooling mom Carolyn places velcro on all of the spaces on the game boards and on the game pieces so that they stick together.

★ Dana keeps a wipe-off marker in the van that she uses to keep track of game scores on the window. It eliminates the need for paper and pencil, and the scores and tally marks wipe right off when the game is over.

★ Card games can be difficult to play in the car because it's hard for small hands to hold onto the cards. Carolyn gives each of her kids a clothespin—the clothespin easily clamps onto a set of cards and makes them easier to hold and keep together. Another trick she suggests is to punch holes in one corner of the cards and use a metal ring that opens and closes (available at office supply stores) to hold the cards together. The kids can fan out their cards and keep them from flying around on bumpy roads. Carolyn discovered that a plastic baggie taped to the back of the front seat will hold a deck of cards neatly until it's ready for use.

Carschooling mom Carolyn also provided some creative ideas for little ones who are strapped into car seats.

★ Tape pictures on the back of seats to give the kids something interesting to look at.

★ String rattles (and pacifiers) onto the car seat so the kids can use them without losing them.

★ Hang miniature mobiles and toys from the ceiling of the car.

★ String a large magnet from the car seat for the kids to use. They can try to make the magnet stick to parts of the car that are metal.

Now let's look at some carschoolers' recommendations for toys that are not only portable but provide many hours of fun.

## Sewing and Lacing Cards

Young children really seem to enjoy sewing and lacing activity cards. They are extremely portable and provide a great way to pass the time in the car. You can purchase them at most toy stores, but they are easy to make as well. Use sturdy poster board and cut it into pieces (squares, circles, triangles, animal shapes, and so forth) that are sized to be easily handheld. Use a hole-punch to punch holes in the card about one inch from the edge and one inch apart all around the card. Take a piece of yarn and wrap some tape around one end to make it easier to poke through the punched holes (or use a shoelace). Tie a big knot in the end of the yarn that doesn't have the tape on it (make it large enough so that it will not go through the punched holes). Now let your carschool tailors "sew" around each and every shape. (*Note:* You might want to make several "laces" of different yarn colors for variety and as backup in the event one starts to fray or unravel.)

## Magna Doodle

Use Magna Doodle by Fisher-Price to make all kinds of designs on the magnetic drawing board. The deluxe version includes the drawing board, eight magnetic stamps of varying shapes, stencils, and a "Spiral Artist" for creating artistic patterns. The board has a built-in handle and snap-in storage for all of the parts. Available wherever toys are sold. (Ages 3 and up.)

## LEGOs

LEGOs are great toys to bring along in the car for impromptu building sessions. Little pieces are less likely to get lost if you keep them in a ziplock plastic bag; the clear plastic makes it easy to see which piece you want to use while building. Challenge the kids to design and build their own LEGO-Car. For inspiration, tell them to look at the passing cars on the road.

## Colorforms

This classic toy by Colorform is used in much the same manner as flannel boards except that the pieces are made from thin, flexible plastic that cling to a playing board. Colorforms also cling to car windows, making them ideal for road trips. The pieces come in every shape and color you can imagine, and there are a variety of Colorform theme kits to choose from. The Beginner's Kit is a good place to start. Available wherever toys are sold. (Ages 3 and up.)

## Make-Your-Own Magnet Toys

Carolyn passed along an idea she borrowed from another mom. Buy sheets of magnet at a craft store. Glue pictures to the nonmagnetic side, and then cut them out into separate pieces. Use a cookie sheet for an activity board—the magnets stick to it in a similar manner to a flannel board. Carolyn also made a tic-tac-toe grid, along with Xs and Os. She also discovered that she could glue playing cards to the magnet strips so that the kids could play matching games on the cookie sheet like AC/DC or Concentration.

# Car Bingo

Bingo is one of the great car games. You can buy prepackaged Car Bingo games, but it is easy to make your own. Use a piece of plain paper, or better yet use graph paper. (A tablet of graph paper is a great thing to keep handy in the car for all kinds of games and activities. When you need to draw rows, columns, and so forth, the graph paper has them ready-made, imprinted right on the paper!) Each player draws a grid containing 16 squares (4 rows of 4 squares across, and 4 squares down). Carschoolers fill in each square on their grids with the name of something they see on the road. For example:

| | |
|---|---|
| Speed limit sign | Gas station |
| Yellow VW bug | Cow |
| Billboard | Fast food restaurant |
| Telephone pole | Tree |
| Ambulance | Truck weigh station |
| Road kill | Toll booth |
| Exit sign | Bridge |
| Men working sign | Trailer |
| Crosswalk | Boat |
| Call box | Parking meter |

When everyone has all 16 squares filled, stop. Collect all of the papers and shuffle them, face down. Each player chooses a grid at random. Then players try to find each of the things on their grid, marking them off with an "×." As soon as someone has 4 ×s in a row in any direction, the player shouts "Bingo" and wins the game.

## Ready Resources

Donna T. prints out auto bingo game cards for free at these Web sites:

**Kids Domain** (www.kidsdomain.com/craft/auto.html). All of the instructions are provided, and you can print the cards with or without road kill options! You will also find some neat ideas on how to make the boards reuseable—from lamination to magnetizing!

**Crayola** (www.crayola.com/parents/travel/bingo1.cfm). A variety of auto bingo game cards can be printed out. They also suggest designating one person to be the Caller. This person looks out the window and calls out objects he or she sees, and the other players mark them off on their boards.

## Wake Up Giants

This game is played within a wooden game box, making it ideal for travel. Roll the dice to determine how many "giants" (wooden pegs) you get to flip. For one or many players. Available from Hearthsong online at www.hearthsong.com. (Ages 8 and up.)

## Monopoly Junior

This version of the classic Monopoly game is designed specifically for car travel. The playing pieces will stay put on rough roads, as items like the game spinner and monopoly money are tucked into the lid. The gameboard unfolds from the convenient travel case. Monopoly Junior is made by Parker Brothers and is available at toy stores. (Ages 5 and up.)

> **From the Information Highway**
>
> More Monopoly money is printed daily than U.S. currency.

## Clue Jr.

This travel version of the who-done-it detective game has been toned down from the murderous plots of the original version to one small children will enjoy. (They search for children and pets hiding in the mansion.) The portable game board holds the game pieces for easy storage. Clue

Jr. is made by Parker Brothers and is available at toy stores. (Ages 5 and up.)

## Action Figures

A carschool mom said that her kids pooled their money on a recent car trip and bought some inexpensive action figures at a store along the way. She remarked, "They spent many happy hours fighting military battles in the backseat—which was better then fighting each other!"

## Handheld Electronic Games

There are lots of electronic (battery-operated) games on the market. You probably already have a few of these handheld gadgets. Here are some carschool favorites that are available at most toy stores:

**Gameboy:** This handheld electronic game by Nintendo has a variety of game options (delivered via game cartridges). Kids will spend hours giving their thumbs a workout as they press keys to play and modify the games. Carschool parents have observed that some children become overstimulated and cranky if they are allowed to play with these games for too long a time. Apparently, moderation is the key. In measured doses, parents agree that Gameboy is a fun way to pass time in the car.

**Battleship:** In this version of the classic game by Hasbro, you line up your battleships on a small display screen and try to out-strategize your opponent—the computer in your hand! The game is designed for individual play. (Ages 7 and up.)

**Yahtzee:** This version by Milton Bradley is just like regular Yahtzee except you "roll the dice" by clicking a button. The score is automatically calculated for you. (Ages 8 and up.)

**Simon:** In this Milton Bradley game, players rely on their memory of a series of notes and colors to repeat patterns. Up to four players can use this miniature version of the original game in the car. (Ages 7 and up.)

**Pocket Tic-Tac-Toe:** You can play this version by Radica the regular way or set the pocket calculator to more challenging levels that up to two players can enjoy. (Ages 8 and up.)

**Wheel of Fortune:** This travel version of the TV show made by Tiger Electronics is similar to Hangman and has more than 400 puzzles to solve. The kids will be engaged for miles! Additional puzzle cartridges can be purchased as well. (Ages 8 and up.)

## Magnetic Games

Magnetic Games is the name of a series of classic games that are magnetized to make playing while traveling a breeze. Each game comes with a history of the game's origins. They are available at toy stores and online at amazon.com. Here are some classics your carschoolers are sure to enjoy:

**Solitaire:** A French nobleman imprisoned in the Bastille invented this game to pass the time.

**Chess:** This game has its origins in India and Persia. This version has 32 magnetic chessmen and a special chessboard that keeps the pieces in place while you play.

**Checkers:** Popular in the Middle Ages, this easy but challenging game has magnetized pieces to prevent unintentional "jumping."

**Tic-Tac-Toe:** Magnetic Xs and Os update this version of the game that was also played by ancient Chinese and Romans.

# TRAVEL ACTIVITY BOOKS AND GUIDES

Here are some carschooling favorites available at toy and book stores or online at amazon.com.

*The Amazing Book-a-ma-Thing for the Backseat,* by the editors of Klutz Press, is a hands-on book of puzzles and games. (ISBN: 1-57054-169-8) Ages 8 and up.

*The Buck Book,* by Anne Akers Johnson, has instructions for folding seven different items from a dollar bill and comes with a real dollar bill. (ISBN: 1-878257-51-X) Ages 6 and up.

*Cat's Cradle: A Book of String Figures,* by Anne Akers Johnson, has easy-to-understand instructions that teaches not only how to make a "Cat's Cradle" but five other classic string figures such as "Jacob's Ladder" and "Witch's Broom," too. The book also comes with a string so you can get started right away! (ISBN: 1878257536) Ages 6 and up.

*Cootie Catcher Book,* by the editors of Klutz Press, contains 20 preprinted tear-and-fold pages with instructions on how to make your own cootie catchers and the fortunes to go inside. (ISBN: 1-57054-131-0) Ages 6 and up.

*The Etch-A-Sketch Book,* by the editors of Klutz Press, comes with the classic drawing toy and 12 see-through pages that cling to the Etch-A-Sketch screen, creating game boards, mazes, drawing patterns, and more. (ISBN: 1-57054-050-0) Ages 6 and up.

*Kids Travel: A Back Seat Survival Kit,* by the editors of Klutz Press, is filled with fun activities you can do in the car and all of the stuff you need to do them! (ISBN: 1-878257-71-4) Ages 6 and up.

*Glove Compartment Guides,* by the editors of Klutz Press, is a new series of fold-out, laminated guides that stash neatly in the glove compartment when not in use. There are guides to backseat activities for science, games, and scavenger hunts. All ages.

*Magic Pen Books,* by Lee Publications, come with a special marker pen. You use it to color in pages in the Magic Pen book where there appears to be no writing or pictures and objects magically appear on the page. Some of the books are filled with trivia questions, and a swipe with your magic pen reveals the correct answer. Some contain blank pages that you color in with the pen to reveal previously "invisible" pictures. They are suitable for all ages and will keep the kids entertained for hours.

> **From the Information Highway**
>
> Comic book character Donald Duck has three nephews named Huey, Dewey, and Louie. Can you name Mickey Mouse's nephews? (Answer: Mortie and Ferdie)

## Comic Books

Karen A. of Massachusetts said that the only time her kids read comic books is when the family takes long trips in the car. She stocks up on comic books, and when the kids get tired of the ride and began to grumble or complain, she produces the comics and buys herself another hour or two of peace and quiet in the car.

## TV-VCR

Most carschoolers will eschew car-compatible TVs and VCRs for games and conversation. However, long trips or unbearably long traffic jams can be eased with a favorite video. There are plug-in devices to turn your automobile cigarette lighter into an outlet for your TV-VCR. Some companies rent complete car TV-VCR systems for those who just want to use them for occasional trips and forgo them as a standard feature. Try www.autobarn.com for more information.

# SNICKERS WITH SNACKS

Having a snack at recess is traditional on most school playgrounds. Snack time in your carschool can be lots of fun, too. Try these ideas.

## Gum Taste Test

Bring along a supply of gum in as many flavors and varieties as possible. Juicy Fruit, Spearmint, Doublemint, Peppermint, Cinnamon, Watermelon, Strawberry, Grape, Sour Apple, and so forth. Have a taste test to determine which one is the best. Give everyone a stick of gum and ask for opinions on its flavor and chewiness. Let everyone buy a pack of his or her favorite gum at the next stop.

Here's another bubble-popping idea. Bring samples of various bubble gums (Bazooka, Double Bubble, Bubble Tape, Big League Chew, Bubble Yum, Fresh Squeezed Bubble Gum, Bubble Jug, and so forth), and instead of a taste test have the kids grade the gums for bubble-blowing ability. Once you determine a winner, buy everyone some of the winning bubble gum and have a bubble-blowing contest. The winner is the person who blows the largest bubble. What do they win? More gum!

### HOW TO BLOW A BUBBLE
★   Chew at least two sticks of bubble gum for about five minutes.
★   With your tongue, flatten out the gum a bit by pressing it against your front teeth.
★   Open your mouth and teeth just a little bit and use your tongue to push a section of the gum into this space, creating a little pocket of gum.
★   Slowly blow air into the gum pocket until a bubble starts to form.
★   Keep blowing until the bubble gets big or pops.

Don't forget that practice makes perfect. If you keep trying, you will be blowing gigantic bubbles in no time. (*Note:* Keep a jar of peanut butter in the car—it helps remove bubble gum from hair.)

## Animal Cookie Car Safari

Here's an idea that I used with my own children. Recess in our car always involved a snack, and my kids loved animal cookies. Whenever we went on a trip to the zoo or a nature preserve where I knew we would see animals, I brought along a box of animal crackers for each child. On the ride home, I'd give everyone a box of cookies. Before they ate each cookie, however, they had to hold it up, identify the animal, and tell one interesting fact about it. If my carschooler couldn't remember anything about that animal, he or she could ask the other passengers for help. It really helped to reinforce what they had learned at the zoo and made the ride home a pleasant and tasteful experience.

## Apple Fortunes

My grandmother introduced this folksy tradition to me. Give carschoolers an apple with a stem. Tell them to twist the stem of the apple to the right while reciting the alphabet until the stem breaks off. Whatever letter they are reciting when the stem breaks will be the first letter of the first name of the person they will marry.

## Cereal Necklaces

Give each carschooler a plastic sandwich bag filled with Cheerios or Fruit Loops, or the

**From the Information Highway**

Some of the oldest pieces of "chewing gum" are 6,500 years old. Archaeological sites in Northern Europe have produced samples of chewed up pieces of birch bark with tooth impressions of people of all ages.

generic or organic equivalent, and a piece of string about 15 to 16 inches in length. (You might want to wrap a piece of tape around one end to make it easier to string.) Have carschoolers make a cereal necklace by stringing the cereal loops onto the string and tying the ends closed when finished.

Recess is over—time for more carschooling.

# INDEX

〜〜〜〜〜〜〜〜〜〜〜〜〜〜〜〜〜〜〜〜〜〜

# MORE CARSCHOOLING?

~~~~~~~~~~~~~~~~~~~~~~~~~~~~~~~~~~~~~~~~~~~~~~~~~

I WOULD LOVE to hear your comments on the carschooling activities and resources you have read about in this book. Please let me know what your favorite carschooling ideas are and how your family reacted to them.

I also invite you to send me your favorite carschooling activity, resource, or story that you would like to see published in future editions of *Carschooling*. You can send your original activities, resources, and stories or those created by others that you have enjoyed. Your submissions may be up to 1,000 words and must be educational, easy, fun, and/or inspiring. You may submit something original or a clipping from a newspaper, magazine, newsletter, e-group, or e-newsletter. It could be your favorite educational car game that your family has played for years, or it could be a personal experience story about learning in the car that made a real impact on you and your family.

Send submissions to:

Carschooling
Attn: Diane Flynn Keith
180 El Camino Real, Suite 10
Millbrae, CA 94030
E-mail: ideas@carschooling.com

I will make sure that both you and the originator/author of the activity, resource, or story are credited for your submission.

I invite you to get news about new activities and resources by visiting the Carschooling Web site at www.carschooling.com.

For information about speaking engagements, workshops, other books, articles, and audiotapes contact Diane Keith directly at (650) 365-9425 or www.carschooling.com.

I hope you enjoy reading *Carschooling* as much as I enjoyed compiling, editing, and writing it.